NSU Ro80
THE COMPLETE STORY

TITLES IN THE CROWOOD AUTOCLASSICS SERIES

Alfa Romeo 105 Series Spider
Alfa Romeo 916 GTV & Spider
Alfa Romeo 2000 and 2600
Alfa Romeo Alfasud
Alfa Romeo Spider
Aston Martin DB4, 5, 6
Aston Martin DB7
Aston Martin V8
Austin Healey
Austin Healey Sprite
BMW E30
BMW M3
BMW M5
BMW Classic Coupes 1965–1989
BMW Z3 and Z4
Citroën Traction Avant
Classic Jaguar XK – The Six-Cylinder Cars
Ferrari 308, 328 & 348
Frogeye Sprite
Ginetta: Road & Track Cars
Jaguar E-Type
Jaguar F-Type
Jaguar Mks 1 & 2, S-Type & 420
Jaguar XJ-S
Jaguar XK8
Jensen V8
Land Rover Defender 90 & 110
Land Rover Freelander
Lotus Elan
Lotus Elise & Exige 1995–2020
MGA
MGB
MGF and TF
Mazda MX-5
Mercedes-Benz Fintail Models
Mercedes-Benz S-Class 1972–2013
Mercedes SL Series
Mercedes-Benz SL & SLC 107 Series
Mercedes-Benz Saloon Coupé

Mercedes-Benz Sport-Light Coupé
Mercedes-Benz W114 and W115
Mercedes-Benz W123
Mercedes-Benz W124
Mercedes-Benz W126 S-Class 1979–1991
Mercedes-Benz W201 (190)
Mercedes W113
Morgan 4/4: The First 75 Years
Peugeot 205
Porsche 924/928/944/968
Porsche Boxster and Cayman
Porsche Carrera – The Air-Cooled Era
Porsche Carrera - The Water-Cooled Era
Porsche Air-Cooled Turbos 1974–1996
Porsche Water-Cooled Turbos 1979–2019
Range Rover First Generation
Range Rover Second Generation
Range Rover Third Generation
Range Rover Sport 2005–2013
Reliant Three-Wheelers
Riley – The Legendary RMs
Rolls-Royce Silver Cloud
Rover 75 and MG ZT
Rover 800 Series
Rover P5 & P5B
Rover P6: 2000, 2200, 3500
Rover SD1
Saab 92–96V4
Saab 99 and 900
Shelby and AC Cobra
Subaru Impreza WRX & WRX STI
Sunbeam Alpine and Tiger
Toyota MR2
Triumph Spitfire and GT6
Triumph TR6
Triumph TR7
Volkswagen Golf GTI
Volvo 1800
Volvo Amazon

NSU Ro80

THE COMPLETE STORY

MARTIN BUCKLEY

THE CROWOOD PRESS

First published in 2023 by
The Crowood Press Ltd
Ramsbury, Marlborough
Wiltshire SN8 2HR

enquiries@crowood.com

www.crowood.com

© Martin Buckley 2023

All rights reserved. No part of this publication may be reproduced or transmitted in any form or by any means, electronic or mechanical, including photocopy, recording, or any information storage and retrieval system, without permission in writing from the publishers.

British Library Cataloguing-in-Publication Data
A catalogue record for this book is available from the British Library.

ISBN 978 0 7198 4174 3

Acknowledgements
Firstly, thanks to Phil Blake, my 'guru' on all Ro80 matters, who read and corrected my draft of this book and was also hugely helpful with pictures and illustrations. The vast majority of images reproduced here are from Phil's archive. Andreas Meyer of the German Ro80 club also devoted a lot of time to looking through my words and putting me straight where necessary. My editor at *Classic and Sports Car* magazine also helped with pictures. Finally, I am indebted to Stuart Bladon and Ray Hutton – formerly of *Autocar* magazine during the time of the Wankel Spider and Ro80 – for access to their archives of pictures and original notes on these cars.

Typeset and designed by D & N Publishing, Baydon, Wiltshire

Cover design by Blue Sunflower Creative

Printed and bound in India by Replika Press Pvt Ltd

CONTENTS

	Preface	6
	INTRODUCTION: AN ELEGANT VISION OF YESTERDAY'S FUTURE	7
	NSU Ro80 Timeline	14
CHAPTER 1	THE LITTLE PRINZ OF NECKARSULM	15
CHAPTER 2	THE FLAWED GENIUS OF FELIX WANKEL	37
CHAPTER 3	LEAP OF FAITH: THE WANKEL SPIDER	47
CHAPTER 4	CAR OF THE YEAR, CAR OF THE DECADE?	59
CHAPTER 5	LAST CHANCE SALOONS 1968–77	95
CHAPTER 6	BUYING YESTERDAY'S FUTURE	157
APPENDIX	THE WANKEL 'CLUB'	169
	Sources and Further Reading	174
	Index	175

PREFACE

This is probably the first book published in English on the NSU Ro80 and it is long overdue. For this reason, I have avoided the temptation to get too distracted by the Wankel-engined vehicles that paralleled the Ro80 or came after it, because these have been well covered in English and really only have the engine in common with the NSU.

While the Wankel rotary engine is integral to the character of the car, this book is a look at the life and times of the NSU Ro80 rather than a history of the engine itself.

The many intrigues that swirled around the Wankel engine in its early years have been well covered by other writers.

This book is not intended to be a detailed history of the complicated politics surrounding the Wankel rotary or even a really deep look into the technical mysteries of the engine (although inevitably both topics are touched upon as the story of the car unfolds). Rather, it is an appreciation of arguably the most interesting Wankel rotary-powered car of all, and the only one designed to take full advantage of what the Wankel had to offer in terms of packaging and refinement.

I hope you find out a few things that you did not know in the pages that follow and, even if you don't end up acquiring an example of what I consider to be the last great bargain in the world of 'significant' classic cars, you can at least enjoy reading about the NSU Ro80 as much as I enjoyed writing about it.

Martin Buckley
Gloucestershire, December 2021

INTRODUCTION: AN ELEGANT VISION OF YESTERDAY'S FUTURE

The NSU Ro80 is the most celebrated motoring lost cause of the second half of the twentieth century, out-ranking the likes of the Edsel and the DeLorean. This is because, unlike those statements of misplaced optimism and ego, it was a good car. Not just good – the NSU Ro80 is one of the *great* saloons.

Launched in September 1967, the NSU Ro80 was an all-new four door, five seater car from a West German company that, post war, had never made anything other than economy runabouts, motorcycles and mopeds. This in itself would have been enough of a risk, but the NSU Ro80 ('Ro' for rotary, '80' the factory design number) was also the world's first purpose-built twin-rotor Wankel-engined family saloon. This compact, refined and elegantly simple power unit was the first really new concept in the realm of internal combustion engines for ninety years to achieve mass production. It was a bold statement of confidence in this new technology from a company that had been developing the engine since the 1950s and had already partly proved the idea in its low-volume, single rotor Wankel Spider of 1964–67. Based on the Sports Prinz coupé, just 2,375 of these rear-engined roadsters were produced. However, the Ro80 represented a step change in the firm's commitment to Dr Felix Wankel's brainchild. This was a prestige car created from scratch around the advantages the engine had to offer, packaged for maximum interior space and wrapped in a futuristic and slippery five-seater body that pointed the way to the best styling of the 1980s and 1990s.

The shape is another major element of the car's appeal. Breathtakingly well proportioned, with no unnecessary fuss, somehow it did not look German, even if the beautiful Fuchs alloy wheels – similar to those of the early Porsche 911 – are a clue.

Yet a car like the Ro80 could only really have come from Germany, where there was a passion for research and a pride in engineering not found elsewhere in Europe. In the

Felix Wankel, inventor of the rotary engine that bears his name, approved of the Ro80 but was not closely involved with its design.

1980s it was calculated that the German motor industry spent more on research and development than the French, Italian and British motor industries put together.

Today's BMW and Mercedes products are as susceptible to faults as anything else; but in the era of the Ro80, the German car industry was steeped in an almost militaristic discipline. Moreover, Germany offered high standards of technical education, fostering a belief in the ability of its products to break new ground while maintaining customer confidence. The reliability of German cars was rivalled only by Japan, which probably explains why the Wankel rotary engine only prospered in these two fastidious engineering cultures.

Much was made at the time of the Ro80's aerodynamics – the fact that it had been designed in a wind tunnel. It *was* a slippery shape, but the profile for the Ro80 was instinctively aerodynamic. It was not in fact put into a wind tunnel at the Stuttgart Technical Research Institute (Europe's first wind tunnel, opened by Dr Kamm in 1930) until the design of the

■ INTRODUCTION: AN ELEGANT VISION OF YESTERDAY'S FUTURE

ABOVE: **NSU reinvented its branding for the futuristic Ro80.**

The world gets its first view of a car that still captures imaginations 55 years on.

car was virtually complete. The drag coefficient was found to be 0.355, which was 30–40 per cent lower than most modern saloons in 1967.

The list of technical niceties did not stop there: front-wheel drive, superb power steering and four-wheel disc brakes gave the Ro80 top-drawer handling and driver appeal; long-travel strut suspension endowed it with a comfortable, absorbent ride. To mask the Wankel's poor low-speed torque, NSU specified a three-speed, semi-automatic transmission with no clutch pedal. Instead, there was a micro switch in the gear knob that operated a vacuum system.

The car was a masterpiece, considered by many to be the finest vehicle of its type in the world. However, it had one fatal flaw: its engine.

Plain steel wheels, no headrests and contrasting black paintwork under the front bumper on the pre-production Ro80.

INTRODUCTION: AN ELEGANT VISION OF YESTERDAY'S FUTURE

Claus Luthe (left) and Ewald Praxl with the famous scale model of the Ro80.

Gerd Stieler von Heydekampf with the Car of the Year award given to the Ro80 by the English magazine *CAR* in 1968.

Early examples of the NSU Ro80 suffered from acute wear of rotor tip seals, meaning that after 15,000 miles (24,000km) – or even fewer – owners of early models began to notice a lack of power and increased fuel consumption, which was never a strong point of the Wankel at the best of times. When this happened, engines became difficult to start and smoked heavily. As a result, NSU were generous with

After the merger with Audi, the Ro80 became the flagship of a much larger range of cars between 1969 and 1977.

LEFT: **The Ro80 was also awarded car of the year by the Dutch magazine** *Autovisie*.

9

■ INTRODUCTION: AN ELEGANT VISION OF YESTERDAY'S FUTURE

DRIVING THE Ro80

The handling and roadholding of this substantial saloon set new standards in 1967.

It would be fatuous to claim that the Ro80 'drives like a modern car'. In almost every measurable way it cannot hope to match the standards of performance, cornering power and refinement – let alone fuel consumption – that are routinely expected of the 21st-century automobile. It does not have airbags, anti-lock brakes, stability controls or any of the other safety factors that make accidents so much more survivable than they were fifty years ago. It is roomy and well packaged, but rather narrow for a car of this class in today's world.

Yet, judged as an individual entity, it is hard not to be impressed by the feeling of calmness, capability and composure that pervades this amazing motor car. It is very much a case of not what the NSU Ro80 does but the way that it does it that makes it such a special experience even today, fifty-five years on.

The manner in which the doors shut gives a first impression of good build quality without being in any way lavish or heavy: finish is of the order of a BMW of its time, but not quite so rich as a Mercedes or as rugged as a Volvo of the 1960s and 1970s. Only the cheap grey carpet in the huge boot grates slightly, and perhaps you will miss the electric windows to be expected on such a prestigious car.

Under the bonnet the compact Wankel engine is smothered by the ancillaries, making the point that while NSU had successfully built a tiny, powerful engine, the component makers were still only providing large, heavy full-sized alternators, starter motors and carburettors. NSU missed a trick by not putting the dipstick on the same side as the oil filler, given how regularly you need to check the oil: but otherwise there is not much to see other than the big inboard brake calipers.

The driving position seems just right – commanding, with a perfect wheel-to-pedal relationship. All-round vision is certainly superior to most modern vehicles with their massively wide roof pillars; and the cleanly designed dashboard with its orange and red 'pilot lights' and pull/twist switch gear is refreshingly free of distractions.

The seats are soft and comfortable, although your neck will feel oddly vulnerable in an early car without headrests. The vinyl seats found in some cars are sticky in hot weather, and later types tend to hold you better in corners. Newcomers usually notice the way the seat belts attach is at odds with the uniformity of modern cars and that the front floor is flat and obstruction free. The

warranty claims – perhaps too generous – and many cars had as many as nine new engines.

The huge costs associated with these failures sent NSU into the arms of Volkswagen–Audi in 1969 and, as word got around about the Wankel engine's woes, sales plummeted. Rather than hitting the planned 15,000 cars a year break-even point, by 1973 production had plummeted to only five Ro80s a day.

10

engine should start immediately and will not be spectacularly quieter – or all that much smoother – than a reciprocating unit at tickover.

With your foot on the brake pedal select a gear: the initial acceleration will seem almost ponderous as the torque converter churns, and there is no question of spinning the wheels. However, by the time you are going 30 or 40mph (48/64km/h), there is more of an impression of liveliness as the revs build and smooth out.

If the gear change is well adjusted, you can whip smartly into second (do not rest your hand on the gear lever, and tuck your left foot away so as to resist the temptation of mistaking the brake for a clutch pedal), floor the throttle and swish turbine-like up to 80mph (129km/h) or more with no sign of vibration or strain.

Three-figure speeds are arrived at quickly in top from here and you can cruise virtually at the Ro80's maximum – any good one will easily show 115mph (185km/h) – but 90 is a good compromise if you want to keep the fuel consumption in check.

Two things are now evident. First, the car is really exceptionally stable and impervious to side winds: the sense that the NSU steering does not require any guidance at high speed makes it very relaxing. Second, wind noise is generally low, so you can listen to the radio even at very high speeds.

The strong, progressive brakes are so confidence inspiring that you don't give them a thought. The car just stops. Firm-ish at low speeds but impervious to speed humps, the long-travel suspension does not bounce or pitch. The steering is delightfully consistent in feel. It is light, but precise, so that you know exactly what is going on and with no 'lumps' in the flow of servo assistance, so that the fact that it is powered is not conspicuous. This was perhaps the first true assistance rather than power take over, the best of its type in the world. The fact that an Ro80 generates more roll than modern drivers are used to is in some respects a function of the huge amount of cornering power it has; you cannot change its attitude by throttle position, or upset it with the brakes. In a tight corner taken very, very fast the car will find its limits in the form of massive understeer, but in general fast driving it conducts itself magnificently, the silky feel and turbine response of its engine merely an important highlight of a superbly conceived saloon.

For once the car lived up to the hype: it really was something different.

At a lower level, sales lasted until 1977, when the NSU marque died and Ro80's place on the production lines was taken by the Porsche 924. Its legacy survived in several generations of large aerodynamic Audi saloons of the 1980s and 1990s, but the Germans seemed content to let the Japanese car firm Mazda carry the torch for rotary technology into the future.

■ INTRODUCTION: AN ELEGANT VISION OF YESTERDAY'S FUTURE

KEY PLAYERS IN THE WANKEL AND Ro80 STORY

Bercot, Pierre Citroën boss who championed the Wankel.

Pierre Bercot, Citroën boss and champion of the Wankel concept.

Brockhaus, Herbert Head of testing, NSU.

Herbert Brockhaus, head of testing at NSU.

Bunford, Max Financier: Creator of Comobil/Comotor.

Cole, Ed GM engineer/executive and Wankel enthusiast.

Ed Cole of General Motors.

Fiedler, Fritz Austrian-born Rolls-Royce engineer who developed the 'cottage loaf' rotary diesel engine.

Frankenburger, Victor Technical Director of NSU, played a major role in the development of the Wankel engine.

Froede, Walter Head of research at NSU, key figure in creation of a practical, commercially-produced Wankel engine.

von Heydekampf, Gerd Stieler NSU executive and engineer, former Opel boss.

Hoeppner, Ernst Felix Wankel's assistant and 'right arm'.

Hurley, Roy President of Curtiss-Wright Corp., first Wankel licence holders.

Roy Hurley of Curtiss-Wright Corporation.

Hutzenlaub, Ernst Businessman who formed a patent management company with Felix Wankel.

12

INTRODUCTION: AN ELEGANT VISION OF YESTERDAY'S FUTURE

Keppler, Wilhelm Advisor to Adolf Hitler and mentor of Felix Wankel.

Wankel's mentor, Wilhelm Keppler.

Lotz, Kurt VW's second post-war CEO (succeeding Heinrich Nordhoff) during the merger of Audi and NSU in 1969.

Kurt Lotz, chairman of Volkswagen from 1968 to 1971.

Matsuda, Tsuneji president of Toyo Kogyo (Mazda).

Paschke, Dr NSU chief engineer.

Praxl, Ewald NSU chief designer and 'father of the Ro80'.

Rowland, 'Tiny' Controversial South African-born businessman and Chairman of Lonrho who bought Felix Wankel's interests in Wankel Gmbh in 1971 for DM 100 million.

'Tiny' Rowland, the colourful tycoon who bought out Felix Wankel's interest in Wankel Gmbh in 1971.

Wankel, Felix Mechanical engineer, inventor of the Wankel rotary engine.

Felix Wankel in his workshop.

Yamamoto, Kenichi Engineer and Mazda executive who supervised the development of the Wankel engine for Mazda.

Luthe and Praxl with their creation.

Yamamoto Kenishi, Mazda's Wankel supremo.

13

NSU Ro80 TIMELINE

1949 NSU restart motorcycle production with the 98cc Fox.
1951 Felix Wankel makes first contact with NSU, working as a consultant.
1953 NSU motorcycles win the first of five world championships for 125cc and 250cc motorcycles.
1954 Development of the rotary engine begins at NSU.
1956 Works team of streamliner motorcycles breaks multiple world records at Bonneville, including 50cc record (at 121mph/195km/h), boosted by Wankel-type supercharger.
1957 First DKM Wankel engine runs. Prinz baby car introduced.
1958 First KKM Wankel engine runs.
1960 $8 million now spent by NSU on Wankel development.
1961 Dr Froede publishes his engineering paper on the Wankel rotary engine. Toyo Kogyo (Mazda) and Daimler-Benz become Wankel engine licensees. Planning of Wankel-engined Type 80 saloon begins.
1962 Production of Wankel Spider sanctioned by NSU board.
1963 Wankel Spider production begins (first customer deliveries 1964); basic design of the Ro80 approved by NSU board.
1965 NSU shows twin-rotor Wankel engine design at Frankfurt Motor Show.
1966 First working Ro80 prototype begins testing. Wankel Spider wins German GT Rally Championship.
1967 Ro80 launched at Frankfurt show. Wankel Spider and NSU motorcycle production ends.
1968 NSU Ro80 voted Car of the Year by international panel of judges. First right-hand-drive UK imports: four x circular headlamps.
1969 Peak sales year for Ro80. NSU merges with Auto Union Audi, to become part of the Volkswagen group. The K70, cheaper, piston-engined sister model to the Ro80 launched as an NSU at Geneva but withdrawn.
1971 K70 relaunched as a VW.
1972 Felix Wankel sells his interest in design to business magnate Tiny Rowland.
1973 Last small, rear-engined/air-cooled NSUs produced.
1974 VW K70 production ends.
1975 Revised Ro80 with bigger rear lights shown at Frankfurt.
1976 Testing of Ro80s with a bigger KKM871 engine begins. Twenty Audi 100s fitted with KKM871 built for evaluation.
1977 NSU Ro80 production ends.
1985 Audi NSU Auto Union officially becomes simply 'Audi AG'.
1988 Dr Felix Wankel dies aged 86.

CHAPTER ONE

THE LITTLE PRINZ OF NECKARSULM

'Obviously this new German challenger has been produced only after enormous thought: and in the minds of designers as well as buyers in all parts of the world it will provoke a very thoughtful reaction.'

The Motor road test of the NSU Prinz, 25 February 1959

Not far from Stuttgart, in the German state of Baden Wurttemberg, the city of Neckarsulm is located where the river Neckar meets the Sulm. It was a settlement of fewer than 4,000 hard-working, thrifty Swabian inhabitants in 1892, the year when Heinrich Stoll's Neckarsulmer Radwerke adopted the acronym 'NSU' as the brand name for its bicycles. The original shield-shaped badge depicted the heraldic stags' antlers of the former Kingdom of Wurttemberg and the cross of the Knights of the Teutonic order, who had a castle at Neckarsulm in the middle ages. Today, home to 26,000 residents, Neckarsulm is still a base for car manufacturing in the form of one of Volkswagen's main German assembly plants, where it builds the larger Audi models on a 1.3 million square metre site to the tune of 160,000 cars per year.

The roots of NSU, like so many other turn-of-the-century car manufacturers, lie in bicycle making. Having established its engineering credentials as a maker of sewing machines in 1900, the firm built the first of the motorcycles that contributed so much to the fame of the marque around the world in the coming decades. By the mid-1950s NSU would become the largest producer of motorcycles in the world.

Yet, before the end of the following decade, NSU would be part of the VW group. At the time of this uneasy merger (which was really a takeover), a few may have recalled that in the early 1930s it was NSU who had commissioned, in prototype form, the first iteration of Dr Porsche's rear-engined wonder car. Others may have ruminated on the fact that the

The 1956–62 250cc Supermax was derived from the Max and Spezialmax and featured improved rear suspension. In the 1950s NSU were the biggest motorcycle manufacturers in the world: production peaked in 1955 at 350,000.

15

■ THE LITTLE PRINZ OF NECKARSULM

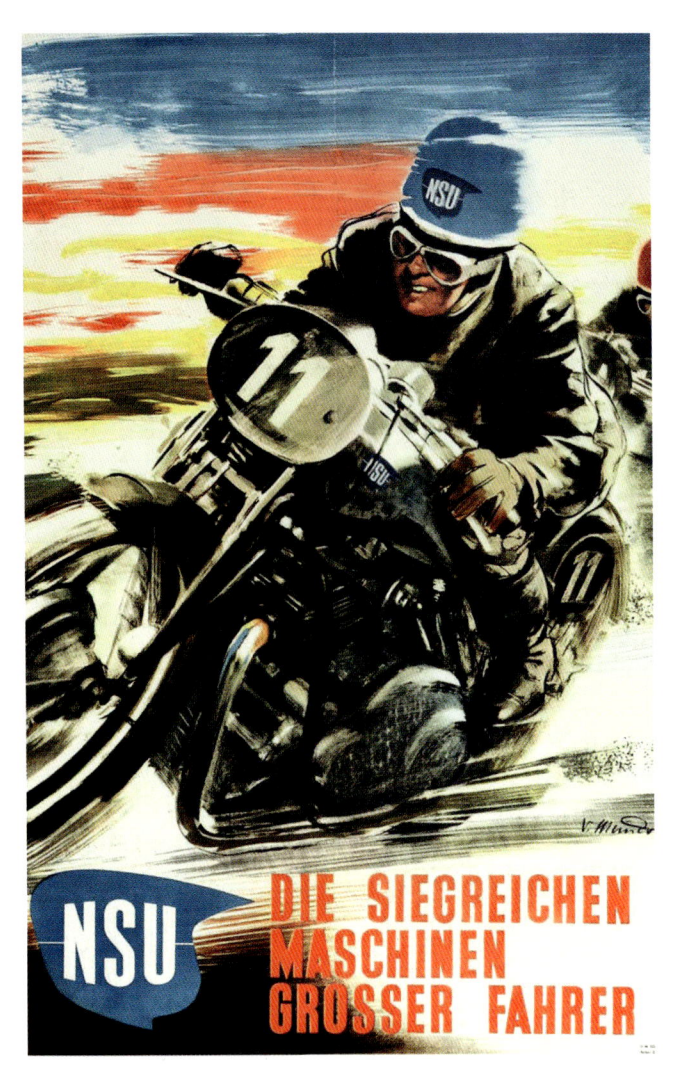

NSU promoted its two-wheelers widely in competition through to the mid-1950s. Its unsupercharged 125 and 250cc Rennsport racing bikes were the fastest of their type in the world and won five world championships between 1953 and 1955.

Surprisingly, NSU continued to produce pedal bikes until the 1960s.

VW Beetle was not even a twinkle in Adolf Hitler's eye when, in 1905, NSU supplemented the success of its two-wheelers (six different models were offered by 1904) with automobile production.

The first Neckarsulm-built four-wheelers were to a Belgian design called the Pipe and produced under licence.

However, the first true all-NSU motor car did not appear until 1906 – the original 6/10 PS being quickly joined by the more powerful 15/24 PS.

These were conventionally engineered and relatively light four-cylinder, side-valve touring cars of between 1.3- and 4-litre capacity, which gave a good account of themselves in reliability trials and, after the 1914–18 war, in racing. A works team of three 5/15 NSUs won the 1923 Avusrennen; three years later, at the same venue, the six-cylinder, 30bhp cars swept the board with a 1/2/3/4 class win at an average speed only a few miles per hour short of Caracciola's straight-eight Mercedes.

THE LITTLE PRINZ OF NECKARSULM

GERD STIELER VON HEYDEKAMPF 1905–1983

Gerd Stieler von Heydekampf is the man behind the wheel.

Born in Berlin, Gerd Stieler von Heydekampf was an engineer of Prussian military background whose wisdom and guidance were highly instrumental in bringing the Ro80 to fruition. Having gained his engineering doctorate in 1929, he spent the formative years of his career working in America, first with the industrial boiler makers Babcock and Wilcox and then at the Baldwin Locomotive Works before returning to Germany in a management position at Adam Opel in 1936.

The car and truck maker had been acquired by GM in 1929. Its new Brandenburg Works was Germany's largest truck-making plant, producing 130,000 of the famous Opel Blitz commercial vehicles between 1935 and August 1944, when the plant was virtually obliterated by an RAF raid. These vehicles, thought latterly to have been built by forced labour, were used extensively by the German military during the war and were most infamously deployed as 'Gas Vans' during the holocaust, although there is no evidence that von Heydekampf knew anything of this – or could have done anything much about it if he did.

Already on the board of Opel, von Heydekampf was General Manager at Opel by 1938 before being hand-picked by Albert Speer in 1942 to run the Tank and Locomotive commission at Kassel, succeeding Dr Porsche, whose complex designs and constant technical changes were holding up production. As a *Wehrwirtschaftsführer* with responsibility for 60,000 workers, von Heydekampf was an important figure whose wartime activities guiding German tank production did not go unnoticed by the occupying Americans post-1945. When interrogated by the Combined Intelligence Objectives SubCommittee in June 1945, von Heydekampf was able to give a great deal of detail about the why and how of wartime German tank design and construction, even down to Hitler's preference for air-cooled engines. He claimed that he had only joined the Nazi party in 1940 when it was suggested he did so by the local Nazi *Gautier*: other accounts say he joined up as early as 1933.

Towards the end of the war he conspired with Albert Speer against Hitler's industrial 'scorched earth' policy. After the war – and a short spell in prison due to his well-known Nazi sympathies – von Heydekampf joined NSU as a consultant in 1948 then as a full employee in 1950, with responsibility for purchasing. In 1953 he joined the board, where he remained until a heart attack forced his retirement in 1971.

With his big cigars and mid-Atlantic accent, the good-natured and approachable von Heydekampf had a strong whiff of Detroit about him. Anxious to change NSU's image he guided the firm not only through the highs and lows of the Wankel adventure – and merger with Audi – but also kept the production lines of the relatively small Neckarsulm factory humming in the face of seemingly irresistible 1950s and 1960s competition from the ever-greater strength of VW and the bottomless pockets of GM-funded Opel.

THE VW CONNECTION

By now NSU had a dedicated facility at Heilbronn making private cars, taxi cabs and light trucks. However, the economic situation in Germany had become so dire by the end of the 1920s that NSU were forced, in 1928, to sell the factory to the Italian manufacturer Fiat, which agreed to keep building NSUs on the site until 1932.

From 1930, alongside NSU models the Italians produced local versions of established Fiat vehicles on this site. During World War II they also assembled NSU/Fiat-badged cars for export markets, sometimes to specifications not found elsewhere in the Fiat empire.

When NSU built three prototypes of the Porsche-designed KdF VW in 1933 – the true predecessor to the eventual Wolfsburg Beetle – they fell foul of the contract

■ THE LITTLE PRINZ OF NECKARSULM

A works team of NSUs won at Avusrennen in 1923 and 1926.

THE NSU-FIATS

When NSU, instructed by its backers the Dresdner Bank, aborted its plans for car production at its new factory at Heilbronn in 1929, the facility was sold to Fiat for one million Deutschmarks. Located a mere 7 miles (8km) apart from each other, NSU Automobil AG and NSU werke AG co-existed somewhat peacefully, the motorcycle makers even – briefly – making parts for the Heilbronn factory. They did fairly good business with locally produced versions of the Fiat 500 and 1100 (under licence from Fiat in Turin) pre-war, but post-war the situation became more uneasy, particularly when the NSU Werke at Neckarsulm began to feel that the car makers were beginning to profit from the successful image of its race-winning motorcycles. Relations turned sour – and legal – when it was announced that the Neckarsulmers planned to build an all new car in the same class as the soon to be released NSU-Fiat 600 and badge it as an NSU. However, a judge threw Fiat's complaints out of court, stating that the rather casual 1929 agreement carried no legal weight and was 'against the public interest'. After this ruling the NSU-Fiats became simple 'Neckars': the 'Jagst' was the 600, while the German 500 baby car was known as the 'Weinsberg'. Its version of the 1100 was badged Europa and in all cases trim levels were a little ahead of the basic Italian Fiats. Neckar production lasted until 1971.

NSU TYPE 32, FATHER OF THE BEETLE

When in 1935 Adolf Hitler commissioned Ferdinand Porsche to create a 'people's car' for working-class Germans, he was almost certainly aware of the small saloon that Dr Porsche had designed for NSU a year earlier. Although rather larger than the eventual KDF Wagen, the Type 32 had a rear-mounted, air-cooled boxer engine and torsion bar suspension. It presaged the general outline of what would become the famous VW Beetle and thus played a large role in maturing the designer's ideas on the matter of a true every-man small family saloon. Only three NSU Type 34s were built – rather noisy 1.4-litre cars that were good for 55mph (88km/h) on 20bhp; the one surviving example had managed 200,000 kilometres before being put out to grass, post-war, as a museum piece. Given that motorcycle sales were on the up, and fearing the displeasure of Fiat (who had the right to use the NSU name on its own cars in Germany) NSU thought better of the idea of going back into the car business. Hitler's concept was for a smaller and almost impossibly cheap people's car to thrum along his new autobahns. The three Type 60s that Dr Porsche delivered to the Fuhrer's brief were put through their paces – in the Alps, forests and on autobahns – by the Research Institute for Motor Vehicles. One of the young testers was a certain Walter Froede, key progenitor of the Ro80.

they had with Fiat not to go into direct competition. So the original NSU corporate entity concentrated on making motorcycles, encouraged by the technology-focused Nazi regime to find advanced solutions, as evidenced by the overhead camshaft, supercharged machines it displayed at the Berlin motorcycle show in 1935.

During the war, NSU's contribution was to build half-tracked Opel Olympia-engined motorcycles for the army called the *Kleines Kettenkraftrad* or NSU HK100.

The factory avoided bombing damage until two weeks before the cessation of hostilities. After serving briefly as a repair facility for the allied forces, the Neckarsulm works returned to two-wheeler production with the 98cc Quick and the 4-stroke 100cc Fox, both of which were single-cylinder machines. NSU assembled Italian Lambrettas under licence between 1950 and 1956 and then built a successful range of scooters of their own design that stayed in production until 1964. NSU reintroduced its pre-war Konsul I and

THE KETTENKRAFTRAD

This remarkable and highly thought of military off-road vehicle, designed by Ewald Praxl, was not a motorcycle or tricycle but really a small car with tracks. Patented in 1939 as a vehicle small enough to be delivered by the Junkers JU 52, it was arguably the first ATV (all terrain vehicle) as we know them today. With room for two passengers, the Kettenkraftrad HK101 was powered by a 1½ litre, 36bhp Opel Olympia engine – identical to the private car unit other than the sump pan and the 'off road' Solex carburettor – that sat behind the driver and drove through a three-speed high/low ratio gearbox that would give a somewhat terrifying 44mph (70km/h) maximum in the highest of those gears. Sitting on a sprung saddle the driver had a speedometer, rev counter and even a heater. Of the six torsion bar-suspended interleaved wheels each side only the fronts were driven: the extreme rear wheels tensioned the tracks, which had forty individually lubricated links each side. The front motorcycle-like forks could cope with shallow, low-speed turns but for anything more acute they operated a hydraulic system that stopped or slowed the tracks, depending on which way you wanted to turn – like a tank. Off road, the Kettenkraftrad was exceedingly agile and its qualities were much appreciated on the Eastern Front, where they first saw service in 1941. They were also used for laying communications cables and as aircraft tugs. All but 10 per cent of the total 8,500 output were produced by NSU, continuing until 1948 for agricultural use. In fact many of the military versions ended up being used on farms post-war and the survivors are now highly sought after.

Konsul II 350 and 500cc models from 1951 to 1954, but found worldwide fame with its little 50cc Quickly moped, which at the height of its popularity was being built at the rate of 1,000 units per day.

NSU promoted its two-wheelers widely in competition through to the mid-1950s. Its unsupercharged 125 and 250cc Rennsport racing bikes were the fastest of their type in the world (with 125bhp per litre) and won five world championships between 1953 and 1955, before the factory bowed out of Grand Prix activity in the face of growing costs and a flagging domestic motorcycle market.

Record breaking was seen as a cheaper way of capturing attention: in 1956 the works team decamped to the Bonneville Salt Flats for a remarkable assault on six different capacity class motorcycle records with a set of cigar shaped streamliners, the 50, 100, 125 and 250cc machines deploying

THE NSU QUICKLY

More than one million of these 49cc/35mph mopeds were built between 1953 and 1968, making the Quickly Neckarsulm's most famous contribution to affordable mass transportation. Based around a pressed steel frame, it featured leading link front suspension and, with a mere 1.4bhp, the pedals were often required when going up hills as well as for starting. Fondly remembered (usually by people who have never heard of the Ro80), most Quicklys were produced in basic 'N' form. Against a background of falling sales a variety of attempts were made to widen its appeal in the early 1960s, with fancier 'styling', higher compression or luxury features such as a kick starter and a speedometer.

hammock-type seating positions. At 211mph (340km/h) the 500cc twin took the absolute world speed record for motorcycles by a full 26mph (42km/h). The 250cc Delphin III crashed at 195mph (314km/h), but the 350 was timed at 189.5 mph (304.9km/h), the 125 at 150.3mph (241.8km/h) and the 100cc bike at 138mph (222km/h).

That the 50cc Baumn streamliner topped 121mph (194.7km/h) is possibly the most amazing achievement of all. Eight times more powerful than the production NSU moped at 12.8bhp (256bhp per litre), its secret was a belt-driven supercharger based on the as yet unheard-of rotary Wankel engine.

■ THE LITTLE PRINZ OF NECKARSULM

(Left-to-right) NSU works riders Ruppert Hollous and Werner Hass with NSU engineer Ewald Praxl.

RIGHT: **NSU** bikes were hugely successful in competition in the 1950s with their 125 Rennfox and 250cc 4-stroke Rennmax, the latter a **DOHC** 135mph (217km/h) machine with a six-speed transmission.

In 1956 NSU made record attempts at Bonneville in six capacity class records with cigar-shaped streamliners: the 211mph (340km/h), 500cc twin took the absolute world speed record for motorcycles by a full 26mph (42km/h).

22

THE RETURN TO CAR PRODUCTION

When NSU produced its last motorcycle in 1967, it had already been back in the motor car market for nine years with its Prinz range of economy runabouts. These cars now represent a long-lost world of euro-austerity motoring, in vehicles that were not sterile blobs of well-honed international 21st-century uniformity but had a strong national character and identity.

In late 1950s Germany, with the economic miracle well underway, NSU decided the time was right to go after a piece of the sub-Beetle domestic market, with a car that was as fast as the ubiquitous VW on half the engine size, but a lot less ponderous to drive. An initial attempt was a three-wheeler called the Max-Sabine designed by the firm's two-wheel design chief, Albert Roder. Work started in the summer of 1954 on the 250cc rear-engined three seater with a teardrop-shaped body.

The prototypes were ready for the firm's financial backers to inspect a year later, but when one of the VIP bankers got his little Kabine stuck on the marked-out test course, it was deemed prudent to have a re-think. Enter, in 1957, the Prinz: here was the firm's first four-wheeler since the 1920s, its intriguing engineering somewhat undermined by its comic styling and the motorcycle connotations of a two-cylinder, 600cc air-cooled engine that shared its oil with the gearbox. It came complete with dynastart (combined starter/generator) and an overhead camshaft driven by concentric links, like a vintage Bentley. The body was unitary, a completely alien technology at Neckarsulm that the engineers had to learn from scratch.

Fiat had been building NSU-badged versions of its own cars in Germany since 1930 and fell out badly with NSU over this proposed new car that was entirely of German conception and was in direct competition with its Heilbronn-built 600. However, a judge threw out Fiat's claims and the Italians renamed their German-built cars 'Neckar'.

The detractors of the baby NSU – of which 150 were built in pre-production form in 1957 – dismissed it as yet another oddity of West German austerity motoring in the 1950s. Those that drove one of the nearly 100,000 built between 1958 and 1962 realised that the first Prinz was a 'real' 60–70mph (97–113km/h) car, ideal for the young family trading up from a motorcycle and sidecar combination, but who didn't relish the indignity of driving a bubble car. Unlike many of its small car-making competitors, NSU had real credibility.

Front view shows independent suspension. The Prinz was intended to appeal to families who wanted to upgrade to a 'real' car rather than a 'bubble'.

Although tiny by modern standards, the Prinz was a well-engineered baby car.

■ THE LITTLE PRINZ OF NECKARSULM

DRIVING THE BABY NSUs

A common factor with all of these cars is that the imposition of the front wheel-arches impedes entry and cramps the foot well, slewing the pedals to the left. On the two-cylinder cars the soft engine mountings mean less vibration than you might imagine and they are really quite sweet from 2,000rpm up to as much as 7,000 – not that you would know, because there was no rev counter. The NSU's 'twins' are surprisingly lively at a mere 30bhp, because they weigh in at a mere 1,200lb (544kg). Despite the presence of swing axles, the two-cylinder cars have none of the handling problems linked to tail-heavy rear-engined cars. Clutches are light, as are the delightful steering and gear change, but the drum brakes – with no servo, as you would expect with such a featherweight car – need quite a heavy shove. Low-slung with two seats and additional luggage space, the dainty Sports Prinz coupé is a car for slim, slinky people – but they thrum along cheerfully in much the same way as the saloon brethren and cruise at 65mph (105km/h) with another 10mph (16km/h) in hand.

The 1000 and 1200 are smoother and faster although still quite noisy. It was possible to get a semi-auto in the 1200 – like the one found in the Ro80 – but the standard four-speed 'box was so sweet that you wonder who preferred this slightly clunky arrangement with a noticeable gap between second and third.

Most exciting of the breed by a huge margin are the TT models of course, with quad headlights, rev counter and a sports wheel. With no water jacket, there was an urgent ring to the engines in these cars and a constant whine from the transmission.

The gear change was fingertip light, fast and a joy to use. Accelerating through the gears, these aggressive little cars pulled hard from 2,000 to 6,000rpm with another 1,000 to go; 70mph (113km/h) comes up quickly before you have to change into top. The gear change felt fingertip-light, fast and a joy to use. Slightly more peak torque at much lower revs probably made the TT a nicer road car than the highly strung and much rarer, more specialised TTS, but the handling of both versions was very agile.

The 1961 Prinz 4 became popular throughout Europe.

Agile and fun-to-drive, the 583cc Prinz sat chest high to an average-sized man, could accommodate a (young) family of four and had a particularly nifty turning circle. Its single overhead camshaft, vertical-twin power unit was considered rather noisy (at least to British ears), but as a really compact car that refused to drop below 40mpg (7.8ltr/100km), would top 60mph (97km/h) on just 20bhp and had modest maintenance requirements, there was a lot to be said for the Prinz. Stirling Moss had one as a London run-about registered 'M 7'; in fact Moss was the first honorary President of the then recently formed NSU Prinz Owners Club of Great Britain. The astronaut John Glenn used his Prinz in preference to

The Prinz 4 was styled in house by Claus Luthe and built for twelve years.

■ THE LITTLE PRINZ OF NECKARSULM

The success of the Glas Goggomobil had shown NSU there was a market for something more grown up than a bubble car in Germany in the 1950s.

NSU opened a Lido at Cavallino in Italy in 1955.

the Corvette that GM had donated, simply because he had a longer commute and preferred to use the money he saved on fuel for his children's college fund.

The Prinz II and III were modestly refined versions of the original version with synchromesh gears, better trim and a little more power. In 1960 and 1961, the NSU Prinz II model achieved class victories in the Tour d'Europe and scored a third successive class win in the *Gran Premio Argentino*.

With the introduction of the Prinz 4 in 1961, the marque gained international appeal with a much more refined suspension and a far roomier and more modern body. This would be stretched and remodelled through various stages of development and achieved overall sales of more than one million units. It was popular all over Europe – particularly in Italy, where the Prinz was the most successful imported car; in Rome they were particularly favoured by nuns, in the 1960s and 1970s. The firm's Italian connections were so good that in 1955 the local importers opened the NSU Lido, a campsite at Cavallino near Venice, to which both two- and four-wheeled NSU owners were especially welcome.

The Prinz 4, launched at Frankfurt in 1961, was the mainstay of the range that accounted for over half those sales and stayed in production right through to 1973, by which time its rear-mounted parallel-twin power unit was looking distinctly outdated in a world of four-cylinder, BMC Mini-inspired, water-cooled front drivers. On the other hand, with such 'luxury' touches as a separate fuel gauge, windscreen washers and adjustable front seats, the Prinz must have looked positively lavish compared to the similarly priced Austin/Morris Mini 850.

26

THE LITTLE PRINZ OF NECKARSULM

Early 1970s UK advertising for the rear-engined NSU range pitched the car at economy-minded buyers in the Mini 850 class.

"£580 can solve balance of payments problem."

What with the rising costs of petrol, oil, licences and the like, car ownership has become pretty pricey.

And as a result your motoring budget has probably been moving deeper into deficit.

But you needn't worry any more. We've the answer to your problem.

All you need do is buy one of our NSU Prinz cars. At £582 it's just about the thriftiest four-seater in the business.

It'll take you 50 miles on just one gallon. And as the Prinz goes beautifully on two-star petrol, you'll have rock-bottom running costs.

You'll also discover that the Prinz needs very little servicing. So you'll save more here. Especially as many dealers give free servicing for the first year.

Then again, as the engine's air-cooled, you'll save on anti-freeze, radiator hoses, fan belts and such like. And the paintwork's so tough you can even save on garaging.

Mind you, the Prinz doesn't economize on everything. When it comes to performance, its 70 mph is as easy as being caught in a radar trap.

And you won't have to pay a penny extra for the extras. They come standard. The fully adjustable front seats, built-in heater-demister, cigar lighter, screen washers and electric clock. To name but a few.

On top of which, the Prinz is compact yet roomy, nimble and manoeuvrable. (That's why it's known as the Town Car.)

So if the future looks black, buy the NSU Prinz. The one car that won't drive you into the red.

NSU (Great Britain) Ltd, Harbour Way, Shoreham-by-Sea, Sussex.
Other models in the NSU range are as follows: Super Prinz £612, 1000c £694, 1000c Super £714, 1200c £797, 1200c Super £816, 1200TT £858, Ro80 £2280. (Approximate prices including PT.)

On just 30bhp the Prinz felt surprisingly lively because it was incredibly light for a four seater car (1,200lb/544kg) and despite the presence of swing axles it had none of the handling problems linked to tail-heavy rear-engined cars, by virtue of the fact that NSU had craftily inclined the cylinders back 45 degrees so that they were only just aft of the axle line.

It was hard to reconcile the pretty Bertone-styled Sports Prinz coupé with the shopping car image of the little bathtub-shaped Prinz saloon. Low slung with two seats and additional

■ THE LITTLE PRINZ OF NECKARSULM

Early British sales and marketing literature for the Prinz 4 and 1000L.

NSU-PRINZ 4

Series production of the NSU Prinz 4 began in September 1961. By the end of 1963, in little more than two years, NSU had built 150,000 of this model alone. The NSU Prinz 4 has successfully established itself on the international market as a compact car with a surprisingly large interior (the Prinz 4 is officially rated as a five-seater) and with a good performance. NSU will continue to produce this car, which has been fully developed for series production and which NSU engineers will nurse very carefully and improve still further in detail over the coming years, without change in design.

Happy is he who owns a PRINZ!

NSU-PRINZ 1000 L

It is natural for NSU engineers to develop cars with basically sporting lines. It is therefore not surprising that the NSU Prinz 1000 L continues this feature — it offers the driver liveliness and road holding that is seldom experienced in its class. Enthusiast who take pleasure in driving forcefully and skillfully, will enjoy taking the wheel of the Prinz 1000 L. Its particularly well chosen equipment and its superlative springing guarantee above-average travelling comfort. The economy of the NSU Prinz 1000 L is particularly gratifying. The spirited 1,000 c. c. four-cylinder engine does 36–42 m. p. g.

A first class car!

28

THE LITTLE PRINZ OF NECKARSULM

Increasing West German affluence turned buyers from motorcycles to cars but would also begin to leave Prinz behind, as rear-engined, air-cooled vehicles fell out of favour.

luggage space, the dainty Sports Prinz was first shown in 1959 as a glamorous coupé alternative to the utilitarian Prinz 30 – the most developed version of the original 1957–62 Prinz saloon. The first 250 bodies were actually built in Italy by Bertone, the remainder being produced in Germany by a coach builder local to NSU. Production finished in 1967 at 20,831 cars. Later examples had a 598cc engine and improved suspension of the Prinz 4; from 1965 front discs were fitted.

Mercedes-Benz had pioneered serious crash testing and it was rapidly becoming a necessity for those who wanted to sell cars in North America.

■ THE LITTLE PRINZ OF NECKARSULM

FROM TWO TO FOUR CYLINDERS, BUT STILL AIR-COOLED

The NSU 1000 of 1963 – with its distinctive lozenge-shaped headlamps – was the first of the 4-cylinder cars with which NSU could square-up fully to VW in the marketplace. The light alloy engine, with five main bearings and chain drive overhead camshaft, was slung transversely between the rear wheels but – as with the Prinz 4 – the centre of gravity was only just behind the axle line.

This was one of the few in-line air-cooled engines in a production car. Each of the cylinders had its own individual rocker cover and the exhaust manifolds fed directly into the exhaust heat exchanger. A selling point of these little NSUs was that they only had two grease points compared to the six of a Mini. Semi-trailing arm rear suspension was a refinement on the four-cylinder NSU and the 1000C's handling held no nasty surprises. It cruised at 70mph (113km/h) easily with another 10 miles per hour in hand, although economy suffered when you drove any of these air-cooled cars hard. Most of its additional length was accounted for in the wheelbase, so the 1000 was a genuine four-seater that looked and felt more grown up than the Prinz 4. This 45bhp middle child of the NSU babies was launched as a 1000 L or LS, depending on the level of trim, but was later re-badged C or CS.

The most famous and charismatic of the baby NSUs were the 1965–72 TT and TTS models, which with their trade-

The most famous of the baby NSUs were the 1965–72 TT and TTS models. With quad lights, propped engine covers and wide wheels, they were Germany's answer to the Mini Cooper S.

THE LITTLE PRINZ OF NECKARSULM

The twin Solex TT had 69bhp, but the 100bhp TTS – the fastest 1-litre production car in the world – was a homologation special, highly competitive in sub-1-litre racing and rallying.

The TT was a usable family car, but not an especially economical one if driven hard.

31

THE LITTLE PRINZ OF NECKARSULM

mark propped-open engine covers (not a pose but a real aid to cooling) and wide wheels – with hefty negative camber – were Germany's answer to the Mini Cooper and Cooper S. The TTS had the added distinction of an oil cooler slung in the air stream below its front bumper and was even bereft of hubcaps. The quickest way to spot one of these hot versions was by its quad headlamps.

The 4-cylinder engine's rugged build hinted at the fact that it had been designed as a 1500cc unit, so there was plenty of meat left in it to extract more power; the twin Solex TT had 69bhp while the TTS homologation special with forged pistons, extra high compression ratio and wild cam timing had as much as 100bhp if you opted for the Group 2 tuning kit. Even in standard 89bhp form, NSU claimed that the 100mph-plus TTS was the fastest 1-litre production car in the world with a wide range of gear and final drive ratios depending on customer requirements.

For the not quite so wild 1000TT, in 1968 NSU upped the capacity to 1177cc to make the 1200TT but kept the TTS at 998cc so as to maintain its competitiveness in sub-1-litre racing and rallying. Slightly more peak torque at much lower revs probably made the TT a nicer all-round road car than the TTS.

The 1200 range was a move in another direction. Germans were becoming more affluent and wanted bigger, more impressive-looking cars. NSU's response (the only one they could afford pending the introduction of the water-cooled, front-drive K70 in 1969) was to stretch the 1000 by 8 inches (203mm) in its wheelbase and give the front a fake 'grille'.

Launched as the 1085cc Type 110 in 1965, it became the 1177cc 110SC in 1966. NSU added to the confusion by almost immediately renaming this flagship rear-engined derivative the 1200C. It was available with semi auto (like the one found in the Ro80) with a micro switch in the top of the gear knob that operated the clutch via a vacuum unit.

The noble failure of the Ro80 was underpinned by the success of these rear-engined NSUs, which were respected for their engineering and had a fine competition pedigree; however, NSU was also at home in hill-climb racing. The 1962 season was a triumph for Karl-Heinz Panowitz, as he became the German Touring Car Hill Climb champion in all of the classes. Just a year later, Siegfried Spiess took the German Hill Climb title, and in 1965 the German GT Hill Climb champion at the wheel of an NSU Prinz 1000. Altogether, six German championship titles went to NSU cars between 1961 and 1968, and on the international scene the company won no fewer than twenty-nine touring car championships between 1962 and 1967. However, by the early 1970s the fate of the baby rear-engined NSUs had already been settled.

The 1200 was a longer wheelbase NSU1000 with a fake 'grille' created to keep interest in the rear-engined cars alive pending the introduction of the K70.

THE LITTLE PRINZ OF NECKARSULM

Extended nose allowed greater luggage capacity.

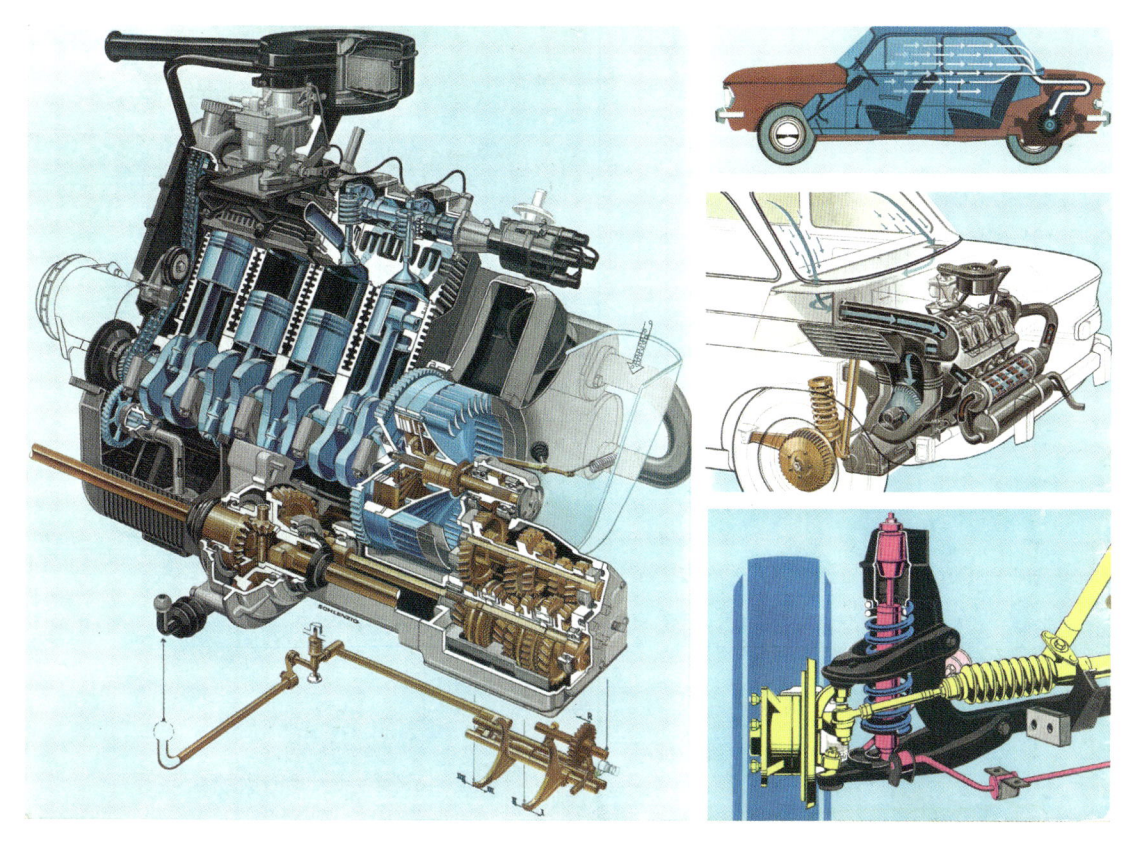

Brochure artwork shows a 4-cylinder, air-cooled engine's compact installation and front disc brakes.

33

THE LITTLE PRINZ OF NECKARSULM

Air-cooled, rear-engined cars were increasingly out of favour with environmentalists because their emissions were more difficult to control. The same applied to safety legislators, because these cars' handling – post Ralph Nader and his book *Unsafe at Any Speed* – was not deemed to be as 'safe' as that of conventional cars. Even if that was an unfair criticism of these nimble baby NSUs, nobody could deny it was a slightly wayward feeling car on a windy motorway, like most of its ilk. Worst of all, they were out of favour with the public because rear-engined cars had an image problem that did not sit well with the prosperous new horizons of the 1970s. So when NSU lost its independence in 1969, the fate of the rear-engined range was sealed. Nobody shed a tear when the crisp new 1973 VW Polo effectively replaced the Prinz and its derivatives.

By then technical problems that had beset the Ro80 since its 1967 inception had been widely broadcast and were well understood – although they were, in the main, solved. At that stage there was still some hope for a rotary-powered German luxury car, but it would carry an Audi rather than an NSU badge. The firm's last flirtation with rotary engines was a test fleet of C2 Audi 100s powered by a superb new version of the two-rotor Wankel, but even these failed to convince Audi management. The German adventure with the Wankel rotary engine, and the NSU name, died with the demise of the Ro80 in 1977.

With the departure of General Motors, Citroën and Mercedes licence-holders from the Wankel 'club', it was left to Mazda to develop the engine to an acceptable level of reliability. However, as of 2022 it has yet to build a successor to its last rotary car, the RX8, although it has made a comeback

The six-model NSU range in the early 1970s after the Audi-VW merger. The rear-engined cars would be killed off in 1973.

THE LITTLE PRINZ OF NECKARSULM

of sorts as a compact range extending engines in the hybrid crossover Mazda, the MX-30.

Forty-four years after the last example was built, the NSU Ro80 is defined less by its engine problems and more by its fabulous shape, an elegant rising wedge with a high tail and a low nose from the pen of one of the great unsung heroes of car design, Claus Luthe. Like everything about the Ro80, it showed an astonishingly sure touch from a company that had never built a large car before.

The politics, personalities and engineering that make up the story of this brave and enigmatic machine will be explored in more depth in the following chapters.

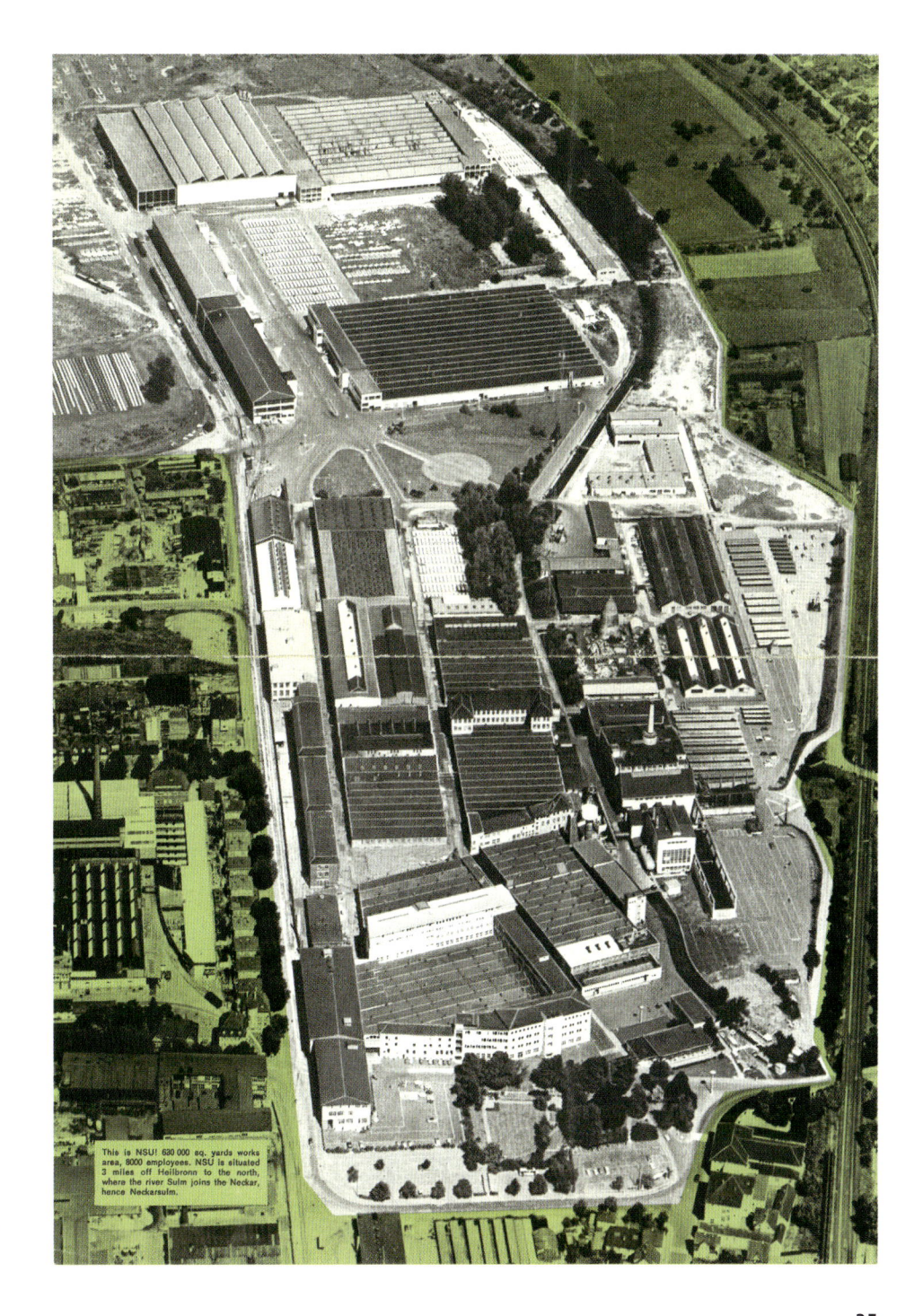

The Neckarsulm factory employed 8,000 people in the early 1960s.

■ THE LITTLE PRINZ OF NECKARSULM

WHAT THE PAPERS SAID

Throughout the range the unit is surprisingly smooth and, above all else, willing. It gives the feeling of being unburstable and, to all intents and purposes, it probably is, because its output has been deliberately restricted, partly in the interests of reliability and partly because in Germany insurance premiums rise steeply when the stated power output exceeds 20bhp.

The Motor, 25 February 1959, NSU Prinz road test

It retains the virtues of economy, small size, manoeuvrability and lively acceleration which made the Prinz 3 appealing as a town car, but to these qualities it adds greater refinement, the ability to seat four people and very full equipment...

Motor, 21 November 1962, road test of the NSU Prinz 4

Bearing in mind that its engine is under 600cc, it provides a high performance. Not only is the body attractive in appearance and in practical layout but its low build and smooth, low drag shape influence performance at medium and high speeds and contribute to sports car handling characteristics.

The Autocar, spring 1961, road test of the NSU Sport Prinz

Few 1-litre family cars can offer as much as the NSU Prinz 1000L. It may not be the quietest or the most comfortable car in this category, but in its performance, handling and equipment it must be one of the top contenders.

Autocar, July 1965, road test of the NSU Prinz 1000L

If there is anything more impressive than its formidable acceleration and 95mph top speed, it is the astonishingly stable way it scuttles round corners.

Motor, 1967 road test of the NSU TTS

Over half a million Prinz 4s were built and were particularly popular in Italy.

CHAPTER TWO

THE FLAWED GENIUS OF FELIX WANKEL

Dr Felix Wankel was the self-taught engineer who patented the idea for a workable rotary engine in 1929, having started work on the concept in 1924 while working at his day job in a publishing house in Heidelberg.

Born on 13 August 1902 in the Black Forest, Felix Heinrich Wankel was the son of a forestry official who was killed in World War I, but little else is known of his early life, about which he was always reticent.

Some have speculated that Wankel had learning disabilities; he was certainly known to be socially and emotionally awkward and may even have had some form of personality disorder. School bored him and he left with minimal qualifications (he only became an honorary doctor in 1969). Unable to afford to take up full-time further education, Wankel taught himself the principles of engineering by attending night school. He was spurred on by the idea for a new type of engine – smoother, lighter, more compact and cheaper to produce – that had first occurred to him as a young man of seventeen; he claimed to have dreamt about riding to a concert in a car he had built himself, powered by an engine that was 'half turbine, half reciprocating'.

By day Wankel worked in the publisher's office, but he spent much of his spare time experimenting with his ideas in a makeshift machine shop he ran with friends, dreaming of the day he could claim unemployment benefit so that he could work on his engineering projects full time. By 1924 Wankel had effectively conceived the engine that would make him famous throughout the world and filed a patent for it in 1929.

Considered a crank by some and a genius by others, Wankel was not a 'hands on' engineer but was gifted with an acute spatial imagination that allowed him to visualise his ideas and think in the abstract. He was evidently not put off by the fact that dozens of eminent engineers – almost since the dawn of recorded scientific endeavour – had attempted to build workable rotary pumps and engines, attracted by their elegant simplicity and inherent smoothness.

As early as 1588 a rotary water pump had been invented and the shipbuilding industry had long since solved the problem for its own requirements in the form of the steam turbine. In aviation, the jet or gas turbine engine was a close relative of the Wankel engine but its automotive applications were limited, as it was thirsty and, at part and medium loads, not suited to the way most people use motor cars on the road.

Although it was essentially an internal combustion engine (running on gasoline and the Otto cycle principles of induction/compression/ignition/exhaust), in most other respects the Wankel engine was an entirely new concept that did away with the limitations of valves, camshafts and cylinder head gaskets in favour of a triangular rotor – a Rouleaux triangle, sealed at each apex – spinning in an epitrochoid housing (with inlet and exhaust ports) and geared to rotate one-third as fast as the eccentric shaft it is mounted on.

As it span orbitally around the fixed shaft, the rotor – with bowed sides to squeeze the mixture and make compression – naturally formed chambers against the sides of the housing, seamlessly expanding and contracting for induction, compression power and exhaust events. The secret of its smoothness and high power to weight ratio compared to a reciprocating engine – which only made one power pulse every two revolutions – was that the Wankel made three power pulses for each full turn of its three-sided rotor. However, because it was geared to drive its output shaft three times faster, this equated to one power stroke per revolution, as in a two-stroke engine. Later this would have a bearing on how the cubic capacity of rotary engines was calculated.

Items such as cooling, fuel delivery and even what materials to build it out of lay in the future – in many cases for other engineers to address – because Felix Wankel dealt in broad

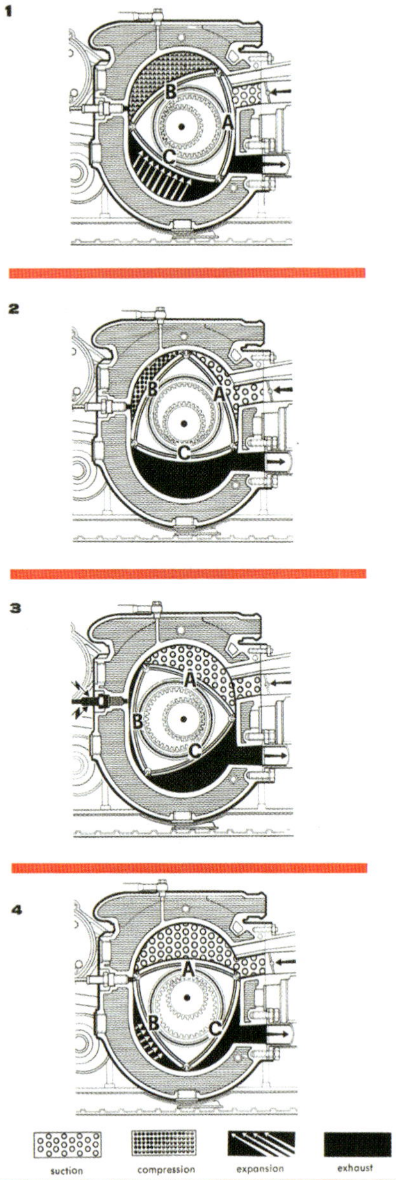

■ THE FLAWED GENIUS OF FELIX WANKEL

Schematic of the operation of the Wankel rotary engine published by NSU in the early 1960s.

Fig. 1
Chamber **A** is at its smallest, denoting the end of the exhaust phase and the beginning of induction.
Chamber **B** is being compressed.
Chamber **C** is expanding-working phase.

Fig. 2
Chamber **A** continues to grow larger, induction continues. Chamber **B** is still being compressed.
Chamber **C** has reached its maximum volume, i. e. end of the expansion phase, and the exhaust port is uncovered.

Fig. 3
Chamber **A** continues to grow larger, therefore, induction continues.
Chamber **B** is at its smallest, maximum compression has taken place, and the mixture is or will be ignited.
Chamber **C** is growing smaller, therefore, the exhaust phase is in progress.

Fig. 4
Chamber **A** has approached its maximum volume, the inlet port is about to be closed.
Chamber **B**, expansion phase in progress, gas pressure acting on the rotor flank turns the eccentric shaft.
Chamber **C**, exhaust phase in progress.

The next figure would be a repetition of Fig. 1 except that the letters will have been moved through 120°, but the phases would continue as indicated. However, the eccentric shaft (equivalent of crankshaft) has made one complete revolution and one complete thermodynamic cycle has occured. Three complete cycles take place during every complete rotor revolution, which requires three crankshaft revolutions.

Photograph No. D 11
Matrix No. D 110 (6 cm)

14

suction   compression   expansion   exhaust

concepts and left the detail for others. But he realised early on that the secret to rotary success lay with the apex seals: so he split his energies between finding a solution to this problem while earning a living as a freelance engineer working on the various sealing issues pertaining to conventional engines.

Ironically – given that the engine that bears his name does not have any – he also became an acknowledged world expert in valves, particularly the disc and rotary type used in aircraft engines produced by Daimler Benz and BMW. Wankel worked for both firms during the 1930s on aero engines in a search for more compact valve trains. By the end of the 1930s, Wankel had taken out patents on methods of sealing that are to this day considered his most important engineering contribution. They were also the basis of his post-war fortune, although Wankel always lived modestly; being extremely short-sighted he never drove and – at least until NSU presented him with one of the first Ro80s – the engineer was happy to be chauffeured around in an elderly Borgward saloon.

Felix Wankel, creator of the rotary engine that bears his name, 1902–1988.

Lightness was one of the big selling-points of the Wankel engine. This one weighs just 11kg (24lb).

An air-cooled 60cc Wankel engine, fitted to a lawn mower.

RIGHT: **NSU** engineers simplified Wankel's concept to produce the first planetary rotation variant of the engine with a fixed housing.

■ THE FLAWED GENIUS OF FELIX WANKEL

NAZI AFFLIATIONS

Wankel was an enthusiastic Nazi. Here he meets with Heinrich Himmler.

It is well established that, in his younger days, Felix Wankel had no problem with Hitler or the National Socialists. In the early 1940s he was briefly an *Obersturmbannführer* in the SS. The loss of his parents' modest family fortune after World War I had laid the groundwork for the sympathies he nurtured as a young man. He even met his future wife, Emma, while a member of Hitler Youth (they were married in 1936 but had no children) and had been involved with various right wing, anti-Semitic organisations from the early 1920s. He joined the Nazi party in 1922 and, after it was banned, led youth groups for a cover organisation teaching paramilitary techniques alongside normal scouting activities.

After the Nazi party was officially re-formed, Wankel renewed his membership and, in 1928, met Hitler to talk about technology and education. Wankel's mother had already helped form a local NSDAP section in Lahr; here Felix met up with regional leader Robert Heinrich Wagner, who invited him to lead the Hitler Youth wing in Baden. Wankel claimed to have resigned from the party in 1932. He was subsequently imprisoned for several months after he supposedly exposed Wagner's corrupt dealings, although it has also been suggested that, as a hardcore 'purist' National Socialist, Wankel took exception to the more commercial elements who wanted to cosy up with big business.

Wilhelm Keppler, the man who had organised Wankel's meeting with Hitler, had the young engineer released and, throughout the war, continued to support his research. Though by no means a savoury individual, Keppler was Felix Wankel's mentor and a key figure in the story of the Wankel engine. A chemical engineer who had fought in World War I, Keppler was introduced to Adolf Hitler by Heinrich Himmler and was an early financial backer of the Nazi party.

In 1936 Keppler, now a Reich Commissioner for external affairs, set Felix Wankel up in a workshop in Lindau where he could work alone on his various projects for the likes of Junkers, Borsig (Germany's largest maker of railway rolling stock) and the piston-

THE FIRST WORKING WANKEL ENGINES

Wankel, still working at Lindau with his favourite engineer Ernest Hoppener, had settled on his *Drehkoibenmotor* or DKM motor. This was essentially a sort of bulbous triangle-shaped rotor circling in a peanut- or dumbbell-shaped housing that is the basis of the rotary engine as we know it today. However, in his pursuit of 'pure' rotary motion, the designer envisaged that both the rotor and the housing would circulate.

Hoppener could realise Wankel's thoughts like nobody else. Seeing that one of the keys to success was the ability

During World War II Wankel developed seals and rotary valves for German aircraft engines built by BMW and Daimler-Benz, like this 24-cylinder DB604.

ring manufacturer, Goetze. At one stage he was working on plans for a rotary-engined hydrofoil torpedo boat – just the sort of fiendish super-weapon that excited the Nazi high command – and a compact torpedo engine for Junkers.

The defeat of Germany in 1945 resulted in the occupation and partial destruction of Wankel's workshops by the French. This setback – along with a term in prison in France – at least gave Wankel the time to get momentum behind his rotary engine ideas, working through dozens of potential combinations of rotor and housing designs that he eventually published in an exhaustive book in 1963.

Meanwhile, Wilhelm Keppler found himself in front of the Americans at the Nuremberg Trials, having become even more deeply embroiled in the Nazi regime, and at his April 1949 sentencing was awarded ten years. Not in the best of health Keppler was released in April 1951, as the American government, distracted by the Korean war, began to take a less bullish attitude towards former Nazis – even those of the calibre of Wilhelm Keppler, who never renounced his Nazi beliefs and who had once enjoyed the use of an office adjacent to that of the führer.

Finding himself hospitalised in Stuttgart in the year of his release, Keppler was placed in a bed next to an NSU executive. Still convinced of Felix Wankel's genius, he mentioned to his fellow patient that NSU might be interested in a design for a rotating disc valve created by his friend and protégé. Thus, Wankel's association with NSU began, initially as a consultant on rotary valves for its motorcycle engines. In fact the company, headed by chief executive Gerd Von Heydekampf, did not agree to fund the development of a rotary engine until 1954; but it was his subsequent total belief in the idea that made it possible for NSU to bring it to fruition. Von Heydekampf had joined NSU in 1949: initially he was merely a 'consultant', but was effectively leading the company by the time Felix Wankel turned up on the scene.

to produce very accurately produced inner housings, he designed a special machine that, by keeping the cutting edge perpendicular to the grinding surface, ensured accuracy.

The first working DKM did not run until 1957. While it matched Wankel's promise of very high revs – 25,000rpm – and smoothness, it was also relatively heavy for its 21bhp (because it needed a second casing over the rotating one) and presented fiendish ignition and servicing complications with its internal spark plug.

If Felix Wankel fathered the new engine, it was NSU's chief engineer Dr Walter Froede, working with his chief engineer Dr Paschke, who tamed and civilized it for commercial use.

THE FLAWED GENIUS OF FELIX WANKEL

It had been Froede who first went to see Wankel at his Lindau workshop in 1951. While cautious of some of the inventor's more extreme ideas, Froede came away impressed and recommended to his immediate superior Dr Victor Frankenberger – head of production at NSU – that the company should make a contract with Wankel.

His KKM *Kreiskolbenmotor* (circuitous piston engine) Wankel engine first ran in April 1958 after experiments with different numbers of lobes and chamber shapes that did not take Felix Wankel's earlier research for granted. He finally came down in favour of a variation on one of Wankel's discarded ideas, in which the casing was static and the rotor moved in a planetary cycle. This not only simplified and lightened the engine considerably (the first running unit weighed just 37lb/16.7kg) but also offered a wider range of porting positions and combustion chamber shapes.

However, Felix Wankel – a difficult character at the best of times – was not happy. In his eyes, this was an engineering compromise that corrupted the purity of his brainchild.

'You have made a cart horse out of my race horse' was Wankel's comment. 'If only we had a cart horse!' was von Heydekampf's response to the tetchy inventor, who had been kept well away from the development of the KKM.

But NSU were funding the research, and at a time when they could ill afford the expense: sales of its once hugely

A marine application from 1962 giving 18bhp from 150cc to power a small boat remotely-controlled by a water skier.

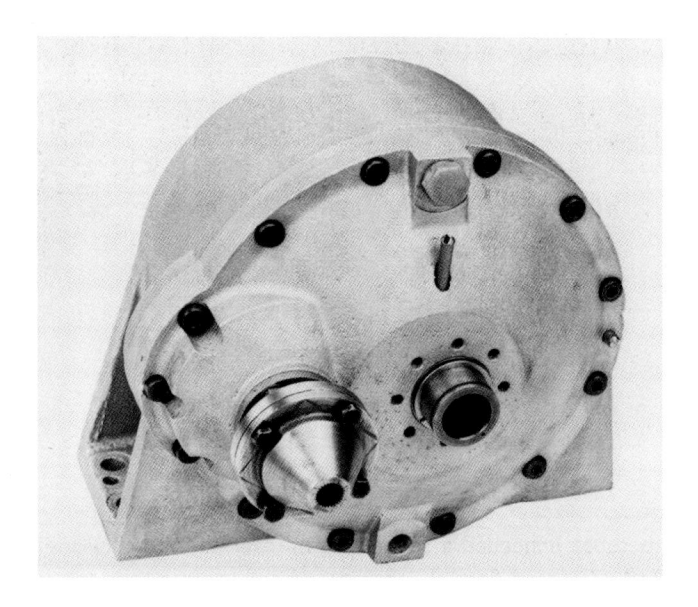

Used as a compressor, this first practical application of the concept allowed NSU's streamlined 50cc moped to set a record-breaking 121.9 mph (196.1km/h) at Utah in 1956.

popular mopeds had flattened out towards the end of the 1950s as increasingly prosperous West Germans turned from two wheels to four. NSU had 40,000 unsold mopeds in stock in 1956 and had to lay off workers. In the background, von Heydekampf had made a deal with the local provincial government to fund the construction of a new factory to build the proposed Prinz small car.

Short term this was to be NSU's saviour, but it was to the credit of the firm's bankers, the Dresdner Bank, that they agreed to release funds for the continued research into the Wankel KKM rotary engine. By 1960, $8 million had been spent on the development and NSU had established thirty patents covering all aspects of the design, thus enabling them to sell licences for manufacturing agreements that would help fund development costs. These came with a generous percentage for Herr Wankel built in (although he contributed relatively little once the KKM engine had established primacy over his beloved DKM), but still added usefully to NSU's coffers. By sharing development informa-

ABOVE LEFT: **This was the first DKM motor from 1957, giving a sporadic 28.5bhp at 17,000rpm.**

ABOVE RIGHT: **Dr Froede's KKM Motor, as fitted to the experimental Prinz cars.**

Despite his insightful imagination, Wankel needed the assistance of many technicians to bring his ideas to life.

LEFT: **The NSU Wankel Spider engine, KKM502 single rotor, single spark plug.**

tion, time and cost were also saved by all members of the Wankel 'club'.

The American aircraft engine manufacturer Curtis-Wright was the first licensee – but jumped the gun, much to the Germans' displeasure, by announcing the production of its own engine in 1959, years before it appeared in the first NSU car. However, it was not until Daimler-Benz got on board with the idea in 1961 – the year Dr Froede published his engineering paper on the new engine – that confidence in Wankel's idea began to grow. The Wankel concept was regarded not only as an engine for automotive use but for commercial vehicles and industrial applications, once it was established that a diesel-fuelled rotary engine was possible.

■ THE FLAWED GENIUS OF FELIX WANKEL

Felix Wankel in the workshop of his research institute with an example of his DKM motor – the 'pure' Wankel engine.
AUDI ARCHIVE

A difficult character to deal with, Wankel was kept at arm's length from the development of the engine for commercial use by NSU.
AUDI ARCHIVE

Felix Wankel remained creative well into later life: he is pictured here at his workshop at Lindau.

In total there were twenty-five licensees, with the Japanese keen to establish the technological credentials of its fledgling motor industry, and the most enthusiastic converts after the West Germans. In the years to follow there would be commercially produced Wankel-powered chain saws, snowmobiles and motorcycles. They would come in all manner of sizes, from tiny 5cc model aircraft engines to huge 4.1-litre industrial power plants producing up to 1,000bhp.

After the demise of the Ro80 in 1977, Toyo Kogyo – better known as Mazda – would end up as the lone champion of the rotary Wankel engine in the coming decades. Ford of Germany would take out a licence quite late in the day, while BMW at one stage threatened to destroy NSU's patents in the courts; however, von Heydekampf called the bluff of the Bavarians and won. In the UK, Rolls-Royce looked at building a multi-fuel military diesel (or compression ignition) version of the Wankel; and a link up with Citroën, through a jointly owned subsidiary named Comotor, seemed like a natural enough fit, given the French firm's commitment to advanced technology.

Meanwhile, the motoring world was looking to NSU to produce the first Wankel-engined passenger vehicle; enter, in 1963, the NSU Wankel Spider.

Marinised two-rotor versions of the Ro80 engine giving 135bhp were produced.

NSU/WANKEL

1962

PLM 150 – The production type rotary piston marine engine

NSU developed a small marine propulsion unit suitable for a new craft for water skiing. The 150 cc (9.15 cu. in.) engine developed up to 18 BHP at 1000 rev/min and gave the small boat, remotely controlled by a skier, a top speed of about 28 mph.

Over 2,400 of these NSU/Wankel marine propulsion units, which include the dynastarter and the bevel drive for the propeller, were produced since October 1962.

Photograph No. D 5 (18x24 cm)

1962

PLM 60 – Experimental completely air-cooled engine

Barely four years after concluding the first license agreement with the Curtiss-Wright Corporation in America, NSU/Wankel developments were pursued on a broad basis. Additional licensees came forward and motor manufacturers in Europe, Asia and the U.S.A. instituted evaluation programmes.

NSU developed, at that time, a small but entirely air cooled 60 cc engine, which relied for rotor cooling upon the induction gases which were arranged to pass through it. Originally this engine was intended for various industrial applications, but eventually it was fitted to a lawnmower which soon raised the lawns around the NSU factory to admirable English standards.

Photograph No. D 6 (18x24 cm)

2,400 NSU Marine propulsion units were sold.

45

NSU/WANKEL

1965

PLM 2 x 500 cc so-called twin-rotor engine

A 100-120 BHP twin-rotor NSU/Wankel engine displacing 2x500 cc per shaft revolution was shown at the 1965 International Automobile Exhibition in Frankfurt. This new engine is to be fitted to a roomy medium class car possessing sporting performance, which will supplement the NSU production programme in the coming years.

Good progress has also been made with a joint venture by Citroen and NSU, which aims to produce the COMOBIL, for which NSU is to manufacture the propulsion unit including the NSU/Wankel engine.

NOTE: For definition of —
- Single rotation machine (SIM)
- Planetary rotation machine (PLM)
- Arcuate engagement

See "Classification of Rotary Piston Machines" by Felix Wankel, published by Iliffe, London.

Photograph No. D 9 (18x24 cm)
Matrix No. D 90 (9 cm)

Photograph No. D 10
Matrix No. D 100 (9 cm)

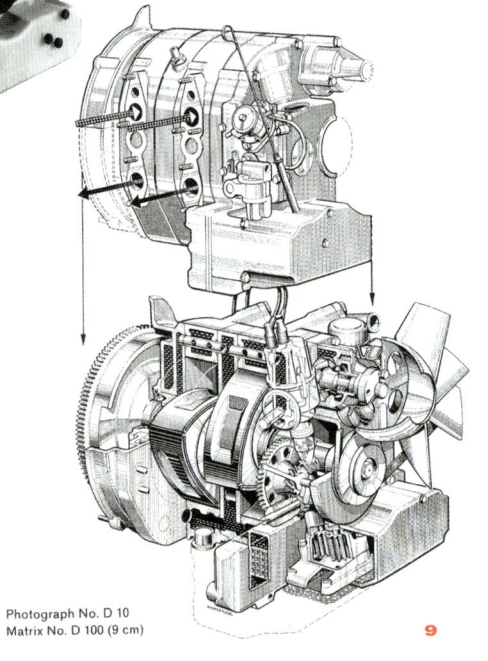

In 1964 and 1965 NSU revealed their first thoughts on a twin-rotor engine, commercially available from 1967 in the Ro80.

BELOW LEFT: **Felix Wankel's** fame spread far enough for him to be immortalised on a postage stamp.

BELOW RIGHT: **Felix Wankel** never learned to drive but was presented with an Ro80 in 1967, painted in a silver colour scheme specially requested by the inventor.

46

CHAPTER THREE

LEAP OF FAITH: THE WANKEL SPIDER

When NSU Decided to market their first production Wankel engine in a small two seater convertible car costing nearly £1400 in this country they presumably neither expected nor wanted a large number of orders. It must be assumed that they regard this as a last stage in a ten year development programme – the stage at which, on the one hand, they could learn something about production problems and, on the other, could get some feedback of experience from the public who, as every manufacturer knows, can always be counted on to discover hidden flaws and to break the indestructible.

Motor road test of the NSU Wankel Spider, 22 May 1965

By 1962 NSU had introduced the buying public to the concept of the rotary Wankel engine in a 'marine propulsion unit': a small, remotely-controlled 20lb (9kg) outboard motor called the 'Skicraft', aimed at the waterskiing frater-

The pretty, compact Wankel Spider in downtown Stuttgart.

■ LEAP OF FAITH: THE WANKEL SPIDER

Rover's 1961 T4 was its fourth-generation gas turbine car.

The Chrysler Turbine car used for research into gas turbine power, bodied by Ghia.

nity. Licence holders Margirus of Ulm were producing a Wankel-powered fire pump. However, the successful take-up of Wankel licences put NSU under pressure to take the lead and put a rotary engine into a production car. Toyo Kogyo (Mazda) was not convinced that the rotary engine was even suitable for use in an automobile: the Japanese firm wanted NSU to commit to making a Wankel-engined production car before it would start paying its licence fees.

Although a large saloon designed specifically around the rotary engine was well under way (the as yet unnamed Ro80), the company saw the value of producing, much sooner, a more specialised product around the technology but based on an existing model. This way they could gauge public reaction and get a sense of how the engine performed in the hands of the public, while using the car as an ambassador for the Wankel engine in international markets.

NSU were by no means the only car manufacturers looking into new forms of motive power in the early 1960s. Both Chrysler in Detroit and Rover in Solihull had been working diligently on the gas turbine concept for a decade. The Americans got as far as building fifty-five Ghia-bodied experimental turbine cars in 1963 and 1964 for the use of customers to see how they fared as everyday vehicles. Rover's programme culminated in a pair of fairly promising Le Mans cars (built in cooperation with BRM) and, in 1961, a saloon named the T4 that was really a sneak preview of the P6 2000: a 140mph, 20mpg (225km/h; 14.12ltr/100km) saloon that they claimed could have gone into production at a price roughly double that of the most expensive Rover 3-litre model.

1962: FIRST THOUGHTS ON THE WANKEL SPIDER

The first Wankel-engined production vehicle, green-lighted by the NSU board in 1962, was to be a specialist open-topped model. The perception that it was a 'sports car' seemed like a good way of distracting critics from the engine's poor low-speed torque (in a vehicle that was likely to be driven using high revs and with free use of its four-speed gearbox), while at the same time making them more forgiving of any reliability problems than they would have been if the Wankel had made its debut in a family saloon.

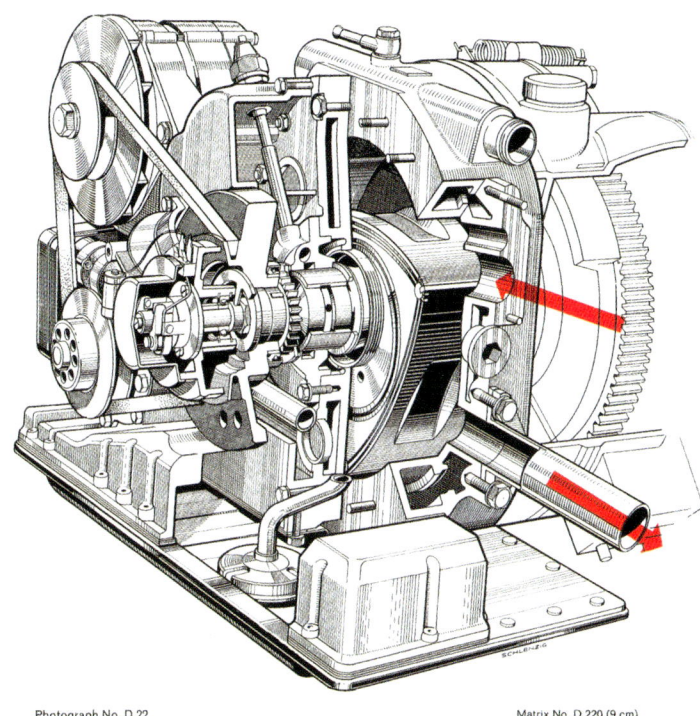

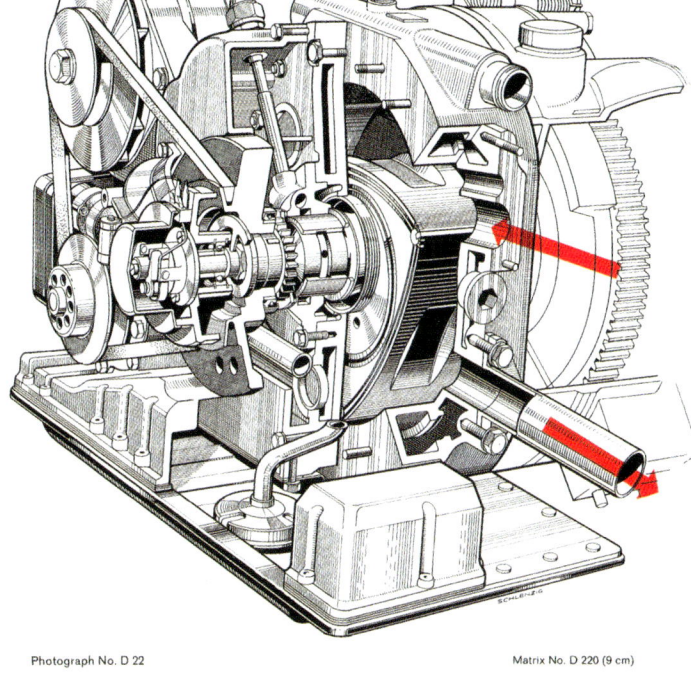

NSU SPIDER

Photograph No. D 22   Matrix No. D 220 (9 cm)

23

NSU-SPORT-PRINZ-COUPÉ

The NSU Sport Prinz has made a name for itself, as a very economical sports coupe. Elegance, maneouverability and gratifying averges on long journeys do not have to be paid for dearly in the case of the NSU Sport Prinz. Its fuel consumption of 45 m.p.g. is a particularly good point in its favour.

The well known italian body stylist, Bertone, designed the elegantly streamlined coupe body.

Easy to handle, elegant to drive and easy to park!

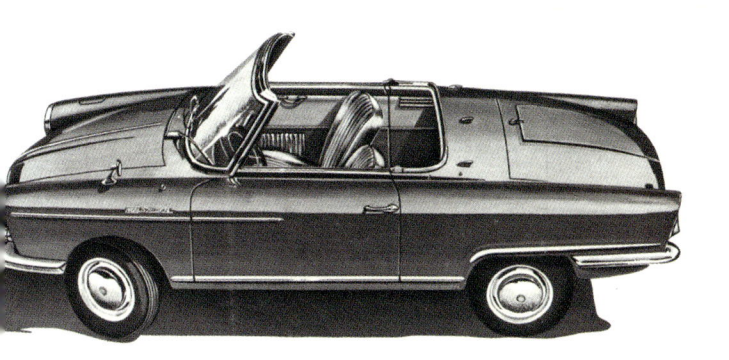

NSU-SPIDER
with NSU/Wankel Rotary Piston Engine

The first car ever to be fitted with the epoch making NSU-Wankel rotary piston engine, the NSU Spider will go into production at NSU in the spring of 1964. Many years of intensive work have proceded this start of a new era in engine making. Now it is here; the NSU-Wankel engine has been bully developed before being put into production. It is initially being used in an exclusive sports car. The NSU Spider will make the heart of any driver who does not want to miss the pleasure of this new and different driving adventure, beat faster.

The first car with the NSU/Wankel engine!

Cutaway of the Wankel Spider's single-rotor 497cc engine, which would easily push the car over 95mph (153km).

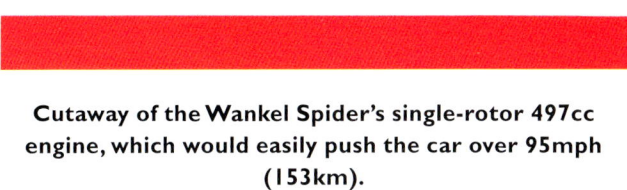

ABOVE LEFT: **The basis of the first Wankel-engined production car was the Bertone-styled Sport Prinz, with 20,831 built from 1959–67.**

LEFT: **The Sports Prinz and Wankel Spider were marketed alongside each other but only the Sport Prinz was available in right-hand drive.**

49

■ LEAP OF FAITH: THE WANKEL SPIDER

The new car was to be based on the little Sports Prinz, the 2-cylinder coupé designed (and at first built) by Bertone in Turin, Italy as NSU's answer to the VW Karmann Ghia.

Modified for water cooling and with an improved form of semi-trailing arm rear suspension from the new 1000 saloon, the Spider body had cruciform bracing underneath that made up for the lack of a roof. A 250cc KKM-type engine had been fitted in two Prinz saloons for journalists to sample as early as 1960. Outwardly identical to the standard cars – apart from cooling vents in the right-hand rear wings and extra instruments inside – these first Wankel road cars were adapted to water cooling with a Fiat 600 radiator and a VW oil cooler. They were crudely converted and not easy to drive – more like a highly tuned two-stroke than anything else – but the potential was obvious. Soon, more rotary-engined Prinz saloons – good for 70mph (113km/h) plus and 37mpg (7.65ltr/100km) – were being tested on the road. Those that broke down 'in the field' were collected in an unmarked lorry by cover of darkness and returned to Neckarsulm to be stripped down and analysed. A larger 400cc KKM was tested in a series of Sports Prinz coupés.

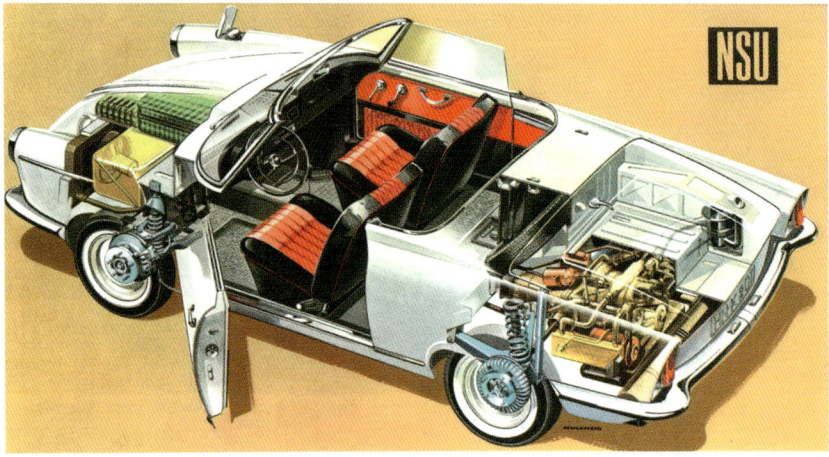

Colour images from the Wankel Spider brochure showing front disc brakes, compact engine allowing luggage space above, and rear suspension of the 4-cylinder NSU saloons.

Claus Luthe reconfigured Bertone's original coupé into the pretty Spider.

LEAP OF FAITH: THE WANKEL SPIDER

The Spider was a promotional tool for NSU to prove the Wankel engine concept in public hands.

Although Bertone, on its own initiative, had created an open version of the Sports Prinz, NSU chopped the roof in-house for the Wankel-engined version, having fallen out with the Italian styling house. They considered that Bertone had recycled the Sports Prinz body style for Simca's 1962 1000 Coupé, and done a better job of it. Nuccio Bertone tried to make amends by proposing a four-seat version of the Sport Prinz, but the Swabians did not take the bait. For the type 56 Spider, NSU's in-house stylist Claus Luthe reconfigured the bodywork for the production drop-head treatment, with a grille at the front for the radiator (in what would be NSU's first post-war water-cooled car) and a hood with irons that projected into the tops of the wings when the top was folded. Driving the Spider with the hood up was, by all accounts, not much fun, mainly because of the wind noise: it was actually much quieter if you went topless.

The Spider shared hardly any metalwork with the closed roof Prinz coupé, which had a shorter wheelbase but was slightly longer overall. Inside it had a completely different dashboard design, with a unique two-spoke 'sports' steering wheel.

The firm had already produced a working two-rotor Wankel engine, but for the new car a compact single rotor/single plug KKM 502 unit was specified after considerable agonising over apex seals, peripheral or side porting and dozens of other permutations. Its casing was water cooled, but the rotor relied on oil cooling with an oil heat exchanger. It sat in a softly-mounted subframe to tame uneven over-run behaviour.

Seven different types were evolved, but the compact 498cc KKM 502 – weighing in at around 200lb (91kg) –

Note the wide, flat sump and alternator. The single spark plug was a special Bosch type designed to run very hot.

Seven different types were evolved before the 200lb, 498cc KKM 502 was settled on. It was almost dwarfed by its bulky exhaust system.

51

LEAP OF FAITH: THE WANKEL SPIDER

allowed the NSU engineers to get a low centre of gravity for good handling. It was almost dwarfed by its bulky transverse exhaust system with twin silencers. With its wide, flat sump, alternator and rather special single Bosch spark plug (which ran very hot) this dinky engine also helped maximise the packaging of the car; there was even room for an additional luggage compartment above the tiny engine in the rear of the Spider. This was in addition to the usual front-end load space, which now also contained the radiator (with a not very reliable thermostatic fan) and the 8 gallon (36ltr) fuel tank. With front and rear lids opened, onlookers tended to enquire 'where's the engine?', but both spaces lacked depth: big suitcases had to go behind the seats above the battery and toolbox compartments.

The spare was relocated from the front (in the Sport Prinz) to a space under the rear deck. Front ATE/Dunlop disc brakes differentiated the Wankel Spider from the 2-cylinder, 36bhp Sports Prinz. On 50bhp, breathing through its specially-designed twin-choke Solex carburettor, the little two-seater would easily top 90mph (145km/h) (98mph/158km/h was quoted by *Motor*), so it probably needed them.

Torque was improved low down by the simple expedient of limiting the recommended rev limit to a mere 5,000rpm. Air for the carburettor came through a vent in the left-hand bottom corner of the top engine cover; petrol station attendants often mistook it for the fuel cap. In fact the fuel filler was under a flap in the right-hand front wing.

FRANKFURT LAUNCH

Like the Prinz saloons before it, the Wankel Spider was brought to fruition by Ewald Praxl, the Austrian-born 52-year-old chief engineer who had joined NSU in 1939. A graduate of the Prague Technical University, Praxl was heavily involved in the development of the NSU's Kettenrad, a half-tracked motorcycle unique to the German military during World War II.

Praxl was deputy chief designer at Neckarsulm from 1949 to 1962, and during the 1950s had responsibility for the motorcycle racing department during its world championship winning years, before settling down to concentrate on motor cars and the baby Prinz. Praxl's first running Wankel Spider was on the road for June 1963 and was launched at the Frankfurt show that year. NSU shares went up 200 points and the event was considered significant enough to feature on German television.

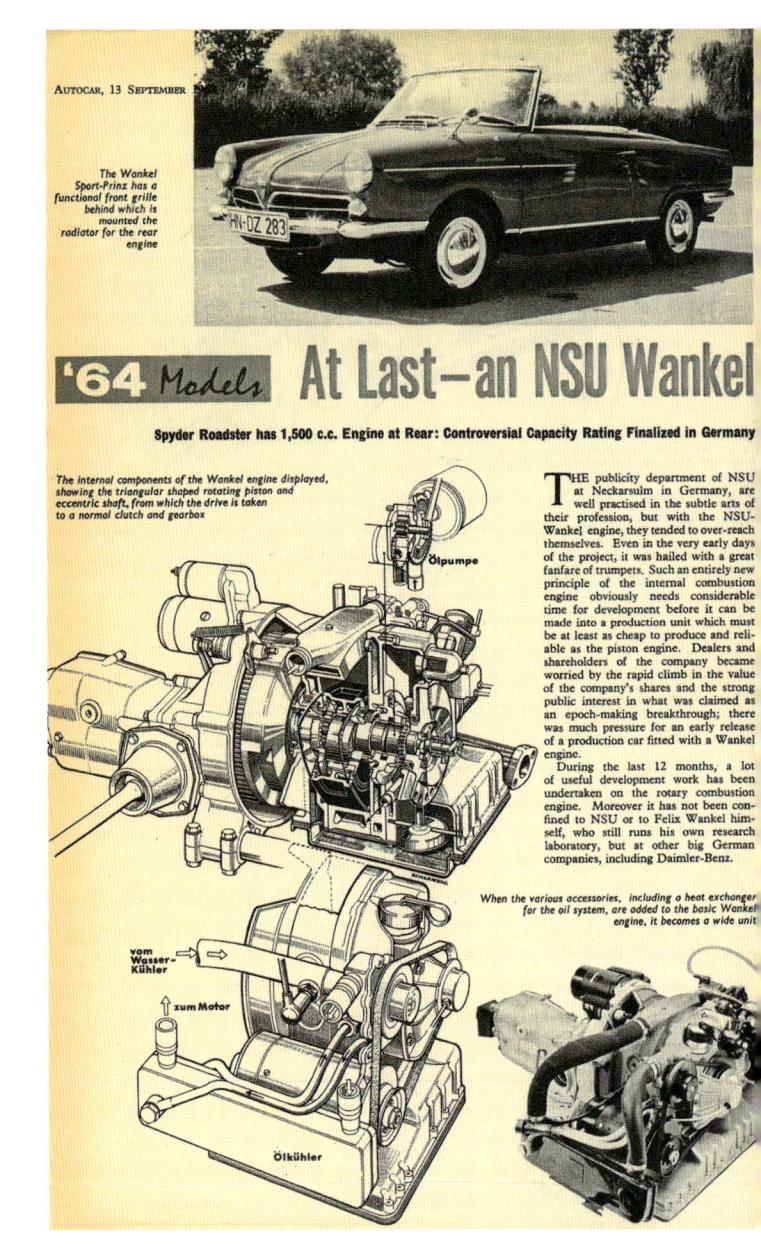

The Wankel Spider aroused huge interest around the world: this is *Autocar* magazine's technical description.

It would be September 1964 before customers took delivery of their DM10,000 baby convertibles. There was a pilot production of thirteen cars, five purely for factory testing purposes.

Colour choice was limited to Alfa Red or Lily White (*Alfarot* and *Lillenweib* in German) at first; two cars were painted a blue named Gemini metallic and just one in silver metallic. Later, there was an alternative white called *gletscheib*.

LEAP OF FAITH: THE WANKEL SPIDER

NSU Wankel Spider

Autocar Road Test NUMBER 2043

AT A GLANCE: Rotary engined sports car with otherwise conventional design. Very smooth power unit once over uneven running at low revs. Good handling and brakes. Interior cramped and hood complicated to erect. Left-hand drive only and price uncompetitive.

motor shows, comparatively few people have heard one running, and fewer still have had the chance to drive a Wankel-powered car. In this test, therefore, it is the behaviour and →

The engine-transmission unit is carried in a tubular sub-frame on soft rubber mountings (right). In the left foreground is the water filler, below the alternator the single sparking-plug, and on the far side the twin-choke carburettor

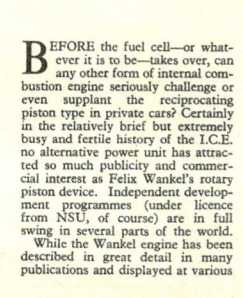

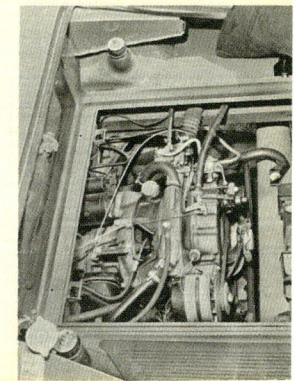

BEFORE the fuel cell—or whatever it is to be—takes over, can any other form of internal combustion engine seriously challenge or even supplant the reciprocating piston type in private cars? Certainly in the relatively brief but extremely busy and fertile history of the I.C.E. no alternative power unit has attracted so much publicity and commercial interest as Felix Wankel's rotary piston device. Independent development programmes (under licence from NSU, of course) are in full swing in several parts of the world.
While the Wankel engine has been described in great detail in many publications and displayed at various

Road testers were cautiously impressed by the smoothness and near 100mph performance of the little Spider, but less so by its highly uncompetitive price tag of nearly £1,400. This was more than enough to buy a large luxury saloon.

The Spider was a cover star in its native West Germany.

The standard specification included heater, steering lock, headlamp flasher and jazzy two-tone seat upholstery, but the factory hardtop was an extra.

Felix Wankel was offered the first production Spider off the line but, still peeved that NSU had developed its own version of his engine, he declined the gift. Instead, it was raffled off to a Neckarsulm employee named Willi Knapp but, being a family man, he swapped it after a short time for a new 1000 saloon. The Spider raffle car survives in almost mint condition.

Many of the 151 cars built in 1964 went to large firms such as Shell and other institutions for technical assessment. Rolls-Royce had two, painted green and fitted with extra instrumentation. One was bought privately from a German owner and shipped off to Detroit for the secrets of its engine to be uncovered.

The first export Spider was sent to Japan – almost certainly for Mazda to inspect – but the German market took about half the 2,375 cars built through to July 1967. Here, at least at first, the government could not decide on how to rate the car for taxation purposes, so early Spider owners went tax free after an initial judgement that they would be taxed at the

LEAP OF FAITH: THE WANKEL SPIDER

DRIVING THE WANKEL SPIDER

These baby two-seaters are very engaging to drive. Although tolerant of low-speed work, they are at their best on the open road, where it is possible to use maximum revs and exploit the gears freely while avoiding the two-stroke-like over-run slight surge endemic to the single rotor engine. Low-speed torque is better than you might expect and the levels of performance out of context with the Wankel Spider's dinky proportions and cuddly looks. Unlike its bigger brother, the Ro80, fuel consumption is not an issue (over 30mpg [9.42ltr/100km] is easy) but the silky pull of the engine as revs soar to 6,000, 7,000 or even 8,000rpm could not be more at odds with the 4-cylinder pushrod engines powering the Sprites and Spitfires with which the Wankel Spider tended to be compared. Perhaps the 10,000rpm capability of the fascinating little Honda S800 sports cars had a similar sort of appeal. The NSU was, in fairness, much more expensive than those cars, but the extra cost bought you a pleasing finish, good comfort and equipment levels and refined high-speed, long-distance cruising capability probably not found in a similarly compact open-topped package. Yet in every sense this was a real sports car, with outstandingly agile handling thanks to accurate high-geared steering, a nifty finger-tip gear change and balanced, potent brakes.

The Wankel Spider was promoted as a fun car for enthusiasts, pictured here among the large American cars then common on European roads.

1500cc rating. This was later set at 1000cc, much to NSU's disappointment, but the judgement was probably fair.

The USA took 230 Spiders, priced at a hefty $2,979 each, specially fitted with laminated windscreens. France had about the same and well over 100 went to Italy, where NSU was a popular make, outselling Volkswagen locally.

NSU had hoped to build Spiders at the rate of 3–5,000 per annum, but 1965 was the Wankel Spiders best year, with 923 built.

After sampling the early cars at an NSU press day at Goodwood in October 1964, the British magazine *Autocar* had a left-hand-drive one on long-term test, having ordered it off the stand at Earl's Court in 1963. At £1,391 the Spider, when the first examples arrived in the UK in the spring of 1965, was double the price of any other small two-seater convertible in the Midget/Spitfire class.

FUN – WHEN IT WORKED...

The fact that the same money bought you a Jaguar Mk II or a Lancia Fulvia saloon, only served to highlight the fact that

THE WANKEL-ENGINED SKODAS, 1964–66

With swing axles at the rear a more potent rotary-engined Skoda might well have been a lethal device.

Skoda, the state-owned Czechoslovakian car maker, came close to signing a licensing deal with NSU in 1964 for the rights to produce Wankel rotary engines of between 50 and 200bhp. The larger of these would likely have been for military applications but engines for road cars were very much on the agenda, slated for use in the new 1000MB rear-engined saloon, in which the compact dimensions would have allowed for a second luggage area above the engine bay. Negotiations reached a fairly advanced stage until the Czechs began to worry about the durability of the engines; with government money they bought two NSU spiders and subjected them to continuous 50,000-kilometre tests. In the background the Skoda technicians – perhaps benefiting from NSU's relaxed attitude to maintaining secrecy around the details of the new engine – were well on the way to producing their own Wankel, without the need to spend millions of deutschmarks on the licences that would give them access to the NSU technology and research. Skoda even planned to land the first legal punch by suing the Germans for infringement of *their* patents, unless the Germans reduced their licensing fee. As the problems with the Spider's engine became more public Skoda began to lose its nerve anyway, but ten Wankel-engined 1000MB saloon prototypes were built powered by a single-rotor, twin-plug engine giving 40bhp, which was only 5bhp more than the production reciprocating engine, the real gain being a 45kg drop in weight.

---

the Wankel Spider was bought for its technical curiosity value rather than as a serious alternative to anything else. When it was running, buyers loved the Spider for its smoothness and speed: using 8,000rpm in short bursts allowed 90mph (145km/h) in third gear, almost 100mph (160km/h) in top and 0–60mph in 14.5 seconds. These factors, combined with superb steering, tenacious grip and its excellent four-speed gearbox (fully synchromesh with a hydraulic clutch), made the Wankel Spider a fun if sometimes nerve-racking car to own. For instance, if the spark boosting transistorised ignition decided to fail, the Spider would come to a halt with very little warning – or indication of what was wrong – but then fire up again half an hour later as if nothing had happened.

Driven quietly, the Wankel Spider might get 30–37mpg (9.42–7.63ltr/100km) – a hefty thirst for a nominal 500cc, but not unreasonable given the performance – and do around 150 miles (241km) to a pint of oil. The system was 'total loss', effectively negating any requirement for oil changes, although every 5,000 miles/8,046km was recommended. Uncontaminated by fuel the oil stayed clean, too. With only two grease nipples to attend to, maintenance requirements were light.

Production hardly got above two or three cars per day, with the first 1,160 examples built in Neckarsulm up to January 1966 and thereafter assembled by body-makers Drauz at Heilbronn. That year production dropped to 581, as the car's engine problems became common knowledge. The later Spiders benefited from a slightly more potent 65bhp engine that owed something to latest advances that would feature in the still secret Ro80.

The Spider was a disaster, but perhaps a calculated one. The public, it seemed, were being used as guinea pigs to test the new technology. NSU were very generous in giving buyers new £550 replacement engines (for free) when they inevitably failed, usually due to cooling problems, causing catastrophic distortion or cracking of the casing. Then there were the inevitable snags with the soft carbon apex seals,

■ LEAP OF FAITH: THE WANKEL SPIDER

FAILURE ON THE ROAD, SUCCESS ON THE TRACK

In 1966 Karl-Heinz Panowitz won the German GT Rally Championship in a Wankel Spider.

The Spider was quick enough to earn itself a very respectable competition pedigree in the 1960s, doing well in hill climbs and short circuit events. In 1966 the Wankel Spider of Karl-Heinz Panowitz, tuned to give 90bhp with new inlet manifolds and a Stromberg carburettor, won the German GT Rally Championship. Siegfried Spiess came second (behind a Porsche) in his Wankel Spider, competing in the 1966 German Hill Climb for GTs and sports cars and won the event in 1967 and 1968.

Private Wankel Spiders in Greece and Belgium also proved that the little car could be a motorsport winner.

In 1966, Al Auger of Richmond California became the first man to race a Wankel-engined vehicle, coming a creditable second place in his Spider in the SCCA (Sports Car Club of America) Class H.

---

which would become brittle in normal stop-start traffic and break up. The fact that a full engine strip took less than two hours was possibly of some comfort to pioneering Wankel motorists.

Few of NSU's 1,400 German dealers had enough experience with the rotary engine to offer much help to frustrated owners and it seems likely that every one of the 2,375 Spiders built had a replacement engine fitted at some stage.

Today, the 736 NSU Wankel Spiders that are known to have survived are highly prized (and highly priced) for their historical significance. As an opening gambit in NSU's attempts to seduce the public with the Wankel concept, this engaging little car was only partly successful. No longer in the two-wheeler business and with $8 million invested in the Wankel dream, NSU could not afford to allow the frustrations and frailties of the Spider dissuade them from pressing ahead with the much bigger gamble that the Ro80 represented.

AUTOCAR'S STUART BLADON ON RUNNING THE WANKEL SPIDER

Nearly 60 years ago, in October 1963, NSU revealed the little two-seater Spider with its revolutionary rotary engine at the London Motor Show. Soon after the Show closed, the Editor of The Autocar, the late Maurice Smith, convinced the managing director that the journal ought to buy one and run it for long-term assess-

The *Autocar* long-term Wankel Spider on a snowy trip up north.

Outside lane cruising on the M6 in 1965 in the Wankel Spider.

ment, and I was delighted when told it would be allocated to me; but delivery was delayed until May 1965.

Even then there was disappointment when I went to collect it from the NSU depot which was then in London, and was told that it could not be released. Why not? I kept asking, only to be fobbed off with assurances that it was nothing to do with the engine. Three years later it was revealed secretly that the manufacturers had 'missed' the welds on the subframe and the engine was in danger of dropping out onto the road. Eventually it was ready to be collected and I was able to drive it for the first time. The little Spider looked very sporty and was fun to drive, but the engine was disappointing. A single rotor unit, it was fairly noisy, lumpy at low speed, and developed little torque below about 2,000rpm. But it was more enjoyable at speed and I used to cruise it above 80mph but needed to keep an eye on the rev counter as there was strict advice not to exceed 5,500rpm. Whenever I parked the little Spider I was invariably asked to reveal the engine, which was a bit of a nuisance when luggage had to be taken out before the rear-engine cover could be lifted, which brought comments such as: 'Is that all there is? It looks so tiny.'

In November of the first year I felt confident enough in the Spider to take it up to Glasgow to cover the 1965 Scottish Motor Show, and a long run seemed to suit it much better than town work. Fuel consumption improved from the usual 28mpg to a more reasonable 33, and oil consumption on the total loss principle was steady at 150 miles per pint. We had a lot of snow in the north, and the Spider proved excellent for traction and control thanks to having the engine weight, what little there was, over the back wheels. After some 4,000 miles the first signs of trouble manifested when the engine suddenly stopped. On removing the solitary sparking plug it was found that the insulation around the electrode was completely burnt away. The sparking plug was a very special type made for NSU by Beru, and fortunately a spare had just arrived. After fitting this the engine ran well until at just over a year old and 11,200 miles covered there was severe smoking on the over-run, some back-firing, and what was very worrying was the evidence of vaporized petrol fumes coming from the cooling system. NSU had by then moved to Shoreham, scene later of the terrible air crash disaster, and I drove the Spider down there to watch the engineer Mike Hoppis remove and then dismantle the engine. It was found that the outer casing had cracked across the sparking plug hole and I was told this was a fault NSU were aware of and had modified the design to prevent recurrence. A completely new engine was fitted and when I drove it away I was impressed to find it was less prone to the jerkiness on the over-run which had spoiled the original engine, and oil consumption had improved to 1,000 miles per pint. The replacement engine was provided free of charge for all owners. The second engine proved less reliable than the first one, often difficult to start, and sometimes it would suddenly stop running then behave normally again. The Editor decided that after two years we had nothing more to learn about the single rotor Wankel engine, so the car was advertised and sold. It had been a lot of fun but not without its many problems.

WHAT THE PAPERS SAID

In size, weight and performance the Spider matches some of the small British sports cars so closely that a detailed comparison of figures is inevitable. It differs from them, however, in displaying a vastly greater ease of travel and also in having considerably greater luggage accommodation.

Motor, road test, 22 May 1965

It would have been interesting to have had a counting device to show how many times the bonnet has been opened in response to the endless requests to see the engine.

Stuart Bladon's second report in **Autocar**, 17 December 1965, on his Wankel Spider long term test car, DYU230C.

We know of few sports cars that can be driven along winding roads so quickly and with so much enjoyment. There is very little roll and the light but high-geared rack and pinion steering gives extremely rapid response and great accuracy.

Motor, road test, 22 May 1965

NSU WANKEL SPIDER 1963–67 (2,375 built, all left-hand drive)

Construction	Steel unitary two seater convertible	Wheels and tyres	Steel 12 inch, 5.00-12 Continental Record tyres
Engine	Wankel, KKM 502 Single rotor 498cc		
Carburettor	Double choke side-draught Solex HHD 18/32	Brakes	Hydraulic, disc front 9 inch diameter, drum rear 7.1 inch diameter
Fuel pump	Mechanical	Electrical equipment	12 volt, self parking two-speed wipers, rev counter, 7 fuses
Fuel tank	7½ gallons (34ltr)		
Compression ratio	8.6:1	Length	11ft 8¾in (3,575mm)
Max Power	50bhp at 6,000rpm	Width	4ft 11¾in (1,517mm)
Max torque	52lb/ft at 2,500rpm	Height	4ft 1¾in (1,264mm)
Bhp per laden ton	60	Wheelbase	6ft 8in (2,032mm)
Transmission	4 speed manual	Weight	1,510lb (685kg), split 40/60 front-rear
MPH/1,000rpm in 4th	16.2	0–60mph	14.3 seconds
Clutch	7.1 in single plate diaphragm type	Standing ¼ mile	19.6 seconds
Suspension Front	Unequal length transverse wishbones, coil spring, anti-roll bar. Telescopic dampers	Top speed	98mph (158km/h)
		Speeds in gears	1st: 26mph (42km/h); 2nd: 46mph (74km/h); 3rd: 70mph (113 km/h)
Suspension Rear	Coil springs, single semi-trailing wishbones each side. Telescopic dampers	MPG	30–37 (9.42–7.63ltr/100km)
		Price New	£1,391
		Extras	Radio; hardtop
Steering	Rack and pinion, 2¾ turns lock-to-lock, 29 foot (8.8m) turning circle		

CHAPTER FOUR

CAR OF THE YEAR, CAR OF THE DECADE?

If a superior being from another planet were to bring with him his own personal wheeled vehicle we would expect it to handle much like the NSU Ro80.

Motor, group test, 19 October 1968

Only very rarely do car designers get the chance to create a new vehicle from scratch. Timing, financial constraints, internal politics and commercial realities usually take precedence over the quest for engineering purity when a complex piece of technology like a new automobile is about to be unleashed on an unforgiving general public.

For good reason, history shows us that few cars are truly born all new: from the Tucker Torpedo and Jowett Javelin to the original Lotus Elite and early Austin Maxi, motoring history is littered with brave all-new designs that looked good on paper but failed in customers' hands.

To save time and ease development pressures, proven components tend to be adapted to fresh concepts: a new bodyshell usually comes with last year's engine to maintain a sense of continuity and customer trust. To do anything else, when a manufacturer's hard-won reputation is at stake, would be commercially irresponsible.

In a sense, the still-independent NSU were immune to these kinds of self-imposed regulations because they did not have a track record to worry about, at least not in the realm of large saloon cars. They had only returned to the world of four-wheelers less than ten years before. Unencumbered by the traditions and preconceptions that tend to fog designers' imaginations when they are tasked with creating 'traditional' large cars, the originators of the NSU Ro80 were literally able to start with a clean sheet of paper and make up their own rules.

THE CONCEPT TAKES SHAPE

Even so, there had to be certain parameters. The original August 1961 design outline for the Ro80 was set down by project engineer and 'father of the Ro80' Ewald Praxl at a meeting at the Wald und Schloss hotel at Friedrichsruhe. With Froede, and his leading production and construction engineers, Praxl established an initial idea for a family two-door saloon, roughly the same size as a Ford Taunus

Early thoughts on a front-end style involved a full-width glass fairing in a style later adopted by Citroën for the SM.

■ CAR OF THE YEAR, CAR OF THE DECADE?

Full-sized mock-up with the shape of the boot not quite settled.

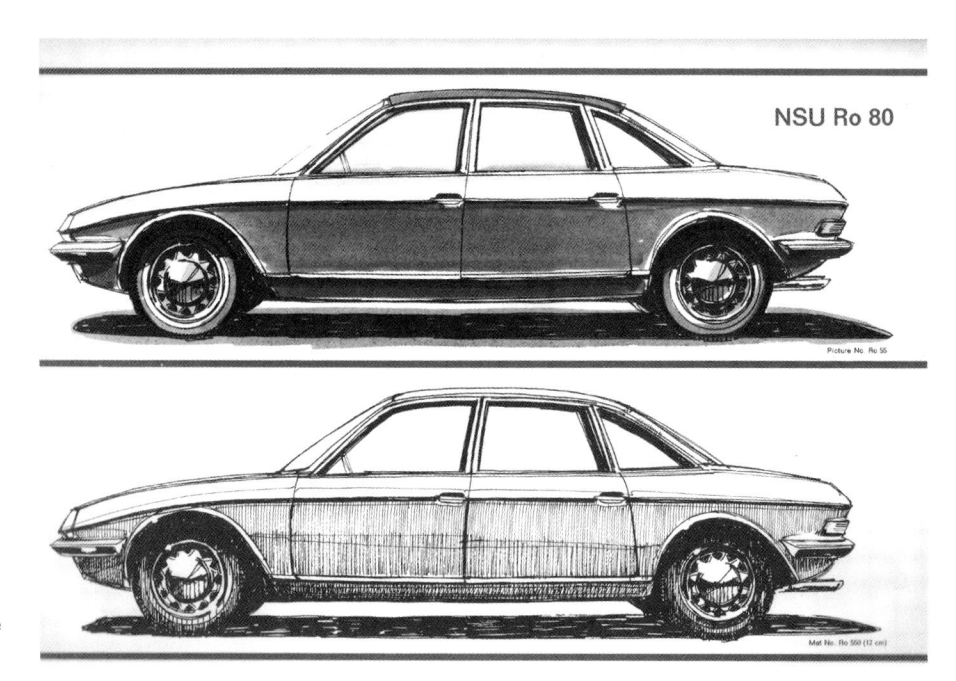

Luthe's bosses were nervous of the high-tailed wedge profile, but attempts at lowering it spoiled the aerodynamics.

with a 2-rotor Wankel engine producing 80bhp (two rotors smoothed out the low-speed throb), driving the rear wheels. They talked about air suspension, disc brakes, fully automatic transmission and even sliding doors.

The only fixed points were the positions of the head lamps and the suspension struts. Weighing in at a projected 800kg (1,764lb) it was hoped that the new car would sell for DM8,000. At this stage the project was referred to internally as the T80, but seeing as memories of a certain Russian tank were still relatively fresh in people's minds (the T34), it was obvious that NSU were going to have to come up with something else as a marketable name for the car.

60

CAR OF THE YEAR, CAR OF THE DECADE?

EWALD PRAXL 1911–1988

Born in Pastelberg, Bohemia (today part of the Czech Republic) the rotund, dark-haired NSU engineering supremo Ewald Praxl liked to style himself 'the father of the Ro80' – and not without justification. A 1937 graduate of the Prague Technical University, Praxl joined NSU in its off-road vehicle department in 1939 and was heavily involved in the development of the NSU Kettenkrad, a half-tracked motorcycle that was exclusively used by the German military during World War II. Praxl was deputy chief designer at Neckarsulm from 1949 to 1962, when he took over from the retiring Wankel sceptic Albert Roder. Perhaps apprehensive about the Ro80's prospects with Wankel power, Praxl supposedly had a V8 waiting in the wings, created out of two NSU in line fours.

From 1951 he had responsibility for the testing and motorcycle racing department during its World Championship winning years, before settling down to concentrate on motor cars; as well as the Ro80, he was responsible for all the small rear-engined NSUs and the K70. Praxl retired from NSU in 1976.

Praxl in 1954 with work team NSU racers Hollous and Hass.

'Delphin' was proposed at one stage – recalling the name of one of NSU's streamlined record bikes – but the name was rejected as sounding too much like Renault's 'Dauphin'. 'Rotary' seemed obvious enough, until it was discovered that the international Rotary club owned the rights to the name. So 'Ro80' it was: easy to remember even if, later on, it failed to reflect the way the ambitions for the car had grown since the early 1960s.

Various body shapes were mooted on paper, any one of which would have been crisp and modern by mid-1960s standards (NSU cheerfully published these musings in the press pack when the Ro80 was launched), but were rejected as being not sufficiently distinctive.

By the time 29-year-old Claus Luthe's low nose/high tail, six-light shape had been evolved in 1:5 model form in May 1963, the new NSU had become a more ambitious vehicle: a luxurious four-door car – 'a comfortable travelling saloon' – aimed at BMW and Mercedes customers with well over 100bhp but offering a more complete specification (power steering, automatic gearbox, fog lights and so on) and with a character sufficiently different from the competition to have a distinctive appeal. It was to be a full five-seater, somewhat influenced by the Citroën DS in general concept.

In many ways the Ro80 *was* the German DS. One of the most audaciously conceived products offered to the public in the twentieth century, surprisingly few of the big Citroën's breakthrough features were adopted by other manufacturers. But certainly no single automobile had ever introduced so much technical novelty in one giant push forward; it almost seemed as if Citroën had attempted to reinvent the motor car from first principles. It floated – and self-levelled – on hydro-pneumatic spheres (when most others still creaked on the leaf springs of the horse and carriage age) and harnessed engine-driven hydraulic power for brakes, steering and clutch/gear change. Its mono-shell base unit was clothed in unstressed panels of such arresting aerodynamic grace that the crowds at its 1955 Paris show introduction stood ten deep to marvel at it. It had frameless door windows, a single-spoke steering wheel, and a mushroom-like button for a brake pedal operating the first disc brakes on a production car. In its adventurous use of new interior plastics, the DS looked, felt and even smelt like nothing anyone had encountered before.

But where the Ro80's appeal centred around – and evolved from – its novel new engine, the big Citroën never truly got the power unit it deserved; conceived with a light alloy flat six, production versions were powered by a variety of dependable but unexciting in-line fours for reasons of cost and the known quantity of a reliable engine. Perhaps not even Citroën were audacious enough to build a truly all-new car in

■ CAR OF THE YEAR, CAR OF THE DECADE?

BMW's 4-cylinder cars were carving out a niche for themselves as fun, practical, but well-engineered family cars.

BELOW: **From Britain came the Rover 2000, one of the pioneering compact executive cars of the 1960s.**

every respect, but it would not be very long before the firm's natural affinity with all things new and unconventional would lead into an alliance with NSU and the Wankel rotary engine.

Those who drove the DS for the first time realised that a new benchmark for comfort had been set. It became the pride of France, a symbol of technological pre-eminence for a nation that prided itself on its sophistication; French president Charles de Gaulle, owing his life to the big Citroën's ability to run on two flat tyres after a failed assassination attempt in 1962, would not ride in anything else.

And yet this car was not intended as a limousine for the elite but an aspirational middle-class saloon that sold to the tune of 1.4 million examples. It achieved maturity in the mid-1960s, just as the Ro80 was about to emerge. They were roughly the same length and weight. Both were front-wheel drive – NSU believed the main weight should always be on the driving wheels, for stability – and had very supple suspension. NSU considered Citroën-style air springs for a while, but were probably discouraged by the trouble Borgward had with its doomed Big Six. Certainly Praxl believed it was unwise to go for a completely new suspension system but rather shop for the best conventional solutions available.

NSU focused on long stroke (7.4 inch front, 10 inch rear) steel springs; inclined MacPherson struts at the front with maintenance free joints, widely spaced anchor points and an anti-roll bar that only did anti-roll duties rather than acting as a locator. The tubular wishbones were chosen as a way of saving on tooling costs as much as anything else. At the rear, the semi-trailing arms were set at 80 degrees to the centre line of the car – for a low roll centre – on a flexibly mounted cross member.

Exceptional roominess was essential, hence a giant wheelbase slightly greater than the big Mercedes 300SEL saloon. This for a car that was 5 inches (127mm) wider than the contemporary Rover 2000 – also inspired by the Citroën DS – but about the same weight.

The move up-market for the new NSU was a result of changing local circumstances. In 1960, the number of private cars on West German roads overtook the company vehicle for the first time, as an increasingly prosperous nation got behind the wheel and embraced the automobile as never before.

CAR OF THE YEAR, CAR OF THE DECADE?

A much less prestigious but more practical and equally comfortable alternative to the Ro80 was the family-friendly Renault 16 hatchback.

The lower echelons of Mercedes S-Class range were in NSU's sights in the form of the 250 SE W108 and the smaller W114 new-generation saloons.

In 1962 Mercedes-Benz built its millionth passenger car, a 220SE saloon. Meanwhile, the growing success of the once doomed BMW firm, with its 'New Class' saloons, was an indication to the managers at Neckarsulm that the future lay with a larger car and a sporty image where the profit margins were higher.

As the Ro80 was being developed NSU bosses could only have looked on nervously as the twin fates of two other medium-sized German car makers – Borgward and Hans Glas – unfolded. Industrial tycoon Carl Borgward had been in the car business since the 1920s, and post-war offered Germany's largest range of vehicles under Hansa, Goliath, Lloyd and Borgward brand names. The bestselling 1½-litre Borgward Isabella range was in many ways a template for the compact, sporty BMWs of the 1960s; but Borgward's financial problems lay with the proliferation of smaller cars built under different names.

With their flat-twin and boxer 4-cylinder engines (with optional fuel injection!) and front drive, these ambitious little cars did not share enough parts to be commercially viable. The autocratic, cigar-chomping Dr Carl ran the firms as private – and separate – entities with no shareholders. However, by the late 1950s Borgward's creditors were circling, and forced him into bankruptcy in 1961, by which time his problems had been compounded by problems with the air suspension on the P100 'Big Six' flagship.

Glas, today best remembered as the inventor of the timing belt, had once been a well-known maker of agricultural machinery. From 1955 they produced a head-on competitor for the NSU Prinz in the form of the popular Goggomobil, before moving up-market in the 1960s with the 1004/1204/1304 range. These begot the BMW-like 1700 saloon and pretty 1300/1700 coupés – both by Frua – but sales did not just justify the investment against the inexorable rise of the Bavarians. It was BMW, in search of production capacity, that took Glas over in 1966.

In the midst of all this, NSU could only forge ahead. In the land of the still largely unrestricted autobahn, they saw a market for a high-speed saloon that could showcase the Wankel's advantages, while appealing to buyers who were excited by new technology. The Germans were, of course, all about leading advanced engineering when it came to cars – and engineering generally – although they were probably better known for the quality of that engineering than for really groundbreaking concepts.

Beautifully finished as they were, Mercedes-Benz made very conservative cars in the 1960s. The firm had pioneered fuel injection on passenger cars but had been slow to adopt disc brakes and had absolutely no interest in aerodynamics. It was even possible to argue that Mercedes clung to flawed concepts such as swing axles in heavy cars with an increasingly middle-aged image. With the exception of the absurdly complex 600, in the 1960s they were effectively making a highly-developed version of a saloon car that they had introduced in the early 1950s.

THE RISE OF THE 'SPORTS SALOON'

The perception of BMW was of a 'younger' company that was more thrusting in its attitude, yet like Mercedes-Benz, its cars were in no sense revolutionary. In many ways BMW, with its 1961 1500 saloon, had merely taken over where the recently departed Borgward had left off.

However, along with cars like the British Rover 2000 and Triumph 2000, the Bavarians had spotted a trend for compact and sporty executive family vehicles that did not rely on sheer size and ostentatious styling for their appeal. They were quick, well finished, fun to drive and reassuringly expensive.

It was at this market that the NSU Ro80 was squarely aimed. With its 7,500-strong workforce, NSU was a small firm in comparison to Mercedes or BMW, but also a bigger operation than Porsche. Yet it could see a day when the popularity of its rear-engined, air-cooled economy saloons would falter. Consequently, much was resting on the success of the Ro80.

It was against this background that the new big NSU evolved. Luthe's 1:1 scale clay model was put together by a small six-man team. It was now officially known as Ro80 – despite the increase in power – and presented to the NSU board in September 1963. Apart from asking for the window line to be raised and the width expanded by 5cm (2in), the design was approved. It was recognisably the car that would be presented to the world at the Frankfurt IAA in 1967.

There were many details to fine tune. The glazed-in nose of the 1:5 model – intriguingly similar to what Citroën would devise for its 1970 SM – had been rejected due to cooling problems, giving way to the trademark oblong headlamp units either side of the narrow, finely drawn grille. For these early Bosch lamps, the horizontal body edge was continued over the headlamp glasses and the grille (aluminium rather than the later, cheaper plastic) was almost flush with the body panels. The later post-1970 headlamps protrude from the bodywork.

Using 978 cotton threads attached to the body, the aerodynamic properties of the shape were established in a two-day session in the wind tunnel of Stuttgart University, emerging at an impressive 0.32cd for the full-size model that Luthe had made slippery by instinct rather than science. He knew from the beginning that the new car had to be aerodynamic to take the edge off the Wankel engine's thirst. The production Ro80 would be a still excellent 0.35, making the big NSU as slippery as a Porsche 911 and 30–40 per cent more aerodynamic than any other saloon car of the time – other than the Citroën DS – and most sports cars, including sleek machinery like the fixed-head Jaguar E-Type.

Stability was another preoccupation of German designers – driving a VW Beetle on a windy autobahn was not a pleasant experience – and Luthe made sure that the Ro80 was outstanding in this respect. Its huge 21-cubic foot/600-litre boot would be a secondary benefit of its high tail/low nose outline that put the centre of pressure just behind the natural steer line for optimal stability. Even the windscreen wipers' arms had pressure plates to keep them on the massively deep, double-curvature windscreen at speed.

There were to be no quarter vents in the doors, whose frames only protruded 1/8th of an inch (3.2mm) from the surface of the glass for clean air flow. The rain gutters were tucked well into the screen pillars of the strong, deeply glazed roof, which seemed to hover above the sculptured

CAR OF THE YEAR, CAR OF THE DECADE?

The long deep 25 cubic foot (708ltr) boot endeared the car to many buyers.

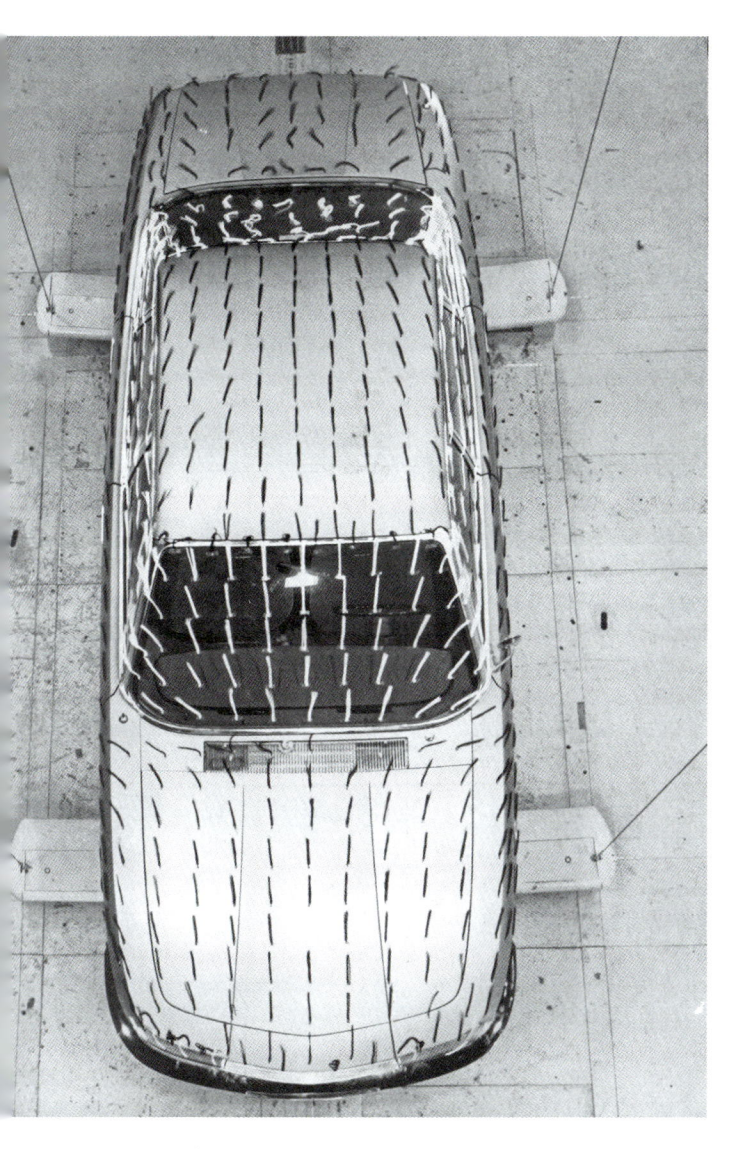

NSU liked to pretend the Ro80 was 'styled' in the wind tunnel, but it was only after the shape was settled on that NSU subjected the car to wind tunnel testing – with impressive results.

flanks of the body. It was clean, almost ethereal and so timeless that, from today's perspective, it seems to get better with the passing years rather than more dated. Only minor detailing, and the slender 175-section tyres, date the Ro80 even today. It is still cited by numerous high-profile design gurus – Bruno Sacco of Mercedes-Benz among them – as the car they would most like to have in their own portfolios.

There was a rumour abroad at the time of its launch that the Ro80 had been designed not by Luthe but a young Italian named Pio Manzu, later responsible for the Fiat 127. The evidence for this is thin and does not really extend beyond the fact that Manzu studied in Germany and, while working on an NSU TT-based sports car project (the Autonova), would have been privy to the goings-on in Luthe's Neckarsulm styling department. As others have pointed out, there is something too intuitive and emotional about the Ro80 for it to have been the work of Manzu, who saw himself very much as an all-purpose industrial designer, and who approached the task of creating an automobile in the same way he would a kettle or the beautiful furniture associated with his name. NSU did not deny these rumours, not out of a lack of respect for Luthe (in fact his authorship remained officially unattributed for decades), but because the company had taken a last-minute decision to avoid glorifying individuals; a refreshingly different attitude to today's personality-led

■ CAR OF THE YEAR, CAR OF THE DECADE?

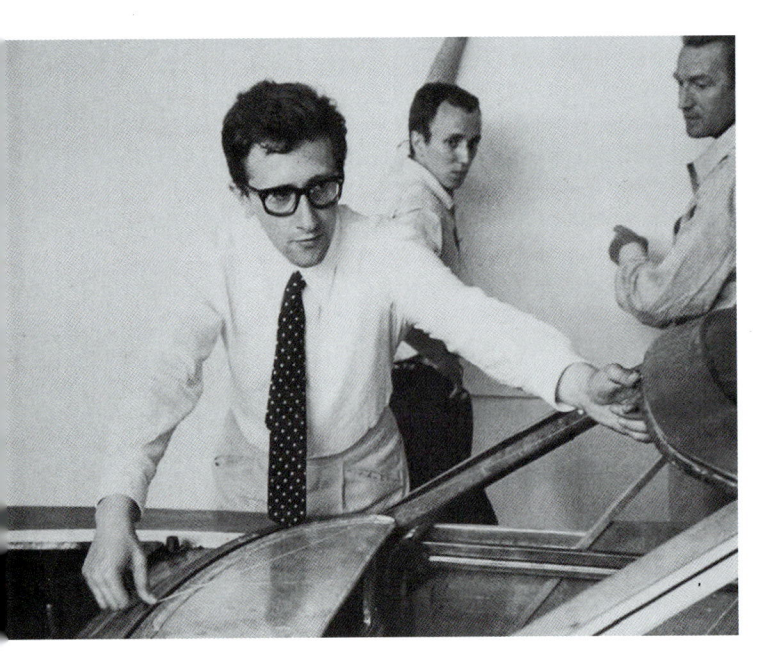

Pio Manzu, later responsible for the Fiat 127, was often cited as the true author of the Ro80's shape…

…but the evidence is thin: he studied in Germany and working on an NSU TT-based sports car project (the Autonova) pictured.

car styling public relations. The designer himself was always fairly relaxed about the matter, although he did point out – with some justification – that the Italians designed beautiful sports cars and coupés but struggled, certainly in the 1960s, to do good saloons.

The origin of these rumours is a story in Britain's *CAR* magazine from 1968. Pitched against the new Saab 99, Vauxhall Victor, Simca 1100, Honda N600 and BMW 1600 Ti, the Ro80 had just won the journal's own '*CAR* of the Year' award, judged by a panel of eighteen judges comprising designers, racing drivers and international magazine editors across Europe, America and Japan. Given this honour, Luthe agreed to a rare interview with Jan Norbye that went well beyond the scurrilous theory about Manzu's supposed input by giving an insight into the German stylist's train of thought at the time. Luthe commented that he did not enjoy the Frankfurt show but liked Geneva and Turin 'for refreshment', although he also told Norbye that he did not have much time for dream cars and that he considered some Italian styling to be 'labour intensive'. If anything, Luthe was more oriented towards Detroit than Italy, freely admitting that he was heavily influenced by the Chevrolet Corvair when designing the Prinz. 'I would like to spend a year in Detroit', he admitted.

Luthe drove a modified NSU 1000 for his own use at the time of the interview and was NSU's sole stylist in a team that comprised two prototype builders and six modellers. He considered that his Ro80 had more Rover 2000 in it than Mercedes-Benz; he drove a Rover around for a few days while finishing the Ro80 and thought the British car a good concept, even if not quite finished in some of its styling details.

Luthe said he was rarely bothered by his bosses but welcomed input from his team, fearing that it was possible to get blinded by your own designs. 'Our first Ro80 was too wild, intentionally: the roofline rose at the back to follow the glasshouse. Then we put an upswing in the waistline to control the glass area.' His superiors voiced disquiet about the high tail at first (it was found that any attempt to lower it increased the aerodynamic drag), but Luthe urged them to wait to see the finished car before making a final judgement. 'The car could be larger inside on the same wheelbase if it was not so sporty in concept, like a BMC 1800. The glass is more angled than it needed to be and you step down into it. My first interior was more sporty.'

Luthe was emphatic that the Ro 80 was not 'styled in a wind tunnel' and that the car would have been even more slippery if the aim was merely pure aerodynamics. 'The wind tunnel people suggested some changes – things like altered wheel arch cut-outs and bulges – but we couldn't accept them for aesthetic reasons.' Most of the wind tunnel work was done to sort out positions of air intakes for the ventilation.

Luthe said he was surprised how much space the engine and its ancillaries took up in the nose. 'We might have been tempted to make the car larger … but an over-large boot is not vital today: handiness on the road is more important.'

CAR OF THE YEAR, CAR OF THE DECADE?

CLAUS LUTHE 1932–2007

Claus Luthe's story does not end with the Ro80. After styling the K70 and Audi 50/VW Polo, he joined BMW in Munich as chief designer in 1976, a time when the company had a reputation for producing boxy, conservative-looking cars. In a fourteen-year career with the firm he maintained the brand's aura of visual restraint while making each successive model sleeker and more elegant. Luthe did not want to be responsible for any design that contributed to 'optical environmental pollution'. Respected as a good engineer and manager as well as a stylist, Luthe created two generations of 3- and 5-Series cars, the 1985 and 1994 7-Series luxury saloons and the 850 Coupé. He is also credited with the BMW K100 motorcycle.

His career at BMW ended abruptly on Good Friday 1990 when he stabbed and killed his deeply troubled 33-year-old son Ulrich in the midst of a violent argument. He was convicted of the murder but did not have to serve his two-year, nine-month sentence. BMW offered Luthe his job back but he soon opted for early retirement, though he remained an external design consultant. Colleagues at BMW knew nothing of Luthe's troubled home life with his eldest offspring. Ulrich was the first of Claus and Gertrude Luthe's four children, born in 1956. Because of Gertrude's multiple sclerosis – which was not diagnosed until 1971 – Claus often assumed the roles of both parents and was particularly close to Ulrich, who suffered from a stutter. However, by his early teenage years Ulrich was becoming troublesome. He did not complete his education and in the 1970s and 1980s became increasingly addicted to alcohol and pills. At the time of the tragedy Ulrich was particularly unstable, his girlfriend having recently died from an overdose. Increasingly immobile in his later years, Claus Luthe was an enthusiastic honorary member of several NSU Ro80 clubs.

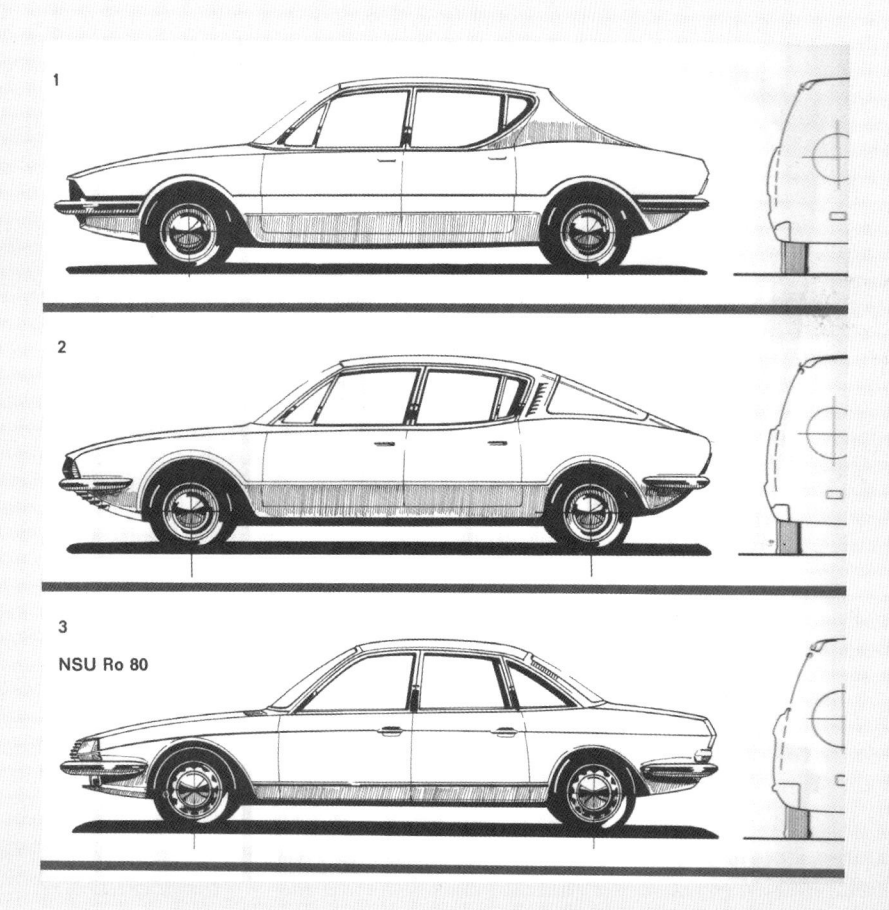

Luthe's alternative thoughts on the Ro80 have a touch of Studebaker Avanti about them.

continued overleaf

■ CAR OF THE YEAR, CAR OF THE DECADE?

CLAUS LUTHE 1932–2007 *continued*

Claus Luthe in his forties while working at BMW.

Luthe with a model of a hatchback NSU, possibly an early K70 proposal.

After the Audi merger, Luthe stayed on to design the first generation VW Polo, originally launched as the Audi 50.

Claus Luthe, born in December 1932, would become one of the most important figures in post-war European car styling but, unlike many design chiefs, was always happy to stay in the shadows. The second of five children, he was born into a deeply religious Catholic family in Wuppertal; his father was a cabinetmaker who died on the Russian front in 1945. Claus wanted to follow his older brother and become an architect. Instead, Luthe completed his apprenticeship at the coach-building firm of Voll in Wurzburg between 1948 and 1954 – working on bus designs – before joining the styling department of Fiat's German outpost Deutsche Fiat AG at Heilbronn in 1954 and then NSU at Neckarsulm from 1956.

By 1960s standards, Luthe's Ro80 had very little jewellery. The anodized bright trim around the screens and door frames was effective in making the roof look light.

The stainless bumpers were slender. There was minimal badging – one 'NSU' badge on the nose and a 'Ro80' script on the boot lid – while a chrome strip along the bottom of the doors broke up some of the bulk in the sculpted flanks. Although the stone-chip painted black section below that chrome trim looked like the sill, it was not; the bottoms of the doors wrapped over the structural member, which was only revealed with the doors open and formed part of the car's interior ventilation system.

In ten years of production NSU hardly raised a pencil to this shape. Like the Citroën DS, the Ro80 could have become a whole range of cars: Luthe schemed a two-door coupé version of his original saloon, but these drawings and models have long since been 'lost' in the Wolfsburg archives. 'The original idea for the Ro80 was a 2+2', he told Norbye, 'but the board began to doubt the wisdom of a sporty version'.

Claus Luthe originally wanted double edges in the roof – as a formal link between those in the bonnet and the boot lid – but this idea had to be abandoned because it made engineering a sunroof difficult. One aspect of the design Luthe was never quite satisfied with was the large gap between the top of the tyre and the front wheel arch, necessary to give the long, supple suspension travel the car was so famous for.

The high, rounded 'bathtub' tail of the Ro80 – which allowed that huge luggage boot – recalled Luthe's earlier work on the small NSU Prinz. The Corvair influence on this earlier design was a last minute re-think when it was discovered, in 1959, that his original proposal looked almost exactly like BMW's new 700. In fact, acceptance of the Ro80's shape at its 1967 Frankfurt show introduction was by no means universal, in an era of sharp, angular styling and when sales of cars like the VW Beetle were still in full swing. As Luthe mingled with the crowds at the Frankfurt IAA in 1967, listening to their comments, he felt that public reaction was mixed, perhaps mostly negative: it was a shape that was going to take some getting used to.

The shell, built at Neckarsulm with final assembly at Heilbronn, was relatively light but fully safety-engineered with front and rear crumple zones. The 18-gallon (82ltr) fuel tank was safely ahead of the rear axle and the engine and gearbox tended to tuck itself under the car rather than intrude into the passenger compartment in an accident. Another key safety feature was the very short steering column, with a bulkhead-mounted power steering rack.

A twin V-belt-driven vane-type ZF pump took hydraulic fluid to a valve behind the rack, which distributed the pressure to the left or right of the piston in the slave cylinder according to which way the steering was being turned. Assistance cut in with 2.2lb (1kg) of effort at the steering wheel.

As well as being considered just about the finest power steering system fitted to any car at the time, the fact that it came as standard added to the sense that the NSU was a 'complete' car with very few extras; bear in mind that PAS

The all steel body/chassis unit was strong and relatively light – but fully safety-engineered.

■ CAR OF THE YEAR, CAR OF THE DECADE?

was an expensive extra even on the lesser versions of the full-size Mercedes S Class. It was virtually unheard of – even as an option – on most 2-litre saloons, although Lancia was offering a good system on its Flavia. The floor was relatively flat, with double box-section side members either side, and the front seats were securely anchored to box-section cross members, tucked well in to help avoid injury in the event of a side impact.

ENGINE DEVELOPMENTS

Meanwhile Dr Walter Froede, head of research, was working through more than 400 combinations of apex seal and housing materials in a quest to find one that had the least harmful properties of abrasion. Rather than the Spider's hard carbon apex seals – on a very hard housing surface – the KKM612, running an 8.8:1 compression, had cast-iron IKA seals (IKA being a type of piston ring alloy developed during the war), running on a silicon surface developed by Daimler-Benz.

The rotor housings would be aluminium for heat dispersion requirements around the very hot spark plugs areas: exhaust gases ran 1700–2000°F compared with 1100–1400°F in a four-stroke reciprocating engine.

The cast iron apex seals ran spring loaded against the rotor bore, which was electrically deposited with a nickel and silicon carbide surface. With two specially developed Beru plugs per rotor firing simultaneously, the ignition system comprised twin contact breakers and twin coils. The Solex carburettors had twin chokes: 18mm for low speed running and 32mm for top end power.

There were separate exhaust manifolds for each rotor, which were rated individually at 497.5cc for a nominal displacement of 995cc. The West German road tax authorities, arguing on the basis that there were three firing strokes per revolution of a single rotor, did not quite agree with NSU's calculation. In any case, they had come up with a scheme to tax any car without conventional pistons on weight rather than cubic capacity. Weighing in at 2,668lb (1,210kg) with a full tank of fuel and a 992lb (450kg) payload, the Ro80 came under the 1,600–1,800kg class for a 198DM/£17 a year tax bill. Elsewhere, the Ro80 was subject to an FIA ruling on rotary engines used in competition that stated that a 500cc rotor was equivalent to a 1000cc in a

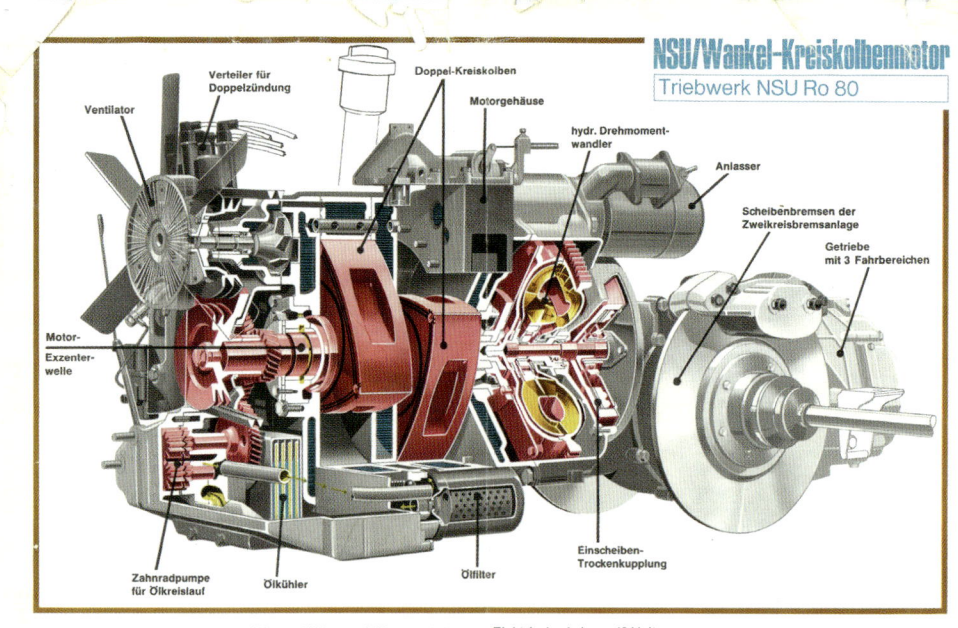

The simplicity of the light, compact Ro80 power pack shows here, good for 115bhp and giving a low bonnet line.

70

CAR OF THE YEAR, CAR OF THE DECADE?

WALTER FROEDE 1911–1984

Born in Hamburg, Froede completed an apprenticeship at the Blohm and Voss Shipyard before taking up studies at the Berlin Technical University in 1935. He wrote his dissertation on constant time-controlled fuel injection for two-stroke engines and, after a spell as a research assistant at the Research Institute for Motor Vehicles (he was an engineer observer on early testing of the VW Beetle) Froede joined NSU – as a fuel injection specialist and head of the test department – in the late 1930s.

Briefly interned after the war, Froede worked as a logging contractor before rejoining NSU in 1948, initially working in the Repair and Maintenance Department on American Military vehicles. By 1950, Walter Froede was head of the racing department – designing NSU's amazing record-breaking 'deck chair' motorcycles – but then moved to research in 1953.

Working with his chief engineer Dr Paschke, Froede was now focused on creating a commercially saleable Wankel rotary engine, the real breakthrough coming when the complicated – if theoretically 'pure' – DKM as schemed by Felix Wankel was usurped by the much more workable KKM with a stationary housing. Some NSU shareholders wanted Walter Froede ('a relaxed character with a natural sense of humour cloaking a shrewd engineering brain and an internal outlook' according to Ronald Barker writing in *CAR* magazine in 1968) sacked due to the huge sums of money being lavished on the Wankel programme. However, he kept his job and in December 1960 was even given a modern research and testing facility with nine test rooms operated by a team of twenty-five engineers, ten testers and eighty factory workers. Froede's daughter, Kirsten, worked in the public relations department at NSU. Having laboured tirelessly on the development of the Wankel engine, his final task was helping to perfect the KKM871 engines. Walter Froede retired from NSU in January 1975.

four-stroke piston engine on the basis of air consumption when the output shaft rotates three times as fast as the rotor. In other words, the Ro80 was rated at 1990cc – not unreasonable given its 115bhp (net) power output. Revs were officially limited to 6,500rpm, but NSU admitted that they could have extracted another 50bhp if wear and fuel consumption had not been a consideration. Occasional brief excursions into the red section of the rev counter were considered permissible.

The subject of exhaust emissions was only just starting to become an issue for firms that wanted to sell cars in North America. NSU certainly did, but they were confident they could get to grips with this ever-present bogeyman of the rotary engine with its high surface area-to-volume combustion chambers.

This Schlenzig press illustration shows two rotors on eccentric shaft, shallow sump with small oil filter, torque converter and inboard brake discs with ATE calipers.

■ CAR OF THE YEAR, CAR OF THE DECADE?

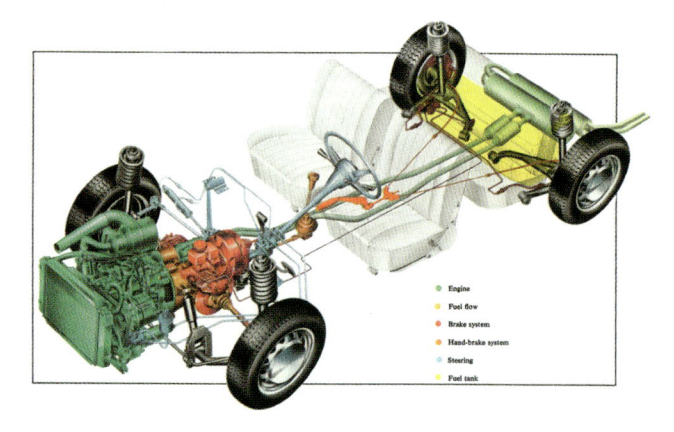

From the back cover of the early brochure, a simplified ghosted layout of the Ro80 shows how compact the engine and gearbox were.

Engine bay of an early car showing the aluminium engine fan and steel cowling.

The NSU engineers – 450 of whom were devoted to the Wankel project alone, tending to 100 bench-tested engines – consoled themselves in the belief that the compact size of the engine meant there was plenty of room for air pumps and the associated paraphernalia of the emissions' requirements. With far fewer moving parts than a conventional piston engine the Wankel could, in theory, be up to 60 per cent cheaper to make than a comparable 6-cylinder, 2-litre unit, at least once the high costs of machining the epitrochoidal housing had been tackled.

NSU had been testing two-rotor Wankels, with rotors offset at 180 degrees to each other, since 1961, and would show its first at Frankfurt in 1965. Weighing in at 265lb (120kg) with all its ancillaries, this 21 inch (533mm)-high, 20 inch (508mm)-long miracle of German engineering was to be mounted well forward of the front axle, putting 60 per cent of the car's weight on the driving wheels.

With its hefty inboard disc brakes (pioneered by the DS to reduce unsprung weight and improve the handling) and gearbox attached, the 470lb (213kg) drive train would result in power steering being made standard equipment, as the manual turning effort became too high without it, particularly when radials were fitted.

Initial testing of the twin-rotor engine was carried out in a DKW Munga off-road vehicle – using high and low ratios only – and then in a series of sixteen heavily disguised prototypes with bug-eyed single head lamps and incongruous tail fins to hide the advanced wedge-shaped profile.

The twin-rotor engine was tested in DKW Munga off-roaders.

72

CAR OF THE YEAR, CAR OF THE DECADE?

Rig testing a prototype: note the chain around the front cross member.

THE FIRST DRIVEABLE PROTOTYPES – BUT WHICH GEARBOX?

A driveable prototype was finished in April 1966 and the cars – giving about 110bhp at this stage and capable of idling at 700rpm – were tested at first with conventional four-speed gearboxes with a manual clutch pedal.

As well as failing to hide the over-run snatch – or 'three stroking' – endemic in the peripheral ports of the Wankel engine, these transmissions had synchromesh problems. Also, when tested in the mountains with a caravan in tow (or in one case a Renault 16, which ended up towing the failed NSU back to base under cover of darkness), they destroyed their clutches because of the poor low-speed torque.

The Simca hydrostatic semi-automatic was briefly considered as a possibility before being rejected as too noisy. Although a British made Borg-Warner fully automatic gearbox was tried in an Ro80, it seems that the Porsche Sportomatic-inspired semi-automatic was established as the only practical alternative quite early on. If NSU intended to stick with the peripheral ports (for top end, autobahn-storming power) rather than the side porting favoured by Mazda (for its Cosmo 110S), no other system would give the Neckarsulm boffins the combination of refinement and versatility that they were seeking.

Drive from the engine's eccentric shaft went through a torque converter that boosted torque at low speed but effectively locked up to become a straightforward and more efficient coupling when cruising above 2,200rpm. A microswitch in the top of the gear lever operated relays in the vacuum control unit to actuate the single dry-plate clutch on the three-speed Fichtel and Sachs transmission. There was a 'Park' position and NSU liked to call the forward speeds 'Performance ranges' rather than gears.

The Ro80 was designed to be easy to look after. It was possible to adjust the fierceness of the clutch operation by turning a screw on the vacuum control unit – mounted on the right-hand side of the engine bay. The headlamp bulbs could be swapped simply by removing plates on the back of the headlamps and the rear lamp clusters were held in by two threaded mountings for easy access to the bulbs. It was possible to slide the front seats off their runners for cleaning.

The Ro80's brakes were extensively tested on the Grosseglocker pass, a 30-mile (48-km) long high Alpine road in Austria famed for its thirty-six hairpin bends. ATE/Dunlop discs were used all round, 11.8 inch front and 10.7 inch rear – with an integral drum for the hand brake – inside 14-inch wheels. The front discs were on the gearbox end of the drive shafts to save on unsprung weight (the twin-cylinder front calipers were heavy) but still subject to a good breeze to keep them cool: and you did not have to take the wheels off to change the pads.

A tandem master cylinder operated twin independent circuits, one on all four wheels and one on the secondary cylinders of the front calipers (which had four pistons each), leaving 75 per cent of normal efficiency in the event that one circuit should fail. The servo acted directly on the master cylinder and, as a further refinement, a compensator regulated the braking effort on the rear wheels to help prevent them locking up too quickly in a crash stop. Gold was used to coat the electrical contacts on the brake warning light circuit, because gold cannot corrode or oxidize.

THE LAUNCH

It was in this form that the NSU Ro80 was launched at the Frankfurt Motor Show in September 1967, although the

■ CAR OF THE YEAR, CAR OF THE DECADE?

The public launch of the Ro80 was at the Frankfurt Motor Show in September 1967, although the press launch took place a few days earlier at the Solitude Palace – the Rocco hunting retreat near Stuttgart, shown here in the background.

A silver car at Frankfurt in 1968 wearing the new alloy wheels from Fuchs.

74

CAR OF THE YEAR, CAR OF THE DECADE?

press launch took place a few days earlier at the Solitude Palace – the Rocco hunting retreat near Stuttgart – using some of the eighteen pre-production cars that had been laid down earlier in the month. These showed some interesting detail differences, the most obvious being simulated wood on the dash, 'Wankel' on the steering wheel boss and non-tinted glass. There was also a black – rather than body-colour painted – engine bay where the engine fan was aluminium and its cowl iron; later, the fan would be plastic. The headlining on 1967 model-year cars was in grey cloth: white plastic was then standardised with black as a (rare) option.

As a genuine German technical achievement, the car received wide and enthusiastic attention in a country that was showing signs of change. The death of its long-serving post-war chancellor Konrad Adenauer in April seemed to mark the end of an era as ordinary, hard-working West Germans read about student riots over their morning sausages: the shooting of a young protester by an undercover policeman at a Berlin demonstration against the Vietnam war gave an early taste of the public unrest that would spread across Europe the following year.

Against this backdrop, the new NSU was a reassuring example of the nation's continuing technical prowess. Visitors to the forty-third Frankfurt IIA marvelled not only at the extraordinarily clean, low-waisted styling but also at the fact that NSU, purveyors of humble rear-engined, air-cooled runabouts until this point, had performed such a giant leap in their aspirations in that the car was not only beautifully styled but also superbly finished inside and out with doors that shut with Mercedes-like solidity.

Unsurprisingly, the Ro80 was the star of the Frankfurt show, where it competed for attention with the new Ford Escort, the Opel Commodore and the Saab 99. Freshly hatched 1967 exotica such as the ISO Fidia, Ferrari Dino 206GT, Aston Martin DBS and the Toyota 2000GT were so remote from the financial and practical requirements of most people's lives as to be almost irrelevant. But the moderately affluent middle classes could dream about owning an NSU Ro80 – or one of the new Fiat 124 coupés. Many Germans also got their first look at cars as diverse as the Citroën Dyane, the fuel-injected Triumph TR5 and the mid-engined Matra 530, but few could take their eyes off the elegant vision of the future the big new NSU represented.

Production was set to begin at the end of September. At DM14,000, the Ro80 went nose-to-nose with the BMW 2000 and Mercedes 230. It was considerably more expensive than a big Opel Commodore yet it was considered a bargain, so much so that NSU could not cope with the demand at first. A Saturday shift had to be brought in at Neckarsulm to boost output from forty to fifty cars a day to a full 100 to keep up with orders in 1968, against the backdrop of an improving German economy with full employment and zero inflation after the tail-off in growth in 1966 and 1967.

The well-known problems with the Spider's engine, as well as the 3,000 troublesome outboard motors NSU had sold, had not exactly boosted public confidence in the Wankel. So the price of the new car included a generous 25,000 kilometre (15,534 miles) guarantee on the engine at a time when 10,000 kilometres (6,214 miles) was more usual.

The sophistication of the Ro80 astonished everyone in 1967: front-wheel drive; in-board front discs; semi-automatic transmission; fully-independent suspension; and roomy, slippery body. A great car even without its revolutionary Wankel rotary engine.

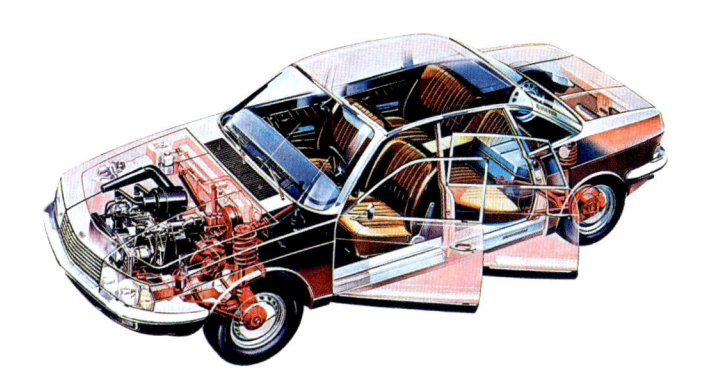

■ CAR OF THE YEAR, CAR OF THE DECADE?

Initial demand for the car was strong thanks to rapturous press reports. Here the early Ro80's near completion at Neckarsulm.

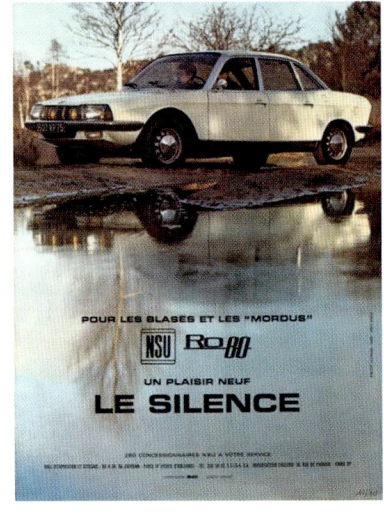

RIGHT: **French advert for the Ro80.**

FAR RIGHT: **The Ro80 was reasonably popular in Italy, where NSUs sold in greater numbers than VW.**

Promotional material combined soothing reassurances about NSU's ever-expanding fully trained service network and freely available spares, although the more eagle-eyed might have been alarmed that the very special Beru 280/1862 spark plugs cost three times as much as a normal plug.

Chatter marks on the bore surface, apex seal wear and high oil consumption were now all 'things of the past' according to NSU's launch press material. Early engines were dyno tested, stripped and inspected by the factory experimental department before being reassembled and dyno tested a second time.

The Ro80, as launched in 1967, was an extraordinarily complete package that included radial tyres (Michelin XAS), twin fog and reversing lights, reclining seats and a heated rear window; features that usually cost extra even in expensive cars at the time. Felix Wankel was sufficiently impressed with the Ro80 that he was even willing to accept one, this time, as a mark of respect from his former employers: but only if he could have it painted in a special silver-grey colour.

CAR OF THE YEAR, CAR OF THE DECADE?

The Ro80 was designed to meet all up-coming safety regulations. In a front smash, the engine and gearbox tended to be driven underneath the car; at the rear, the fuel tank was mounted safely behind the rear seats.

BELOW RIGHT: **Claus Luthe's vision of a sportier dashboard than the one settled on.**

Von Heydekampf of NSU was keen to point out that Herr Wankel had nothing to do with designing the car. Then again, neither had the recently released Albert Speer, Hitler's former Minister of Armaments and Munitions. The ex-Nazi was also quietly gifted one of the early Ro80s: he was still running his third one when he died in 1981. Two cars were sent to Russia as diplomatic offerings. Given that the communists were busy cheerfully copying the Wankel design without bothering to take out a licence, this was a pretty generous move.

The spacious flat-floored interior of the Ro80 was luxurious, safe – but in no way ostentatious. For the dashboard design, Luthe worked through a variety of ideas on the subject that included a variation on the Mercedes vertical thermometer speedometer style, a chrome-laden, American-inspired interpretation and various sporty and/or futuristic ideas including a tightly grouped binnacle that was rejected by the board as being too radical for traditional buyers. Luthe finally came down in favour of a plain and functional arrangement fully in keeping with the character of the car. A simulated wooden facia featured in the first brochure for the model, but a leatherette covering was adopted when production got into full swing and stayed throughout the model's life.

The four-instrument display clustered in front of the driver comprised classic white on black VDO speedometer and rev counter flanked by smaller instruments either side: fuel and engine temperature in the left-hand gauge and a clock on the right. Lights for low fuel/brake fluid/oil and handbrake 'on' plus choke and ignition warnings were spread across the top of the instrument panel, with pull out crash-safe knobs for lights, heated rear window – nine wires on the early cars – fog lights and four-way flasher (hazard lights were a rare standard item at the time outside Germany, where they had been a legal requirement since 1967) along the bottom. Headlamp flashing, indication, windscreen wash/wipe and horn were all on column stalks. The big glove box contained the eight easily accessible fuses and there was a storage shelf underneath the dash on the passenger's side, a feature that did not make it on to right-hand-drive versions.

■ CAR OF THE YEAR, CAR OF THE DECADE?

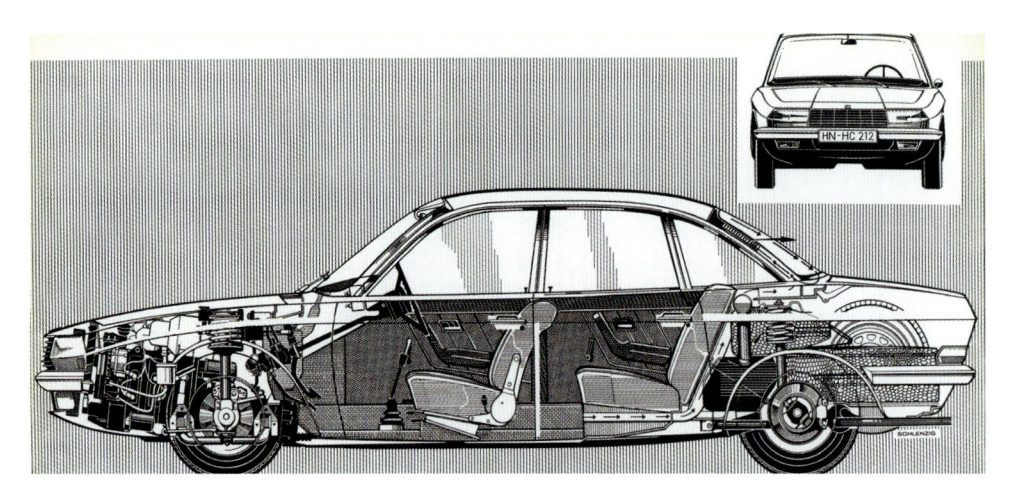

LEFT AND MIDDLE: **NSU** put a lot of effort into the fresh air ventilation of the Ro80 with a low pressure area in front of the screen. Efficient aerodynamics tended to mitigate against air flow inside: big windows did not help either.

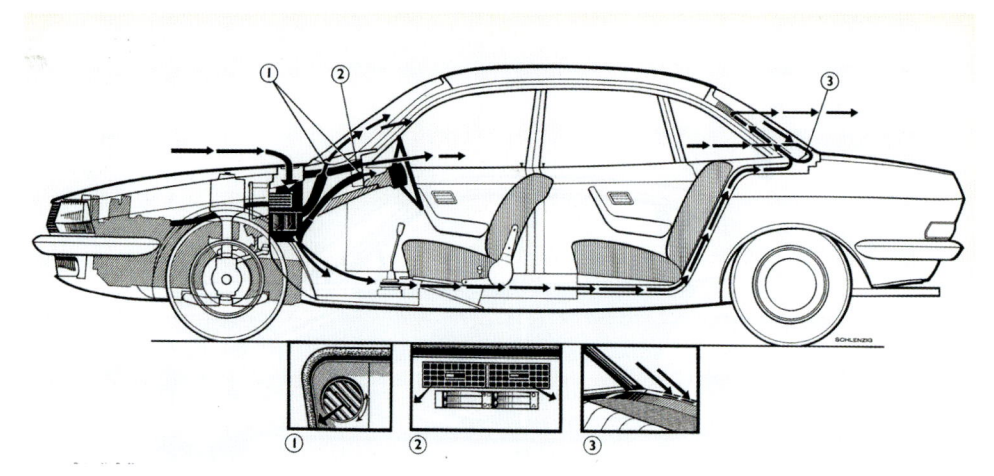

Early (first year only) dashboard with wood finish and the **Wankel** logo on the steering wheel boss.

CAR OF THE YEAR, CAR OF THE DECADE?

A much more familiar version of the Ro80 dashboard used through to the end of production – simple and clear.

Slide controls for what NSU called its 'Air Comfort System' were in the middle of the dash. This consisted of independent heating and ventilation systems, with driver and passenger having individual fresh-air grilles. There was a two-speed blower and, behind the side windows and on the front edge of the rear windows, extractors to change the air. However, none of this really took into account the greenhouse effect of the Ro80's huge windows, which could turn the interior into a furnace on a really hot day. Strangely an air conditioning option was never offered by the factory, or the electric window lifts you might have thought such an expensive car would have as standard.

There was ample room for five people inside, where passengers enjoyed nylon velour carpeting under foot, doors with combined armrests/grab handles and leatherette, wool cloth or velour trim on the seats. Leather was a rarely specified option and, in all cases, the colour choice was restricted to black, dark blue, beige, red, green and grey. In the front the plush fully reclining seats – with height adjustment on the driver's side for left-hand-drive cars – were supplied by Recaro.

The rear seats had 170–280mm (6.7–11in) of leg room thanks to the long wheelbase. The back rests of the seats could be unhooked to give clear access to the boot, giving more than 7 feet (2,134mm) of length for skis. Front seat belts were not a standard fitting until August 1972: when seat belts became obligatory in Germany in 1976, the older cars had to be retrofitted with them, which is why early 1970s cars have such a variety of systems.

The beautiful Fuchs alloys that became such a visual trademark of the Ro80 did not become available until 1968. Fifty per cent lighter than the pressed steel wheels, they were of a forged heavy-duty type with no welding or rivets.

The radio with an electric antenna would cost you extra. A full range of sets from Blaupunkt and Becker were available on request – you could listen to any of them at 100mph without having to turn the volume up – but bodywork colours for the first year were restricted to Sepia metallic (9 per cent) Sagunto blue (55 per cent) and glacier white (31 per cent) while 5 per cent of cars had special order colours such as Derby Red and Silver Metallic for shows or important customers.

79

■ CAR OF THE YEAR, CAR OF THE DECADE?

MAZDA COSMO 110S 1967–72

Where the Ro80 ultimately failed, the original Mazda Cosmo was the first step towards the huge sales success of the RX7 in the 1970s and 1980s. This was a good-looking car that could somehow only be Japanese in the way it seemed to mix Italian, British and even American styling cues. Production began in 1967, but the design was frozen in 1962 and first seen in public as a prototype at the Tokyo show in 1964. It had been agreed that NSU should reveal its Wankel Spider first.

Eighty pre-production cars were built for dealers (NSU had a Cosmo in its experimental department) and the factory test department and production settled down to a car a day from the end of 1967 in Hiroshima. Officially it was only badged as a Cosmo on its home market: export cars were badged 110S. There were two versions: the original L10A type with 110bhp from a four-plug, twin-distributor, twin-rotor engine breathing through a four-barrel Hitachi carburettor and nominally rated at 2 litres, with each of the rotors worth twice their actual 491cc swept volume. A further 833 L10B Cosmos were built from 1968 to 1972 with 128bhp, five speeds and a longer wheelbase, but still with the De Dion rear suspension and disc/drum brakes, now servo assisted. In the interests of low-down torque, smoother idle and part-throttle characteristics, Mazda had a preference for straight inlet porting rather than NSU's autobahn-friendly peripheral ports and the Cosmo was as happy to potter at low speeds as it was to sing around 7,000rpm with that smooth hum that can only be a rotary engine. Those revs would give you 120mph (193km/h) in top gear.

With a slight rearward weight bias (the compact engine was mounted well back) the Cosmo was a really agile go-where-you-point-it car with light, neutral steering, lots of adhesion and very little body roll plus a firm, flat ride that seemed to confirm its sports rather than GT aspirations.

The Cosmo name was used on many subsequent generations of rotary-engined flagship Mazdas that varied widely in desirability. However, the 1967–72 originals are now regarded as one of the rare jewels among 1960s Japanese classics, and priced accordingly. Meanwhile, the Mazda rotary concept was rolled out on a variety of more affordable models, beginning in 1968 with the little R100, which proved its reliability by coming a creditable fifth on the 1968 Marathon de la Route and sold particularly well in Australia and New Zealand. The 1970 RX2 Capella was based on the piston-engined 616, while the 1975 RX3 Savanna proved to be the most popular Mazda rotary car offered before the RX7 appeared.

The Cosmo was the first of the Mazda rotary cars and still the most desirable.

CAR OF THE YEAR, CAR OF THE DECADE?

Although promoted in the UK, no serious attempts were made to sell the car in any numbers.

All the major motoring magazines tested the Cosmo. *Motor* **extracted 116mph (187km/h) out of its 1968 test car.**

Neatly plumbed-in engine with twin distributors.

Unlike many early Japanese cars, the Cosmo 110S was comfortable for tall people.

continued overleaf

81

■ CAR OF THE YEAR, CAR OF THE DECADE?

MAZDA COSMO 110S 1967–72 *continued*

LEFT: **For a while, Mazda threw its lot in with the Wankel concept, the R100 being one of its more successful rotary models.**

BELOW LEFT: **The 1970 RX2 Capella, based on the piston-engined 616.**

BELOW RIGHT: **The truly bizarre Roadpacer luxury saloon.**

Mazda did not attempt to build a car to rival the sophistication of the Ro80 with these sometimes ornately styled and unexcitingly engineered models. They were quick cars, but too thirsty for most buyers, although a few were tempted by the competitive prices and high equipment levels.

The more up-market R130 Luce was a Bertone-styled coupé aimed at the domestic Japanese market and Mazda's only front-wheel-drive rotary model. A true oddity was the Mazda Roadpacer, a large saloon intended to be the Japanese manufacturer's answer to the big V8-engined Nissan President/Toyota Century/Mitsubishi Debonair formal luxury cars that were built for the local market.

It was actually nothing more than a right-hand-drive Holden Premier bodyshell – bought in from GM's Australian outpost – and fitted with Mazda's 130bhp rotary engine and an automatic gearbox. Slow and thirsty (103mph, 9 mpg; 166km/h, 31.39ltr/100km) only 800 were sold through to its official demise in 1977, mostly to the Japanese government. Mazda's commitment to the rotary idea was best illustrated by the introduction in 1974 of a Wankel-engined pick-up (the Repu, a one-year-only model for North America and Canada built to the tune of 15,000 examples) and a 26-seater bus called Parkway.

CAR OF THE YEAR, CAR OF THE DECADE?

Reclining front seats were standard with vinyl cloth/ velour or (rarely) leather options.

In the boot was a neat tool kit with a plug spanner and two plugs, Beru or Bosch. NSU even provided a special pin for cleaning out the windscreen washer jets.

Smiles all round as von Heydekampf and Frankenberger accept the Car of the Year award for the Ro80 in 1968.

The combination of handling, ride and overall refinement made the Ro80 a strong candidate for the title of best saloon in the world.

AS GOOD AS IT LOOKED

It would be fair to say that the Ro80 caused a sensation not seen in the motoring world since the announcement of the Citroën DS, the BMC Mini or the more recent Lamborghini Miura.

What's more, reports in the press soon confirmed that it was every bit as good as it looked, setting new standards of refinement, stability and all round road behaviour. All this acclaim made its victory in the 1967 Car of The Year awards – presented at the Amsterdam Hilton in February 1968 – almost a foregone conclusion, especially as the opposition that year was hardly sparkling: the Fiat 125 and Simca 1100 came second and third respectively.

The Ro80 was the first German winner of this award, which had been organised by the Dutch magazine *Autovise* since 1963: previous winners had been the Rover 2000 (1963), Austin 1800 (1964), Renault 16 (1965) and Fiat 124 (1966). Many pointed out that had the Ro80 been entered as a new model in 1969 or 1970, it probably would still have swept the board.

Judged by an international panel of forty-four motoring journalists (and chaired by the Belgian writer/Le Mans winner Paul Frère) it was reported that thirty-five of them voted for the NSU.

83

■ CAR OF THE YEAR, CAR OF THE DECADE?

Britain's outspoken and colourful monthly *CAR* had no hesitation in voting the Ro80 Car of the Year.

Even misgivings about the new car's thirst – by 2-litre standards – were tempered by the fact that its rotary engine would run on 3-star/92 octane fuel and was easily as smooth and quiet as any V8.

NSU rather optimistically quoted 25mpg (11.3ltr/100km), but even at 15 to 20 miles to the gallon (18.83–14.12ltr/100km) it compared well with other big five-seaters of the day. Cruising at 90mph (145km/h) it would return 19mpg (14.87ltr/100km) and was less thirsty overall than the soon-to-die 'baby' Jaguar 240 – and not far behind a Ford Corsair. More relevant in those pre-fuel crisis days was the fact that a carefully driven Ro80 – not going over 3,500 revs was a good rule of thumb – might go 360 miles (579km) on a tank of fuel. To some extent the thirst was also offset by fairly modest servicing requirements with, for instance, no suspension grease points. Perhaps mindful of how often owners would

CAR OF THE YEAR, CAR OF THE DECADE?

need to handle it, NSU gave its new flagship a pleasingly tactile polished aluminium locking fuel cap.

Not everybody got on with the semi-automatic gearbox (although many came to love it), while others would have liked to have had the extra power that the Ro80's chassis could so easily have handled. The churning torque converter certainly made the initial acceleration feel more ponderous than it actually was but, even so, the Ro80 was no tyre-smoking rocket ship: zero to sixty times varied between 12 and 14 seconds.

However, it was the way the car swished from fifty to seventy or eighty miles an hour so effortlessly – and then

The Ro80 was the undoubted star of the Frankfurt Motor Show in 1967.

The shape was startlingly futuristic; it took some time for it to become widely accepted.

85

CAR OF THE YEAR, CAR OF THE DECADE?

maintained 100 or 110mph (160 or 177km/h), with its engine getting smoother and quieter the faster it spun – that could not be conveyed in mere figures.

Top speed was anything between 107 and 117mph (172–188km/h), depending on who you believed and how much you were willing to exceed the red line. Some maintain that a car with a strong engine will pull well over 130mph (209km/h). Second gear was good for 80mph (129km/h) if 6,500rpm was observed, or almost 100mph using 8,000rpm in these early four-plug cars, although the speedometers were always a shade on the optimistic side.

NSU freely admitted that wear increased and oil consumption went up if you used very high revs (400 miles per pint [1,133km/ltr] using 7,250rpm, for instance) but at least you did not have to change the oil very often or even run the engine in, although the handbook recommended keeping speeds below 5,500rpm/100mph for the first 600 miles (966km).

Although NSU had limited ambitions for the new car on the American market, they designed its interior to meet all known upcoming legislation on crash safety. There was a feeling quite early on that the unfamiliar technology and the lack of dealer infrastructure would limit sales in this huge and unforgiving territory. Twenty examples were exported in 1968, mostly to be picked-over for technical secrets by domestic car manufacturers.

The British market, always possessed of a healthy appetite for fast, beautiful but also 'different' cars, was another matter.

There were a few left-hand-drive imports as early as December 1967 (thought to be around thirty cars), with launch events at the NSU headquarters at Shoreham and Brands Hatch. Right-hand-drive cars began to appear in October 1968, with the original one-piece headlamps replaced by four Hella circular lamps with halogen bulbs for dipped and main beam fitted in specially-made nacelles. There seems to have been no particular legal reason for this on the UK market, but the quad lights had better output and relieved the importers of the bother of having to modify the reflectors of the original lights, which, in any case, had thick lenses that were prone to distortion. In Italy local rules meant that the rear bumper was divided with the licence plate filling the void.

A TRULY MODERN SALOON

All who tested the Ro80 in 1968 and 1969 agreed that the car's steering, brakes, handling and ride were superb. In fact, there was so little to criticise that pundits were generally reduced to commenting on things like the low-geared window winders or the fact that the wipers, on right-hand-drive cars, were set up for left-hand drive and thus left a large unswept area.

In its classic 1968 road test (undertaken in snowy Italy on an early left-hand-drive factory press car) *Motor* magazine said: 'The steering, handling and road holding are probably better individually and almost certainly collectively than

Not everybody wanted to wait for right-hand drive: here the famous show jumping champion Harvey Smith helps NSU dealer George Cordingly promote the new Ro80 in Yorkshire.

The first officially imported UK market Ro80s had this four-headlight arrangement.

those of any other luxury car we have tried.' Roger Bell, author of that test, also pointed out – as many others have since – that the big NSU would have been a great car even without its rotary engine, so hard had its creators worked to make it a truly complete, truly modern saloon.

Comfort was outstanding; a handful of other cars might have had an even softer ride and lower levels of road noise, but the cumulative effective of the whispering engine, the lack of wind rustle and the absolute stability certainly made the Ro80 one of the world's most restful saloons to drive and travel in as a passenger.

THE FIRST DOUBTS

Unfortunately, like most things that seem too good to be true, the Ro80 was just that. As the applause surrounding the launch faded and the first lucky owners (just 306 in 1967) took to German roads, reports from the field began to make their way back to eager ears at Neckarsulm. And the news was not good....

First came reports of fuel consumption as high as 10mpg (23.5ltr/100km); then it soon became obvious that cars used for short stop-start journeys were showing high levels of wear.

It began to dawn on NSU that its testing had focused on high speed, long-distance endurance rather than the sort of driving a doctor might use the car for on his daily rounds, never getting the engine properly warmed up.

Auto Motor Und Sport's 1968 survey of 191 Ro80 owners found that a quarter of them had broken down on the road at least once, that three-quarters had problems with starting and that half had had catastrophic bearing failures leading to complete engine replacement. In fact, two-thirds of the cars had been given new engines under the generous factory warranty.

So, from being an object of pride and envy the NSU Ro80 became a national joke. The story of the Ro80 drivers routinely holding up three or four fingers when they encountered each other on the road – to indicate how many new engines they had had – probably originated in an editorial cartoon in the German press. NSU themselves even referred to this rare example of German humour in one of its factory films. The subject of that film, naturally, concerned NSU's vigorous efforts to cure the Wankel engine of its ills, which we will explore in more depth in chapter five.

■ CAR OF THE YEAR, CAR OF THE DECADE?

THE SELECTIVE SEMI-AUTOMATIC

Although the Americans – led by GM and Chrysler – had almost perfected the fully automatic transmission for its own large 6-cylinder and V8 cars by the late 1950s (few of which were under 3 litres), these did not adapt well to smaller European vehicles; heavy and power sapping, automatic transmissions were not very suitable for cars under 2 litres. In Europe the focus, at first, was on ridding the driver of the effort associated with operating a clutch pedal rather than of working a gear lever – as illustrated by the system used in the Citroën DS – and thus retaining a degree of control.

BMC offered the Manumatic on its mid-size 1950s cars (supplied by Automotive Products), which still required the driver to select a gear but relieved them of the bother of controlling the clutch in traffic. The Smith's Industries system – marketed as the Easidrive by Rootes on its 1.2 litre Hillman Minx – was fully automatic, using a magnetic clutch and a series of governors and solenoids.

Neither of these systems was a commercial success, but the Ferodo-designed system used by Simca – and Fiat's Idroconvert – found a reasonable audience on small rear-engined models. Renault successfully offered an electromagnetic system named Ferlec on the Dauphine and related rear-engined models.

Thus, there was nothing new about the principle of the Ro80's three-speed 'selective automatic' transmission. It comprised a hydraulic torque converter with the impeller attached to the eccentric shaft of the engine and the turbine impeller for the gearbox and the diffuser. There was a single dry-plate clutch between the torque converter and the three-speed, all indirect gearbox, actuated when the driver touched the gear lever. It was supplied by Fichtel & Sachs, an old established German company with its roots in the manufacture of bicycle hubs and ball bearings. Now part of ZF, Fichtel and Sachs were also Wankel licensees producing single-rotor stationary engines.

The almost flat floor of the Ro80 gave a feeling of space.

CAR OF THE YEAR, CAR OF THE DECADE?

The BMC/Automotive Products attempt to build a semi-automatic never caught on.

The Ro80 transmission shared its principles with the Sportomatic offered in the Porsche 911 from 1967 to 1979 and was also available as an option on the NSU 1200. VW offered it as the Autostick from 1968 to 1976. Its predecessor was the Fichtel and Sachs Saxomat, which was used in the Lancia Flaminia, Fiat 1800, various Borgward, Saabs, Auto Unions and German Fords from 1957 onwards and – under different brand names – by Opel and Mercedes. It was Mercedes who adapted the system to use a hydraulic torque converter rather than a centrifugal clutch and it was in this form that it was adopted by NSU and Porsche in three- and four-speed form respectively. The Stuttgart people wanted to make the 911 more appealing to North American buyers, whereas NSU needed a transmission that would make the best of the poor low-speed torque and mask the over-run snatch (thanks to the cushioning effect of the torque converter) that was endemic in the design of Wankel engine, while at the same time retaining most of the driver appeal of a full manual without sapping too much power or fuel, although it almost certainly had a detrimental effect on mpg.

continued overleaf

■ CAR OF THE YEAR, CAR OF THE DECADE?

THE SELECTIVE SEMI-AUTOMATIC *continued*

Change quality was variable and very dependent on having the correct tick-over and setting on the vacuum servo for the clutch. Although some owners came to love the semi-auto in their Ro80s, it seems certain that the car would have found more buyers if it had offered a fully manual or fully automatic option; not everybody got on with the idea of having three 'driving ranges' and some drivers abused the engine's seeming willingness to pull away (albeit slowly) in top gear as an invitation to treat first and second gears as being optional, even in town driving.

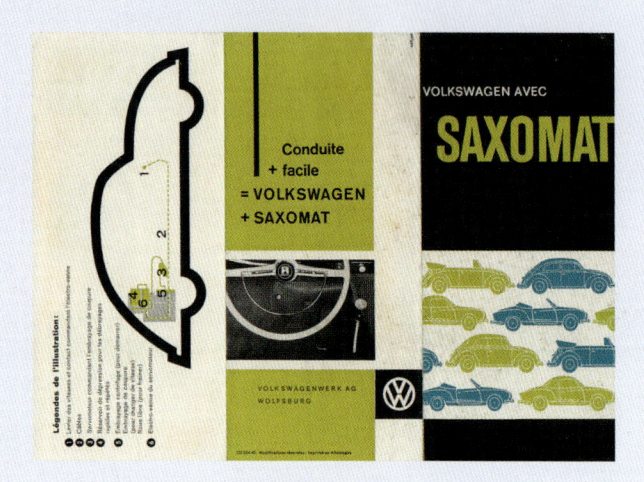

In the UK Borg Warner worked with NSU on a fully automatic Ro80, as reported by former employee John Player of the now disbanded Ro80 Club of Great Britain. Writing in 1999, he explained that the gear shifts were smooth but that it proved difficult to get good initial acceleration without setting the stall speed so high that it made the engine sound fussy in traffic; however, the project was developed to the stage where a gear selector had been evolved that combined detents and a gate pattern similar to the one used by Jaguar years later. John Player considered the calm and civilised NSU team a delight to work with and made the point that, had a full automatic been successfully adapted, many of the engine problems might have been avoided simply because an automatic would have protected the engine from over-revving in the intermediate gears and slogging in top.

ABOVE: **Fichtel and Sachs' Saxomat gained greatest acceptance in the VW Beetle.**

Mercedes-Benz take on the concept, the Hydrak.

THE *MOTORING WHICH?* TEST, OCTOBER 1969

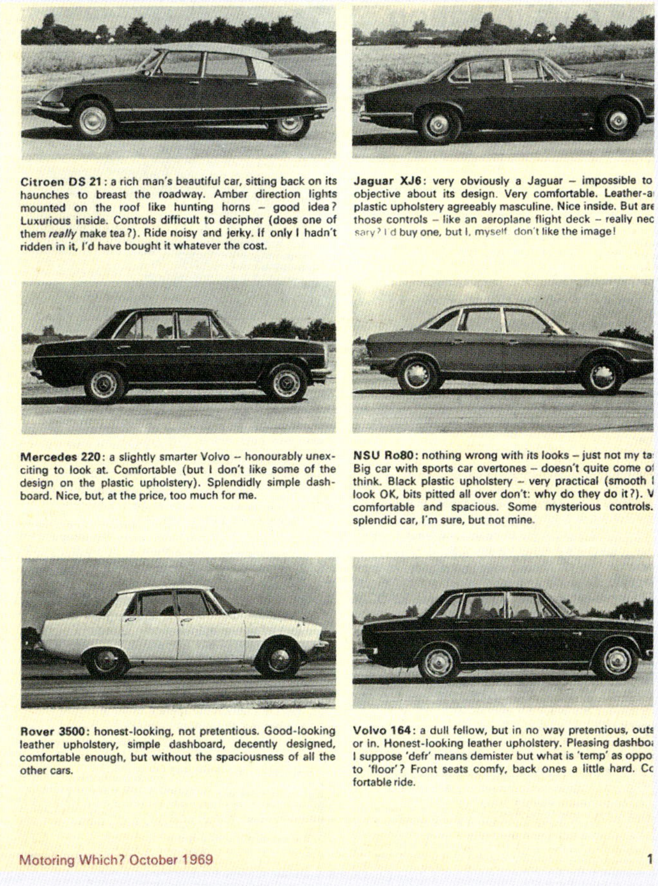

Motoring Which? was a consumer- rather than enthusiast-focused magazine that was unusual in that it actually bought, and ran, the cars it tested. This practice was designed to obtain the magazine what it believed was a more accurate impression of the car's performance, reliability and after-sales service. The October 1969 issue compared the Ro80 against the Citroën DS, Mercedes 220, Rover 3500, Volvo 164 and the Jaguar XJ6: the latter, interestingly, was the troublesome 2.8-litre version that was never released by the Jaguar Cars press office for an official road test. Although a few hundred pounds more expensive than the Volvo, Rover and the Citroën, the £2,280 fully-equipped NSU came in well under the £2,500 Jaguar and (with power steering and automatic gearbox) the near £3,000, 99mph Mercedes. With the NSU proving to be much faster than the Mercedes and as quiet as the Jaguar, *Which?* were as impressed with the Ro80 as the weekly magazines, even rating its gear change and ventilation as 'good'. In contrast to the Jaguar, which was delivered in 'very bad condition' and required an engine rebuild after burning a hole in a piston (a fault endemic to the 2.8-litre XK engine), *Which?* reported that its NSU, apart from weak synchromesh on second gear, gave virtually no trouble and was still in excellent condition after 14,000 miles (22,530km). They voted it 'Best Buy' of the six cars and in conclusion said:

> Our NSU Ro80 impressed us enormously. It was not fantastically fast, it used a lot of petrol and oil and its headlamp dip beam was pitifully weak. But its handling, power steering, ride and quietness at high speeds were outstanding and it did very well in virtually every other respect. So far, like the Mercedes, it has been one of the most reliable cars we have tested.

NSU Ro80 Specifications 1967–1977

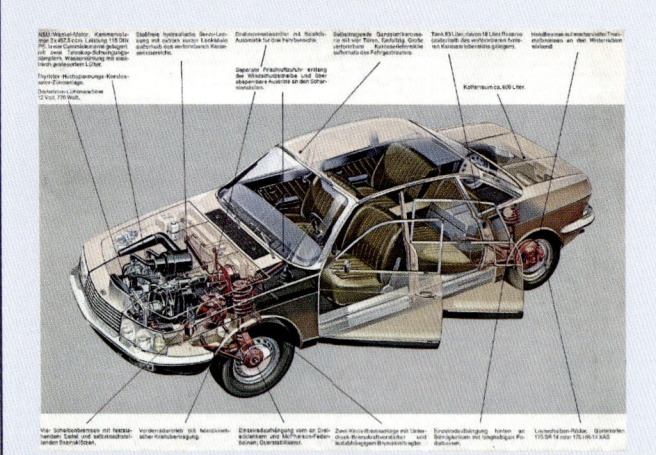

Cutaway showing strut suspension, in-board front disc brakes and forward position of compact Ro80 engine/gearbox package.

Engine
NSU-Wankel KKM 612. Two co-axial oil-cooled rotors with two main bearings in water-cooled housing. Cubic Capacity 2 x 497.5cc equivalent to 1990cc
Compression ratio: 9:1
Motor dimensions: 475/660/555mm (L/W/H)
Engine weight 143kg/315lb (dry, complete with fan and exhaust gas reactor)
Direction of rotation counter-clockwise (seen in the direction of travel)
Compression Pressure 8–10 bar. Idle speed 1,100–1,200rpm
Engine mounting 4-point rubber bearing, supported on both sides with vibration dampers
No valves. Bosch distributor, twin coils. Mechanical fuel pump. Full flow oil filter
4 x Beru 280/1862 spark plugs: 2 x Beru G3/18.

12 pint (6.8ltr) sump; 15 pint (8.5ltr) cooling system; viscous coupling fan and thermostat
Octane requirement: 90
Max power: 113.5bhp @ 5,500rpm
Max torque: 117lb ft @ 4,500rpm

Fuel system
1967–72: Two double choke compound Solex 18/32 HD carburettors with accelerator pumps
1973 model year: Automatic choke carburettor Solex 32DDITS with accelerator pump. Mechanical and electrical fuel pump

Electrical system
12 volt negative earth with Bosch 60 amp hours alternator. Eight fuses
Generator: 12-volt three-phase alternator 770W/55A, driven by double V-belt starter motor: Bosch GE (L) 12V2 HP
Battery: 12V/60 Ah ignition system
Transistorized high-voltage capacitor ignition (HKZ) with single-pulse charging
Bosch single circuit ignition distributor: Bosch PFU 2 Contact breaker points
Ignition coil: ignition transformer, Bosch 0221 121 002
Spark plugs: spark plug with auxiliary mass electrode.

Transmission
Fichtel and Sachs Hydrokinetic torque converter coupled to three-speed synchromesh gearbox with single dry-plate clutch operated by Fichtel and Sachs vacuum servo energised by micro-switch in gear lever.

Top gear (range 3)	0.788:1	= 18.8 mph per 1,000rpm
2nd gear (range 2)	1.208:1	= 12.3 mph per 1,000rpm
1st gear (range 1)	2.056:1	= 7.2 mph per 1,000rpm
Reverse	2.105:1	
Final drive	4.857:1	

Another cutaway from the 1969 press pack shows construction of the floorpan, the firewall-mounted rack and pinion steering and semi-trailing-arm rear suspension.

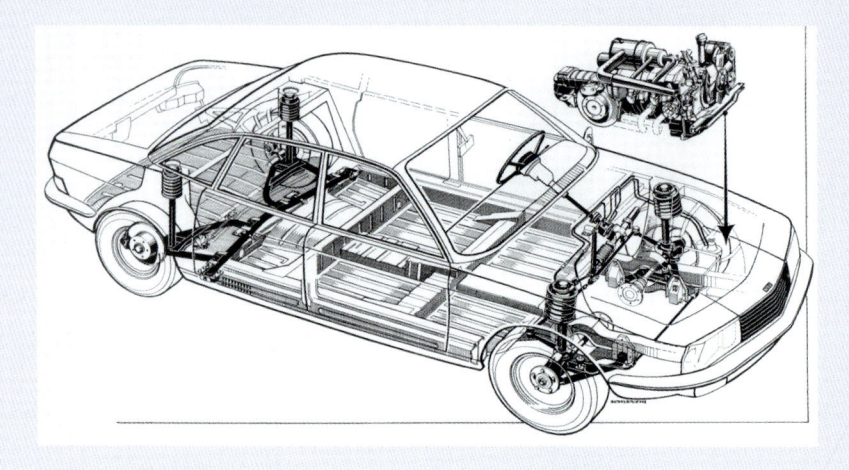

The compact simplicity of the twin-rotor power pack is evident here, with recessed combustion chambers in the rotors, viscous coupled fan at the front, torque converter at rear.

Suspension
Front: Independent suspension, symmetrical wishbones and MacPherson shock absorbers, progressive inclined coil springs, anti-roll bar and additional rubber springs. Total wheel travel: 188mm (spring deflection unloaded 104mm)

Rear axle: Independent suspension with semi-trailing arms, and cross member subframe mounted via silent blocks, 10° linkage angle, coil springs and additional rubber springs. Total wheel travel: 257mm (spring deflection unloaded 148mm) Shock absorption: front and rear hydraulic double-sided telescopic dampers.

Steering: ZF power-assisted rack and pinion with hydraulic servo ram and reduction gears. 3.7 turns lock-to lock, 38 foot turning circle.

Brakes: ATE-Dunlop discs 11.2in front (in board) and 10.7in rear with dual circuits, vacuum servo and load compensator. Handbrake operating on rear drums.

Wheels and tyres
14 inch 5J steel or Fuchs alloy wheels with five stud fixing 175-14 Michelin XAS tyres. Zero front wheel toe-out, camber angle 30 degree, castor angle 0 degrees. Tyre pressures 28lb/sq in front, 24lb/sq in rear.

Body and chassis
All-steel, 4/5-seater, four-door saloon with integral body/chassis construction. Front hinged bonnet. 30 sq ft window area. 20.5 cubic foot luggage space. 83 litre fuel tank. Cloth or plastic trim. Standard heated rear window. Fresh air heater/demister, two-speed wipers with electric screen wash.

Dimensions
Length	4,780mm (15ft 8¼in)
Width	1,760mm (5ft 9¼in)
Height	1,410mm (4ft 8in)
Wheelbase	2,860mm (9ft 4½in)

Cutaway shows that torque converter and gearbox is longer than the four-plug engine.

continued overleaf

NSU Ro80 Specifications 1967–1977 *continued*

Weights
Empty weight: 1,290kg/2,843lb
Payload: 450kg/992.08lb
Admissible total weight: 1,740kg/3,836lb
Axle load distribution: empty 62 per cent/38 per cent (front/rear); occupied 51 per cent/49 per cent (front/rear)

Permissible axle load: front 950kg/2,094lb rear 850kg/1,873lb
Permissible towing capacity: unbraked 640kg/1,410lb; braked 1,200kg/2,645lb

This full-size car with a sliced-off side was shown at the Frankfurt show in 1969.
AUTHOR'S COLLECTION

WHAT THE PAPERS SAID

Driving the Ro80 for the first time since our Italian test earlier this year we again find it difficult to express the depth of our admiration for a car that scores in so many ways over all others…A vehicle worthy of the space age.

Motor, group road test, 19 October 1968

Cruising at speed in the Ro80 is so quiet and smooth one notices the other disturbances, like tyre noise and even luggage moving in the boot.

Autocar, road test, 19 October 1968

In many ways the Ro80 feels more like a jet aircraft than a car. From the matt black of the cockpit, plain functional instruments and careful interior planning to the turbine-like whistle from beneath the bonnet it is a kind of mini Caravelle. It is certainly as smooth, sweet and quiet as one of the better Jets and it rides as well as the biggest of them. A few weeks ago it was voted internationally as the car of 1968: in the new standards it sets, it is also the car of the seventies.

Autocar, road test, 1 February 1968

When the technical pundits examine Germany's Ro80 at the Frankfurt Show in ten days time they may be in for a surprise. For this front-wheel-drive car is one of the most highly sophisticated, best designed – both mechanically and aesthetically – models ever to be placed before the public.

Maxwell Boyd, **The Times**, 3 September 1967

…the best power steering we have tried but also the only one that does not betray itself to the slightest degree. Kick back has been eliminated without affecting feel. But it is not just the lightness and precision of the steering that makes the Ro80 perhaps the world's best-handling saloon. The car's behaviour is so impeccable on twisting mountain roads that without highly skilled or suicidal provocation it is impossible to slide the back wheels.

Motor, road test, 3 February 1968

CHAPTER FIVE

LAST CHANCE SALOONS, 1968–77

The NSU Ro80 gives a combination of road holding and riding comfort which is unsurpassed, and has power-assisted steering which is equally outstanding. Its unconventional Wankel engine adds greatly to the interest of driving it and some may find its high-pitched song of battle inspiring. Cruising at 90mph over almost any road surface it gives one a glimpse of what motoring in the future will be like.

John Bolster, **Autosport**, 22 March 1968

The NSU Ro80 emerged into a late 1960s luxury saloon car market that was more keenly fought than ever, but also more potentially lucrative. Buyers for such cars, as well as being wealthier than hitherto, were generally younger than they had been ten years earlier.

Those buyers were also more discriminating and critical; it was no longer enough that a large, expensive, prestigious motor car should be dripping in chrome and have a big, thirsty 3-litre engine to waft it quietly but unexcitingly along. The ponderous big saloon concepts of the 1950s were making way for the new generation of compact executive cars – 'sports saloons' – that were better packaged and engineered and appealed to people well under fifty years of age: men and women who had a family but

Strong, bright colours and the optional Fuchs alloys were becoming trademarks of the Ro80 by the early 1970s.

Of all the German manufacturers, NSU seemed the least bashful in its use of young women in promoting its cars.

95

■ LAST CHANCE SALOONS, 1968–77

NSU Ro80 *Hailed as the car of the decade. The Ro80, powered by the revolutionary Wankel engine, is designed and engineered throughout to the very highest standards. It is truly a car without peers.*

still wanted a car for business and pleasure that was engaging to drive.

In fact, by 1967 some of these compact executive cars had already been around for a few years and were showing the first signs of looking tired. For example, BMW's boxy 2000 – launched in 1961 as the 1500 – was still a very good machine, but it looked decidedly tall and gawky next to the prophetic NSU. It was not due to be replaced, by the 5 Series, until 1972.

If the New Class range propelled BMW's return to health in the 1960s, then it was the E3, launched in 1968, that would really put them back on the map. For the first time since the demise of the big 3.2-litre V8s in 1965, here was a BMW that could directly challenge the large Mercedes saloons on home ground and would certainly steal sales from the Ro80. The 2500/2800 saloons were leaner, fitter and arguably more handsome than the S-Class range and it would be another four years before Mercedes would produce a car that could truly answer the BMW challenge on every point.

At the heart of the car's appeal was a fabulous new 6-cylinder engine, the M52, which shared certain principles with its 4-cylinder sibling and showed there was plenty of life left in the reciprocating engine. Canted over to keep the bonnet line low, attention to combustion chamber design and an exquisitely balanced bottom end with twelve counterweights and seven main bearings made this the most lusty, efficient and sweetest-sounding straight-six you could buy.

It was common knowledge in 1967 that a successor to the Mercedes 'fintail' was imminent in the form of the 'new

ABOVE: **The Ro80 was now the flagship of the Audi-NSU group.**

In 1978 the Ro80 may have a little competition.

We've spent 17 years developing this car. For the next ten our competitors will be wondering how. Because we've incorporated some pretty advanced ideas in the Ro80. By any standards.

Take the revlutionary Wankel engine. Twin rotors in an epitrochoidal bore. That's two rotors going round and round, instead of four or more pistons going up and down: unprecedented smoothness.

And this smaller engine takes up less space. So there's extra room for five inside, as well as all their bags in the boot.

Surprisingly, this big boot helps the car go faster. It's all part of the beautiful, aerodynamic shaping.

In the Ro80 you feel relaxed because you feel safe. At any speed. Front wheel drive, power assisted disc brakes and all round independent suspension give reassuring stability, always.

In fact it's never been easier to handle such power. There isn't even a clutch pedal. Just a Selective-Automatic transmission. With butter-smooth gears.

To help you out of tight corners there's servo-assisted steering. To keep you in at tight corners, Michelin XAS radial tyres. And the Ro80 offers a very personal comfort. Fully adjustable seats. Heating and fresh air ventilation. Fine carpeting. And wide windows (a de-mister at the back.) The sensible things.

All to be had at a sensible price. £2232 (recommended retail price including P.T.).

This has been just a glimpse of the future.

There's more to the Ro80. Much more. Enough to make you despair over cars as they are today. But unless you buy the Ro80 there's nothing you can do except wait.

It'll be ten years before the others catch up.

Send me full details of the revolutionary NSU Ro80
Name
Address

If you wish to receive details of other NSU cars tick the appropriate box.
SUPER PRINZ £599 □ 1200c £780 □
1000c £680 □ 1200TT £840 □

NSU (Great Britain) Limited, Harbour Way, Shoreham-by-Sea, Sussex. Telephone Shoreham 5281.

British advertising for the Ro80, its best market outside West Germany.

96

LAST CHANCE SALOONS, 1968–77

generation' range. Smaller than the W108 – but visually similar enough to be routinely confused with the bigger, older model – these cars were powered by a variety of 4- and 6-cylinder overhead camshaft petrol engines. In diesel form they would become West Germany's best-loved taxis.

These new Stuttgart-built cars, while less obviously charismatic than the Ro80, came closer to the standards the NSU set, although it depended how much you were prepared to spend on options. Power steering and automatic transmission were extra and you did not even get a rev counter as standard. The light, airy interior was well finished but also slightly bleak and joyless. The W114 Mercedes sold to people who wanted a long-term investment in engineering rather than a short-term thrill machine.

It was often said that the Ro80 looked Italian, yet that country had a poor record when it came to designing good-looking four-door cars. Focused on family small car motoring, coupés and supercars, the Italians seemed totally disinterested in making middle-class saloon cars that, visually, really captured the imagination of buyers. Both Alfa's 1750 Berlina and Lancia's Flavia for instance, were so uncompromisingly angular that few could love them outside their home market. It was not a question of price: at the very top of the Italian saloon pecking order, even Maserati's Quattroporte looked decidedly boxy. It was not that the 1750 and the Flavia were bad cars – far from it. The Alfa was fun (and fast) while the beautifully made – but overweight – Lancia was almost as refined as the Ro80, but more sedate in feel and not such a modern package.

From Sweden, perhaps unexpectedly came the 164, a bid for the 3-litre luxury saloon market first seen in 1968. Visu-

ABOVE: **The 2.8-litre XJ6 was priced to challenge the Ro80; if anything its engine was even more unreliable.**

The 'new generation' Mercedes was a car beloved of the taxi trade in Germany but priced in the luxury class.

97

■ LAST CHANCE SALOONS, 1968–77

Britain's BMC had the opportunity to make an Ro80-rivalling world-beater out of its staid 1800 range, with this Pininfarina aerodynamics proposal from 1967...

...instead they built, in the same year the Ro80 was launched, the doomed Austin 3 litre.

ally the 164 made no attempt to hide the fact that it was a 144-saloon with a nose job. Its understeer-inducing straight-six offered a performance versus mpg equation very close to the Ro80's (107mph, 0–60 in 12 seconds at 17mpg) but with much less driver appeal; yet it was a restful, refined car for those temperate drivers who simply wanted to waft around in leather-lined luxury.

In some ways the British had led the way in sports saloons. The new Jaguar XJ6 – launched in 1968 – represented the state of the art in the manufacture of desirable four-door, five-seater machinery with sporty overtones: it was quieter, faster (as a 4.2 at least) and, arguably, more conventionally beautiful than the Ro80. However, on the basis of size, weight, engine size and price, the Rover 2000 and Triumph 2000 felt like more relevant yardsticks. Dating from the early 1960s, these cars were still in great demand and a hugely aspirational part of the British motoring landscape. The well-engineered Rover 2000 (P6) in particular was a former Car

98

THE SUNDAY TIMES, 3 SEPTEMBER 1967

MOTORING
MAXWELL BOYD

Britain lets the Wankel go by

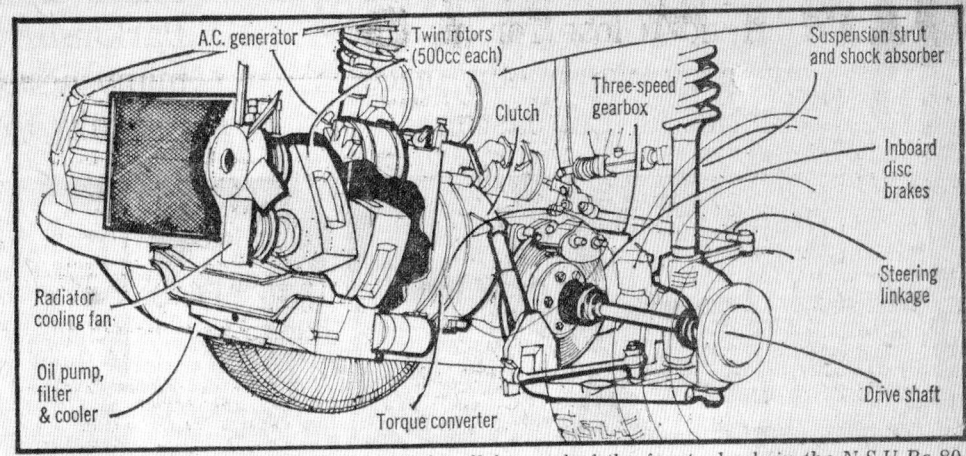

The Wankel twin-rotor engine is mounted well forward of the front wheels in the N S U Ro 80

EVEN THOUGH both Germany and Japan, Britain's deadliest rivals in world markets, now have production models powered by the revolutionary Wankel rotary engine, used to power the NSU Ro 80 announced yesterday, British manufacturers are still reluctant to take the slightest interest in it as a passenger car engine of the future.

They have allowed the impatient Japanese, who bought a Wankel development licence from N S U, to get ahead even of the Germans themselves and launch the world's very first twin-rotor car—the Mazda Cosmo sports coupé, introduced some weeks ago.

The British industry has merely done some work on diesel and military applications. The rotary idea has been pooh-poohed by some of our leading engineers, despite the opinion of others, equally prominent abroad, who consider it to be the only practical alternative to the conventional piston engine.

When these technical pundits come to examine Germany's Ro 80 at the Frankfurt motor show in ten days' time they may be in for a surprise. For this front-wheel-drive car is one of the most highly sophisticated, best designed, both mechanically and aesthetically, models ever to be placed before the public.

It is, I feel sure, a concept showing the way in which the family car will develop in the not-too-distant future, and the manufacturer who is first on the scene with a really mass production Wankel-engined vehicle will surely reap the rich reward of making every normally-engined small car seem obsolete.

In a way the Ro 80 is a mobile shop-window, displaying the capabilities of the Wankel engine with the best of design and high-quality engineering. With dual-system disc braking, power-assisted rack and pinion steering, a three-speed gearbox working both manually and automatically, refined all-independent suspension, and a host of safety and comfort refinements, it is easy to see why the car is expected to cost around £2,000 when it reaches the British market next spring.

The engine is the first European Wankel to use twin rotors. A pair of steel triangular rotors take the place of the six separate pistons, connecting rods and cylinders which would be necessary to drive a conventionally-engined car of similar power and operational smoothness.

The weight of the engine is two-thirds that of a conventional six-cylinder unit of similar power (113 b h p). It is only half the size, has far fewer moving parts and is claimed to be already little more than half as expensive to produce.

With no up-and-down piston movement, it is almost as vibrationless as a turbine. Pulling well over a ton of car, it has excellent acceleration (0-60 in just over 12 sec.), a more than fair turn of speed (maximum: 110 m.p.h.) and reasonable fuel consumption (around 25 m.p.g.). Its exhaust fumes are no more toxic than those of a normal engine and are said to be capable of further "cleaning." Overall, these attributes seem to present an irresistibly attractive proposition. But the British industry's apathy is at least, in part, understandable.

Changing over to the Wankel would mean throwing away astronomic sums invested in existing production machinery, as well as spending further huge amounts on development and factories full of new equipment —all on what is still commercially the biggest gamble since the advent of the car itself. So the British industry would rather wait and see, and let someone else spend the money and make the early mistakes.

Unfortunately this policy might cause us to miss the boat altogether, at least for an appreciable time. N S U is a relatively small firm gambling heavily on the Wankel. Suppose her cars were a technical success but a commercial failure, a combination not unknown in the industry. In the take-over which would doubtless follow, the winning firm would be unlikely to part with any of their Wankel know-how. That way might lie total British exclusion; and that way might also lie the long-awaited new Volkswagen.

The highly sophisticated lines of the new German car

A clipping from *The Sunday Times* bemoaning Britain's failure to embrace the Wankel engine.

LAST CHANCE SALOONS, 1968–77

of the Year winner and seen as a leading player, particularly once it got its twin-carburettor engine.

In this 2000TC form it was as fast as the NSU, nicely finished but nothing like as spacious or refined: the later V8 models came close. If not exactly beautiful, the Rover P6 had a clean-lined authority about it that tended to avoid unflattering comparisons. Triumph's 2000/2.5 Pi range aged more quickly but, as an injected 2.5Pi, they presented a lot of six-pot bang for your buck in a narrow but still handsome Michelotti-styled body.

French saloons were still all about ride comfort and the Ro80 buyer might fleetingly have considered the rather cheaper Renault 16TS – or the soon-to-be-announced Peugeot 504 – as credible alternatives to the NSU. However, the Citroën DS was still perceived as the French car to beat. In some respects the idiosyncrasies of the Citroën DS, and the audacity of its original 1955 concept, tended to blind buyers to its age and its shortcomings. It fared well in comparisons with the German car – it was quite a lot cheaper even in Pallas trim – but was no match for the Ro80 as a quiet motorway mile eater.

If the Citroën's engine sounded harsh and undistinguished, it did at least have lusty torque on its side. The last fuel-injected versions were fast, near-120mph (193km/h) cars.

Like the brakes and steering, the DS's semi-automatic gearbox (if fitted) took some getting used to. With its giant nose and highly sensitive brakes, the big Citroën also tended to feel ponderous around town and could not be flung around country roads with the joyful abandon that the Ro80 encouraged. But its outstanding feature remained its comfort, its gas-and-air, self-levelling suspension setting standards even the NSU struggled to match.

But perhaps of more concern was the new-for-1968 Audi 100, a coldly rational yet thoroughly competent 100mph car, which in many ways established the tone for all Audis to come, setting out to impress with its finish, its efficiency and

Had the fuel crisis not struck, the Citroën CX would have been launched with a Wankel engine.

The Ro80 should have been the natural heir to the Citroën DS, which bowed out in 1975 at 1.4 million sales.

As a more conventional alternative to the Ro80, its Audi 100 stable-mate had a lot going for it.

LAST CHANCE SALOONS, 1968–77

Audi's Ludwig Kraus, designer of the first Audi 100.

The K70, initially launched as an NSU, seemed like at least part of the answer to VW's problems.

The addition of a sportier LS version failed to change the K70's fortunes.

good overall behaviour, rather than seduce you with its looks or driver appeal. Not that the Audi 100 was a bad-looking car. Its greenhouse treatment, and neat tail light design, inherited something from the Daimler-Benz interest in the firm in the first half of the 1960s before selling to Volkswagen in 1966.

The Audi 100's engine, derived from the Super 90 and Auto Union-Audi's first post-war 4-stroke, was unquestionably DBAG in origin. It pulled the Audi along energetically – with good economy – but with none of the serene turbine charm of the NSU's rotary engine.

Even with its engine slung well out beyond the front wheels, the Audi was far from being an understeering pig: it handled and rode with a lack of drama that left buyers impressed but unmoved, which was clearly its designer's intention. Inside, its inviting velour seats and handsome facia showed how the Germans were leading the way in the use of modern, high-quality cabin materials.

THE K70, AUDI AND A LOSS OF INDEPENDENCE

From NSU's point of view the big new Audi was not merely a Ro80 rival but, as of 1969, internal competition: they were step siblings in a marriage of the two firms.

With the West German dominance of the motor industry under threat from the Italians (Fiat had just overtaken VW as the biggest carmaker in Europe in 1968), NSU was look-

■ LAST CHANCE SALOONS, 1968–77

The K70 was a competent modern car, but somehow lacked sparkle.

BELOW LEFT: **VW boss Kurt Lotz about to sample an Ro80.**

ing more vulnerable than ever. It needed capital for tooling and automated transfer lines to increase production of the still largely hand-assembled Wankel engine. Even if warranty claims against the early Ro80 engines had not been crippling the firm, the development costs associated with its piston-engined supposed saviour car, the K70, were potentially ruinous.

It was against this background that Von Heydekampf was given permission by the NSU board to find a partner. Volkswagen were the obvious candidate and by February 1969 an agreement had been settled between VW boss Kurt Lotz and Von Heydekampf whereby NSU would take over the VW subsidiary Audi Auto Union rather than VW absorbing NSU itself. This way VW got tax breaks and 60 per cent controlling shares in the new company, without having to get permission to do the deal from its own shareholders or give dividends to NSU shareholders, whose interest in the new company was reduced to 40 per cent.

To sweeten the deal for the NSU shareholders, they were promised a cut in the profits on the Wankel licences, although only for ten years and only at two-fifths of the income. Neither would they receive any compensation for the costs associated with the development of the K70.

VW boss Kurt Lotz was attracted to the deal not so much by NSU's Wankel expertise, but by the promise of this new smaller and conventionally-engined sister model to the Ro80. Not only did the K70 give VW access to the water cooling

LAST CHANCE SALOONS, 1968–77

and front-wheel-drive technology that it so badly needed; it was also a ready-made entry into the 1½-litre saloon class where its own rear-engined, air-cooled 411 – really a giant but more refined Beetle – was struggling to find friends.

A new company called Audi NSU Auto Union AG came into being in April 1969, with NSU directors taking five of the nine seats on the board. Share prices in NSU stock had been rising ever since rumours of the alliance had begun to circulate in February. Officially the Ro80 would now be known as an Audi-NSU product, although it was never badged as such.

For the NSU stockholders, the appeal of the alliance should have been access to more capitalisation and the fact that, with Audi, it was now the third-largest car maker in Germany. But many of its stockholders were not impressed. Raging against the deal, some argued that VW had been handed a complete range of conventionally-engined cars on a plate – never mind the Ro80 – and pointed out that, in the small print, was a clause that stated VW would be invoicing NSU for VW technology because, legally, the merger was between Audi and NSU (with Audi holding 59.5 per cent of the shares), not Volkswagen.

It was only when better terms for the NSU stockholders were insisted on by the British Israeli Bank – representing 25 per cent of voting shares – that the deal went through, and even then not without incident: the first Audi-NSU-Auto Union AGM lasted a record-breaking twenty-six hours, as disgruntled shareholders – many of whom considered NSU was rescuing VW rather than the other way around – were given a chance to voice concerns.

The new car lurking behind all this fuss was called the K70 ('K' equalled piston or *Kolben* in German and 70 was its bhp) and Neckarsulm had been on the verge of announcing it when news of VW's interest in a deal with NSU broke.

The ungainly 411 was symbolic of VW's difficulty finding a successor to the Beetle.

In fact, the K70 *was* launched as an NSU at Geneva in 1969 but went into production, as a VW, in 1971. This gives the K70 an additional level of historical intrigue: is there another car that can claim the dubious distinction of being born under one brand name but brought to market with another?

Superficially, the K70 seemed to have all the ingredients for success, not least a good engineering pedigree. Neat and well-proportioned with lots of glass area and usable space for people and luggage, the K70 seemed to be precisely the sort of rational one-and-a-half litre Euro saloon VW needed after a rash of 1960s duffers. Here was an ideal front engine/front-drive answer to face the early 1970s where the public (and the legislators) were rapidly turning their backs on the slow, noisy air-cooled, rear-engined cars that had been the basis of VW's post-war success.

The K70 was shown as an NSU-badged prototype at Geneva in March 1969, but promptly dropped from sight again for several months in the wake of Volkswagen's takeover of NSU and its integration into the Audi/Auto Union division. While the rotary-engined car was allowed to continue as the group's NSU-badged technical flagship, it seemed to make sense to realign the almost fully formed K70 as a VW.

After years of struggling to replace the Beetle, here was the water-cooled technology Wolfsburg needed. And with the new technology came the fresh creative blood VW needed even more, principally in the form of NSU chief engineer Ewald Praxl (already in his sixties) and a much younger stylist, Claus Luthe.

In styling the K70, Luthe was tasked with creating a shape that did not need to be particularly aerodynamic but had to be easier to build and have a wider appeal than his edgy, slippery Ro80, while at the same time being visually linked to it; there was certainly a hint of the Ro in the car's flanks, beltline and low waist.

The K70 was at least a cost-effective proposition because its engine was water cooled and a longer stroked development of the old 1200cc engine from the last of the rear-engined cars and, crucially, could be produced on existing NSU tooling. Canted over and mounted well forward above the final drive, its overhead camshaft was driven by a double-roller chain and each cam follower had its own individual pressed steel cover (harking back to the rear-engine cars and NSU motorcycle engines of the 1950s), which gave the unit a distinctive top-end appearance.

Actually, there was less in common with the Ro80 than is generally acknowledged. Shorter in wheelbase and overall length than the NSU, direct commonality with the Ro80 was

LAST CHANCE SALOONS, 1968–77

Luthe considers a new dashboard design and a station wagon K70 concept.

restricted to front strut/rear trailing link long travel suspension and inboard front discs plus a few minor items like outside door handles. The car was productionised by VW, but lost some of its NSU technical niceties along the way, such as the use of pressed steel box section lower wishbones instead of the more elegant Ro80 style welded tubular ones. VW upped the wheel size from 13 to 14 inches and offered Ro80-type Fuchs alloys (actually a cheaper cast rather than forged version of the same design) as an option on the post-1973 LS versions with the 100bhp 1807cc engine, quad headlamps and matt black side flash.

The K70 was almost as roomy as the Ro80, with a similarly enormous boot augmented (as in the Ro80) by rear backrests that folded down to accommodate long loads. The 360-degree vision was equally outstanding and, while you would expect the K70 not to be quite so refined and pleasing in its detail finish, the build quality and materials were by no means bad: pleasing velvet cloth seats and a heavily hooded instrument pod that looked close to what Luthe had originally intended for the Ro80.

However, this is where all meaningful comparisons with the NSU ended. Certainly, there were echoes of the Ro80 in the K70's road behaviour. Its long suspension travel gave a similarly supple ride and it did not descend into run-wide understeer as quickly as its nose-heavy engine layout suggested. But as you twiddled its hefty unassisted steering, pumped its clutch and stirred your way through its notchy and undistinguished four-speed gearbox, the K70 felt as joyless as the Ro80 was spirit lifting.

The original 1607cc cars were criticised for a lack of low-speed torque; the bigger-engined LS was lively enough on paper, but the engine was thrashy and uncouth when asked to deliver performance. All this of course has to be balanced against the fact that the K70 was a much cheaper car than the Ro80 (roughly half the price) and one which, in fairness, it was never intended to be compared with.

Its under-developed and rather thirsty engine is only one component in the story of the K70's failure. In fact, as usual, it was a combination of factors that conspired against it in roughly equal quantities. Without a doubt its confused and hesitant birth stacked the cards up against the car in the public's mind from the off, and perhaps for too many people the link with NSU equalled potential reliability problems. And for those who admired the Ro80, the relatively noisy and slightly over-bodied K70 might have proved underwhelming, especially when you could have the superficial charms of a lusty Cortina 2000 GXL (say) for £300 less.

More to the point, perhaps, the K70 sat awkwardly in the VW-Audi range, where you could buy an Audi 100LS (frankly a much nicer car) for only £150 more.

People often say that the Ro80 would have been a great car even without the rotary engine. The irony is that had NSU produced the more conventional K70 first it might have survived, at least for a bit longer, as an individual marque. When the VW Passat range emerged in 1973, its fate was effectively sealed and only about 800 K70s were sold new in the UK by the time it had faded away in 1974.

Ro80 DEVELOPMENTS

Somewhere amidst the debacle of the K70 and the VW takeover, NSU found time to make some meaningful improvements to the 1970 model year Ro80 for the 1969 Frankfurt Motor Show, where their stand featured a sectioned 'see-through' car with hinged sides.

It was one of the first cars to have a full halogen lighting system – low beam, high beam and fog lights. Inside, its heating and ventilation gained greater throughput (thanks to additional ducts under the dashboard) and the dashboard knobs were now more easily identifiable with clearer markings. The wipers gained an automatic wash/wiper function.

Outwardly the only change, apparently much against the wishes of the stylists, was the addition of a handle for the boot lid.

LAST CHANCE SALOONS, 1968–77

By the time the Ro80 had its first and only styling changes for 1974, it had already been decided it would have no direct successor.

Late brochures for the Ro80 were underwhelming.

In 1970 NSU celebrated the construction of its one-millionth post-war car at Neckarsulm. It was carefully choreographed not to be one of its ageing – and increasingly hard to sell – rear-engined models, but instead the still attention-grabbing Ro80, which had recently passed the 1970 Californian emissions tests after 50,000 miles (80,500km) of trials.

It was hoped that a well optioned de-smogged version with quad lights (and additional driving lights behind the grille) might find favour with discriminating North American customers, priced at $5,995 or $7,500 with leather seats and air conditioning. It's hard to get a sense of how many Ro80s made it to the United States, but given that NSU had little presence in that market, it is unlikely to amount to more

105

■ LAST CHANCE SALOONS, 1968–77

A fussier look for 1975–77 rear styling, with the licence plate above the bumper (which has a rubber insert), new badge and bigger rear lights.

Water sports were fun, but did not do much for the Ro80's famous slippery profile.

than a few hundred cars. Total NSU sales in North America (all models) amounted to 1,582 cars between 1967 and 1971. Federal 5mph bumper legislation would have outlawed the car after 1973 in any event.

Most customers for the rear-engined cars in North America were German immigrants who bought the cars from a smattering of dealers. Plans to invest $10 million in an expanded network probably died with the Ro80's reliability prospects in Europe.

More than 12,000 examples had been built by this stage, over 3,500 exported and production was running at fifty cars a day. Not bad, considering how widely reported the car's engine problems had been since they had first been whispered about in 1968.

Herbert Brockhaus, head of testing, had begged the NSU board for more time to develop the engine: 'The following engine parts are not yet tested' he told them on 23 June 1967; 'The seal inserts, the trochoid, the eccentric shaft and the rotor bearings. Due to engine problems and the extra workload to replace the engines there is not sufficient time to test the other components. Final release is not possible for the start of October.' Formerly an employee of Esso, where he had worked on research into the Wankel engine from 1953, 38-year-old Brockhaus had been invited to join NSU in 1963 after delivering a lecture on his findings. As of June 1967 he believed the two rotor engines required another two years of testing. The NSU board thought otherwise, or at least believed they could make 'on-the-hoof' changes: with the profits from the small cars drying up, they needed the Ro80 in production without further delay. Moreover, German technical pride was at stake (such was Mazda's rate of progress with the Cosmo) and, for the Wankel licence holders, there was a pressing need to come up with a true halo product to put the Wankel engine on the map as a serious alternative to the reciprocating engine for use in motor cars.

There was no magic bullet or instant fix of course, and NSU found themselves in the unenviable position of having to produce, for many months, engines they knew would end up coming back to haunt them, particularly when they were known to put a very generous interpretation on warranty claims. Many owners got new engines when they were well out of the 14,000 mile (22,500km) warranty period (only Rolls-Royce offered a better one), and only had to pay the cost of having them fitted. It was found that two-thirds of the engines returned to the factory in the first eighteen months actually had nothing wrong with them and only needed adjustments. Not all NSU service agents understood the ways of the Wankel it seemed. But, in the UK at least, NSU were quietly simplifying its operations by dealing directly only with the distributors of the cars rather than individual dealers, and at the same time ensuring a steady flow of technicians were being sent on Wankel training schemes at Neckarsulm. They also made sure that all its distributors were fully equipped with the special tools needed to work on the engine.

Eager to show the world that it had cured the Wankel's well-publicised shortcomings, NSU organised a briefing at the Schloss Solitude in 1971 to bring the changes since 1969 to the attention of the press. At the heart of these improvements was a change of apex seal material to Ferrotic, a ceramic-metallic composite of titanium carbide hard enough to cut glass with.

NSU Ro80 PERFORMANCE FIGURES

The top speed of the Ro80 depended on how much the driver wanted to exceed the rev limit: figures of between 107mph and 130mph (172 and 209km/h) have been quoted!

PERFORMANCE FIGURES *MOTOR* ROAD TEST OF FOUR-PLUG NSU Ro80 PUBLISHED 3/2/1968

Maximum speed in top (third)		112.6mph (best one way 117.1)
Maximum speed in second		80mph
Maximum speed in first		47mph

Acceleration (seconds)

0–30 (mph)	0–48 (km/h)	5.1
0–40	0–64	7.1
0–50	0–80	9.8
0–60	0–96	14.2
0–70	0–112	18.6
0–80	0–128	24.6
0–90	0–144	33.1
0–100	0–161	44.3
Standing ¼ mile		19.7

Acceleration in Top (sec)

			2nd
20–40 (mph)	32–64 (km/h)	8.3	6.5
30–50	48–80	9.7	7.0
40–60	64–96	11.2	7.8
50–70	80–112	13.2	8.0
60–80	96–128	14.5	9.3
70–90	112–144	17.0	
80–100	128–161	21.1	
Overall mpg	15.3 (18.5ltr/100km)		
Touring mpg	20.2 (14ltr/100km)		

RIVALS 1967

BMW 2000 TiLux	111mph (178km/h)/£1,999
Citroën DS21 Pallas	100mph (161km/h)/£1,898
Lancia Flavia 1800 Injection	105 mph (169km/h)/£1,997
Mercedes 250S	107mph (172km/h)/£2,724
Rover 2000TC	108mph (174km/h)/£1,547
Triumph 2.5 Pi	109mph (175km/h)/£1,547
Jaguar 420	117mph (188km/h)/£2,268

continued overleaf

■ LAST CHANCE SALOONS, 1968–77

NSU Ro80 PERFORMANCE FIGURES *continued*

PERFORMANCE FIGURES *MOTOR* ROAD TEST 22/6/1974 OF TWO-PLUG Ro80 WITH TWIN DOWNDRAUGHT SOLEX CARBURETTOR

Maximum speed in top (third)	106.2 (best one way 108.2)	
Maximum speed in second	80	
Maximum speed in first	47	

Acceleration (seconds)

0–30 (mph)	0–48 (km/h)	4.4
0–40	0–64	6.3
0–50	0–80	9.2
0–60	0–96	12.6
0–70	0–112	16.6
0–80	0–128	22.0
0–90	0–144	32.0
0–100	0–161	47.6
Standing ¼ mile		19.1

Acceleration in Top (sec)

			2nd
20–40 (mph)	32–64 (km/h)	7.2	5.4
30–50	48–80	8.7	6.0
40–60	64–96	10.4	6.3
50–70	80–112	11.8	7.3
60–80	96–128	12.9	10.2
70–90	112–144	16.0	
80–100	128–161	–	
Overall mpg	18 (15.7ltr/100km)		
Touring mpg	23 (12.3ltr/100km)		

RIVALS 1974

Audi 100S Coupé	112.7mph (178km/h)/£3,070
Citroën DS 23 Efi	119mph (191km/h)/£2,814
Jaguar XJ 4.2	120mph (193km/h)/£4,043
Rover 3500	117mph (188km/h)/£2,736
Lancia 2000 Sedan	115mph (185km/h)/£2,399
BMW 520	105.8mph (170km/h)/£3,499
Volvo 146E	112.5mph (181km/h)/£3,450
Peugeot 504 Injection auto	100mph (161km/h)/£2,351
Mercedes 230/4	101mph (163km/h)/£3,689
Alfa Romeo 2000 Berlina	114mph (183km/h)/£2,499

Still the subject of so much debate, the Ro80's engine went to a single plug per rotor in 1969.

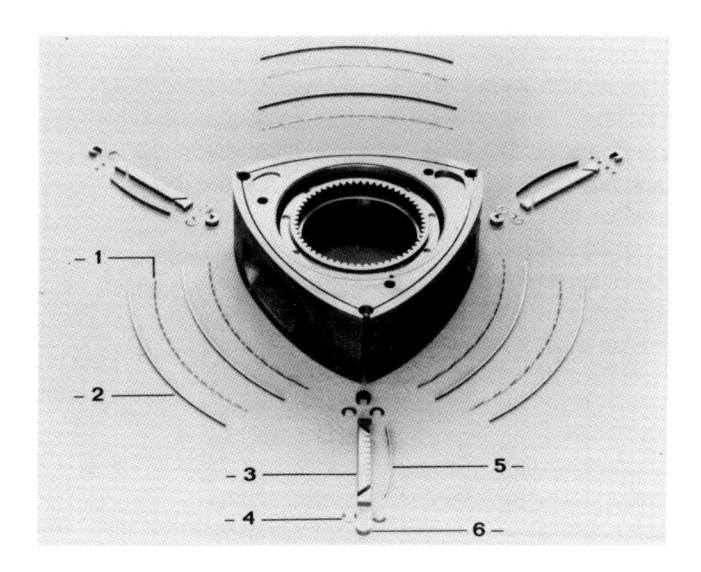

At the heart of improvements to the engine was a change of apex seal material to Ferrotic, ceramic-metallic composite of titanium carbide – hard enough to cut glass with.

It was embedded in high chrome-alloy tool steel and ran on a tremendously hard Nikasil surface – an alloy of nickel and silicon carbide (rather than the previous chromed surface, which was much more time consuming to apply), which was effectively sprayed onto the inner surface of the combustion chambers at 1,000ft per second using molybdenum wire fed through a gun – with acetylene gas and oxygen – at 3,000°C.

Easier to spot was a change over to one plug per rotor with transistorised ignition to replace the twin coils, a decision taken mainly on the basis of cost.

It was fairly well understood that very high revs would shorten engine life dramatically (and in many cases it did), but less well known that pottering around in top gear at low speeds – or treating the gearbox like a conventional automatic and using only top gear – did quite a lot of harm too, even if the engine seemed to tolerate such treatment.

Plug life in urban use could be as short as 5,000 miles/8,047km. They were not very tolerant of city driving and when the plugs fouled up it was not possible to clear them – as in a normal engine – with a burst of high revs due to their position in the chambers. Low-speed driving also tended to build up ash deposits around the plugs that could lead to harmful incandescent surface ignition, better known as pre-ignition. At higher revs, these particles ignited, causing high coolant temperatures and the knock-on effects of excessive wear on overheated components and even cracks in the rotor housings.

The adoption of a single plug per rotor meant better cooling and water flow around the combustion area. The old two-plug per rotor housing used Bosch type MAG310T2SP (lower position) and Beru G3/18 (higher position). The one-plug housing had Beru G3/18 plugs, the same as two-plugs' higher position. A new Bosch thyristor ignition pack replaced the twin coils and it was claimed that this put much less amperage across the points, thus banishing the tendency for them to burn out or go out of adjustment too often, leading to a weak spark and fouled plugs.

The 'Hasenmuhle Programme'

This later design of engine had been subject to extensive cold running tests. Conscious that short trips and low-engine temperatures were a big issue, having studied owners' habits in detail, Froede established four city driving simulators in 1969, set up to operate continually between 30 and 50°C before automatically shutting off on a thermo switch and then restarting again when the coolant temperature dropped back to 30°C. Meanwhile, a dozen Ro80s were driven, around the clock, 1½ kilometres between the factory at Neckarsulm to a village called Easenhall; the incoming car was left with its bonnet raised while the driver returned to the factory in another Ro80. This process went on for days and weeks on end until the engineers were satisfied that the problems of cold start/short journey wear had been conquered, or at least brought within the realms of acceptability. The 'Hasenmuhle Programme' is thought to have consumed 1,000 test engines, but Audi-NSU now claimed 60,000 trouble free miles (96,560km) at least, having discovered – under spectroscopic analysis – that with new Ferrotic seals, wear had been reduced from 65–85 micros to just 5 micros.

A significant number of issues had centred around owners' mistreatment; for instance, fitting extra lights behind the grille could block the radiator and cause overheating, along with the usual over-revving and lack of attention to the oil level. Some owners extrapolated from NSU's long 12,000-mile (19,300km) oil change intervals that the oil did not need checking – or topping up – either, leading to dry sumps and seized bearings. NSU eventually stipulated that the oil level should be checked at every fill up. Another simple way of helping to tackle this was to make the difference between the minimum and maximum level on the dipstick greater.

It did not help that nervous, inexperienced NSU dealers had a tendency to return engines to the factory that had nothing wrong with them. Some owners had as many as nine new engines – although three was the average – and it was not unknown for some of them to take advantage of NSU's generous nature by destroying engines deliberately, just so they could have a new one.

Other improvements for the 1970 model year included more elements in the heated rear window, more padding in the seats and a quieter booster fan for the heating and ventilation system.

The cooling system had an improved thermostat and the heater valve and engine fan had been redesigned. As before, oil changes were not required, particularly now NSU engineers had satisfied themselves that, with no fuel blow by into the sump, the oil stayed cleaner for longer, and only needed to be topped up, albeit quite regularly compared to most piston-engined cars.

Despite the problems owners, besotted with the cars, had a high level of tolerance: that many of those earlier Ro80s were still in the hands of first owners – wealthy people who drove them in preference to all kinds of exotica, including Rolls-Royce Silver Shadows in at least one reported case – says everything about how good this car was to drive. For the most part, it seemed that the problems had been significantly eased, if not entirely resolved, by the turn of the decade. *Moto Journal*, the French motoring magazine, did a 30,000 mile (48,280km) test of an Ro80 and reported no problems. In Britain both the main weekly motoring magazines had Ro80s on their long-term test fleets. *Autocar*'s Stuart Bladon had a second engine in his 1971 car when a crankshaft bearing failed. Conversely, Roger Bell of *Motor* rated his 1974 long-term Ro80 one of the most trouble-free cars he had ever run.

Readers of *Motor* magazine in the UK voted the Ro80 Car of the Decade in 1970, by which time NSU had the engine's problems more firmly under control: so much so that it was claimed that some distributors were issuing full two-year warranties.

After the relative bonanza of 1969, sales of the Ro80 eased off in the 1970s. Figures for 1970 were down 20 per cent and fell a further 50 per cent in 1971, then picked up again in 1972 and 1973 before the ravages of the fuel crisis put sales into a terminal decline.

FACING THE TROUBLED 1970s

Many old certainties were undermined in the 1970s, as the world seemed to lurch from one crisis to the next. Our television screens were filled with war and famine, riots and strikes. In Britain we had the three-day week and, thanks to striking miners, power cuts. So, in some ways the 1973 fuel crisis could be viewed as just another bit of bad news along with many others for beleaguered Brits of the 1970s.

Not so the West Germans. Yes they had there own terrorism problems (the Bader Meinhof group) and dodgy taste in pop music (Klaus Wunderlich springs to mind), but they also built great cars that they could drive as fast as they liked on great roads. And good for them: they had worked hard after the war to build an ordered society that was as much a symbol of success as Britain seemed to be one of failure. In the early 1970s the *Wirtschaftswunder* or economic miracle of the 1950s and 1960s had perhaps levelled off; but Germany was still basking in its afterglow, with high levels of employment and high productivity.

It took the events of October 1973 to shake the Germans' belief in themselves for the first time since 1945 and take a long hard look at their dependency on crude oil.

The background to these conflicts is well known and it still reverberates today. In many ways it probably had almost as much influence on the fate of the NSU Ro80 as its reliability issues. Angered by America's support of the Israelis during the Yom Kippur war, OAPEC (the Organisation of Arab Petroleum Exporting Countries) announced that it would limit, or cut off, supplies of oil to America and any other country that supported its actions.

In the UK we *nearly* had rationing at the pumps (ration books were issued but never used in anger), but in Germany there were five car-free Sundays in late 1973 and early 1974 where driving was banned altogether. A 100km/h speed limit on the autobahn was brought into force by Chancellor Willy Brandt, effective between December 1973 and March 1974. The most severe effects of the crisis continued until the spring of 1974 (when the Arabs opened the taps again), but in the meantime building large, expensive fuel-guzzling motor cars like the Ro80 was not looking like a very profitable or popular business to be in.

But even without the fuel crisis more buyers seemed to know about the Ro80's shortcomings than its strengths and, at the price, there were many less risky alternatives to this troubled if still fresh-looking saloon.

Thirst alone meant that the Ro80 was never an every-man machine anyway, but it continued to appeal to a hardcore of connoisseurs who loved the way it looked, felt and drove. The British were probably more forgiving than the Germans

Audi's soothing noises about the Ro80's new-found reliability fell mostly on deaf ears by the mid-1970s.

of the Ro80's reliability problems and bought the car in relatively large numbers.

If treated carefully from cold but driven briskly when thoroughly warm – and used for long trips rather than stop-start work in heavy traffic – the Ro80 was a dependable means of transport for 50–70,000 miles (80,457–112,654km), at a time when not all that many conventional engines would go 100,000 miles (160,934km) without major work.

Who knows, the Ro80 may even have been dependable enough to be a police car, had it been given the chance. The UK importers sometimes demonstrated the Ro80 to local forces – perhaps encouraged by the inroads BMW had made into a market that had until recently been the preserve of British marques, for obvious reasons – and there is reason to think the Ro80 might have done well if used as a motorway traffic car in round-the-clock use.

■ LAST CHANCE SALOONS, 1968–77

Shown in quad-headlight form in this 1969 ad, whose writer could not have predicted the Ro80's fate a mere seven years later.

LAST CHANCE SALOONS, 1968–77

NSU were not shy of quoting the highly favourable column inches this darling of the motoring press inspired.

MOTOR week ending May 30 1970

THE BEST CAR IN THE WORLD.
Roger Bell, "Motor", 3.1.70.

* I unhesitatingly vote it as one of the world's most outstanding cars, for thorough design, handling, roadholding, comfort and style.
Geoffrey Charles. *The Times.* 5.3.70.

* The Ro80 is technology's nearest approach yet to a fully maintenance-free car.
Michael Kemp. *Daily Sketch.* 1.9.69.

* The Ro80 has achieved some considerable success.
Dudley Noble. *Financial Times.* 23.8.69.

* The high-speed acceleration and silent cruising at 100 m.p.h. put the Ro80 in a class by itself.
Gordon Wilkins. *Observer.* 13.4.69.

* The best thing about this NSU is its roadholding. It has set a new standard for me.
Robert Glenton. *Sunday Express.* 18.4.69.

* There is no doubt in my mind that the NSU Ro80 is an excellent saloon.
Keith Challen.
News of the World. 11.1.70.

The Ro80 was "car of the year" the very year it came out. We could have filled several columns with quotes like these and have become complacent. Instead we have tried to make the best even better. We've simplified maintenance with transistorised ignition and one plug instead of two per rotor. We have improved front seats, heating and ventilation, and identification of controls. We have introduced "cyclic" wiper operation in conjunction with the screenwash.

Safety features we'd hardly want to change are all-round independent suspension, servo assisted dual circuit anti-lock disc brakes, safety steering with hydraulic servo unit and selective automatic (no clutch pedal) transmission with front wheel drive. Our four door five seater body is the latest safety design with a very rigid passenger compartment and crushable zones to front and rear. Michelin XAS radial tyres are fitted.

Many of the 100 or so NSU Ro80 dealers have found the Ro80 so reliable that they have increased the manufacturer's guarantee from 18 months to two years.

Perhaps your NSU dealer is among them (we'd be pleased to send you his name and address). We don't need to say more about the Ro80 than the professionals we quoted as the car speaks for itself.

NSU

For a complete list of NSU dealers write to : NSU (Gt. Britain) Ltd. Harbour Way, Shoreham-by-Sea, Sussex. Tel: 07917 5281.

113

■ LAST CHANCE SALOONS, 1968–77

The Italian importers used modern architecture as a backdrop.

The car's thirsty reputation has perhaps been overstated, even if it is not without foundation. Driven sensibly 25mpg (11.3ltr/100km) plus was possible – with a range of 360 miles/579km or more – and the running costs had to be weighed not only against the fact that it would happily partake of the cheapest available 2-star/90 octane fuel (in fact it had been discovered that the engine would run on an octane rating as low as 79, as found in Turkey) but also that this was not a skinflint's economy runabout but a large, roomy five-seater saloon offering levels of refinement comparable to flagship 15mpg (18.83ltr/100km) Jaguar and Mercedes models.

The Ro80 was a car beloved of architects, lawyers and every other kind of self-determining professional person, especially if they were devotees of Leonard Setright.

114

This bearded, cheroot-smoking aesthete and intellectual of motoring journalism never missed an opportunity to extol the virtues of the Ro80 in print, as it was a car that he firmly believed was the best saloon in the world.

There was talk of a two-door coupé Ro80 – with a four-speed version of the selective automatic – but when asked years later Edwald Praxl maintained that a two-door version was never seriously considered, or the dealers' pleas for a V6 or flat-six version as an alternative to the rotary. Rumours of a bigger 160bhp engine were also much discussed in the early 1970s, and behind the scenes Audi-NSU were looking hard at the possibilities and producing running, driving prototypes.

Thus equipped, the car might have won over early sceptics who may well have been willing to overlook the reliability issues if they could have a big NSU with more authoritative initial acceleration. There were plans for a three-rotor engine called the KKM619, but it soon became clear that a bigger capacity two-rotor unit would make more sense.

A manual gearbox or a conventional leave-it-alone automatic would undoubtedly have enhanced the cars appeal as an executive express, especially if they had been offered alongside features like electric windows and air conditioning, the latter a fairly routine aftermarket fitment in hot territories like Italy.

It was not to be: but at least there was money now to improve the Ro80 in smaller ways as it quietly positioned itself as the flagship of the Audi-NSU range, above the Audi 100LS and recently introduced Audi 100S Coupé.

With no place on the Audi-NSU board, Ewald Praxl now answered to Audi's Ludwig Kraus, designer of the Audi 100. The pair were tasked with making the Wankel engine 'call back safe', with durability and fuel consumption equivalent to a 6-cylinder engine and with the lower production costs that had been promised in 1967 but never achieved.

In 1971, with cars still coming out of Neckarsulm at the rate of fifty a day, an audible warning system was fitted to guard against over-revving. In 1972 there were changes to front suspension with improved shock absorbers and aluminium stub axles.

In 1972 – for the 1973 model year – the front seats were changed to the Audi 100 type with standard head rests but no height adjustment.

More significant was the change to a new down-draught Solex carburettor with automatic choke – the 32DD ITS – in the name of improved cold running manners, better low- and mid-torque (at the expense of top-end power), improved economy and cleaned-up emissions.

From the early 1970s the Ro80 shared its front seats with the Audi 100.

But, as the fuel crisis began to make itself felt, and even Americans began to worry about mpg, the fate of the Ro80 was probably already settled. The future of the Wankel engine in the Audi NSU range was still being pondered, but there would be no tooling money allocated for a direct successor to the Ro80.

It was already the orphan of the range, the baby NSUs having been killed off in 1973 to make way for the Audi 50/VW Polo, styled by Claus Luthe. A decent 4,074 cars were sold that year, 1,021 of those in the UK, the car's best export market, where NSU had boasted a network of ninety dealers in 1970.

At their headquarters in Shoreham technicians were taught the secrets of the Wankel rotary, and it was claimed that changing an engine took just five hours.

Sales of all expensive cars were in the doldrums in 1974 – as the fuel crisis began to bite really hard – and the VW group had more important things on its mind with the introduction of its turn-around car, the Golf. It was styled by ItalDesign, but some believe the basic design was on the NSU drawing boards before the 1969 takeover. Writing in top-shelf monthly magazine *Penthouse* in 1974 L. J. K. Setright was still telling everyone who would listen that the Ro80 was 'probably the best production car in the world.' Certainly, for many in Britain it was still a dream car.

When Gladys and Edward Du Gay won the pools in 1974 the first thing they splashed out on was a brand new Ro80. 'It was such a lovely shape' said Gladys 'I must admit my husband wanted a Mercedes – but he soon changed his mind.' Had the couple consulted the architect Sir George Grenfall-Baines, they might have thought again and bought the Mercedes. Professor Baines had fallen in love with the NSU in the late 1960s and was on his third example by 1975, having been persuaded to buy another one by Audi-NSU's claims that they had the engine problems licked. However, when the car started to lose power – and became difficult to start – his local Audi-NSU dealer proved less helpful than expected and Grenfall-Baines penned an exposé of his experiences. It was published in *Motor* in June 1976, revealing that he had gone through seven engines in seven years.

Changes for 1974 were hardly earth shattering – a new plastic expansion tank, improved automatic choke, integrated voltage regulator and larger markings for speedometer and rev counter – but there was time for one final flourish.

At the 1975 Frankfurt show the first real visual alterations to Luthe's still beautiful shape were sanctioned: larger tail light clusters, rubber-faced bumpers, and a new (rather cheap-looking) badge on the boot lid. The rear number plate was now fixed above the bumper, except in Switzerland and Italy (Italian Ro80 exports ended in summer 1975 anyway) where the rear bumper was split. The boot lock was now in the lid rather than the body.

Improvements to the engine included port liners for the exhaust, so that gases could reach the thermal reactor at higher temperatures in the name of lower fuel consumption (especially from cold) and cleaner air. A 10 per cent improvement in mpg was claimed, with up to 25mpg (11.3ltr/100km) now possible. There was less cold-start smoke too, thanks to improved oil seals.

THE END OF THE ROTARY DREAM

Final 1977 Ro80 cars had a stronger gearbox in anticipation of a more powerful Wankel engine that was never fitted to customer cars. Behind the scenes, Audi-NSU were working on that bigger, more potent unit, but still with two rotors rather than three, as had originally been envisaged. It had been decided that two rotors with a bigger capacity was the optimum way to go, mainly because it reduced the number of expensive machining processes during manufacture, but also because it had been determined that adding rotors added complication rather than smoothness. Enter the KKM871, which was being tested from 1973 onwards. It had 150bhp in carburettor form and 170–180bhp with Bosch K Jetronic injection, using three injectors per rotor – two into the inlet manifold and one into the chamber. In both cases the KKM871 marked a return to two plugs per rotor.

A great deal of thought was put into the question of porting and the choice between side and peripheral types. Having tried a combination of both (side intakes for the first stage of the throttle opening, peripheral for the second stage through to full throttle) NSU came down in favour of double-side intake ports with one intake in each side housing, which gave advantages in idling smoothness and part-load response while also allowing for simpler carburettor and exhaust systems.

The KKM871 (also known as the EA871 in VW terminology) was only 2mm wider than the KKM612 in the Ro80 – remarkable, considering the increased power. One way they achieved this was by reducing the spacing of the eccentric shaft bearings, which made it both shorter and stiffer.

The designers were focused on creating the smallest possible combustion chamber surfaces and, by using less cooling water, getting the engine up to operating temperature more rapidly in the name of emissions, fuel economy and reduced wear.

Another preoccupation was limiting the amount of friction-creating oil swilling around the engine while improving the flow to where it was needed most – the bearings – according to speed and load. A single rotor version of this engine known as the EA866 was mooted for a rotary version of the Audi 80.

There was some enthusiasm for the idea that these improved versions of the Wankel concept would be highly suitable for use with hydrogen power.

The decision to drop the big NSU had already been taken when these engines were being tested in Ro80s in 1976. With 750cc per chamber – equivalent to 1.5 or 3 litres depending on how you calculated the measurement – carburettor versions of this engine were good for 130mph (209km/h) with 154lb ft at 3,000rpm. Fuel consumption was said to be equivalent to a straight-six – better, they claimed, than the BMW and Mercedes sixes – but still running on the cheapest possible low-octane fuel. The cars were fitted with three- and four-speed selective automatics and, along with the beefed-up transmission, only needed wider tyres and a rear anti-roll bar to cope with the extra urge.

LAST CHANCE SALOONS, 1968–77

POPULAR CULTURE, PROMOTION AND FAMOUS OWNERS

The Ro80 Club International (formerly Wankel-Journal) is the quarterly organ of the German and Swiss Ro80 clubs.

continued overleaf

117

■ LAST CHANCE SALOONS, 1968–77

POPULAR CULTURE, PROMOTION AND FAMOUS OWNERS *continued*

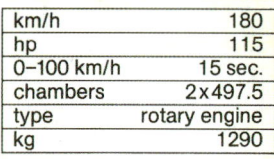

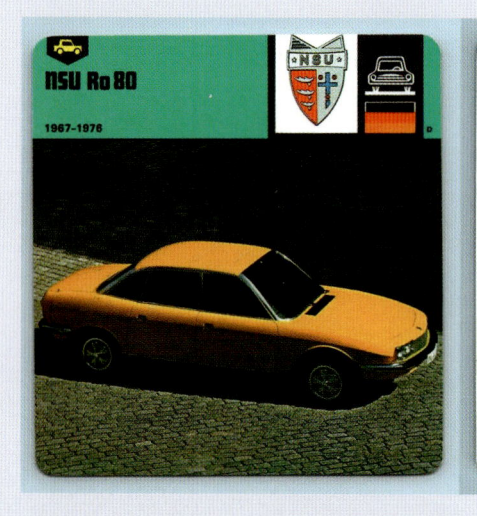

ABOVE LEFT: **The ubiquitous *Top Trumps* card game gave many youngsters their first encounter with the Ro80.**

ABOVE RIGHT: **Italian collector's cards from 1978 featured the Ro80 as a subject. (Phil Blake Collection)**

The early 1970s was a time when foreign cars of any sort were eyed with suspicion in the UK (mostly out of a fear that spare parts would be hard to get hold of) while anything with an unconventional engine – with a vaguely rude-sounding name to English ears – was regarded as witchcraft.

A functional rather than fanciful object, somehow not quite of its own time, the Ro80 was born into a late 1960s world in which Morris Minor production was still in full swing, our television programmes still came mostly in monochrome and hanging for murder had only recently been abolished.

Nevertheless, here was a real-life car of the future that you half expected to see depicted in *Joe 90* or *Captain Scarlet*, the Gerry Anderson puppet-based television presentations. In fact, big or small screen appearances for the Ro80 are few and far between outside of German- and Italian-language thrillers. There was a one-off casting in a Bruce Lee film, a fleeting appearance in a 1980s Vauxhall advert and a part for an early green example in an episode of *The Persuaders*.

Gerry Anderson redeemed himself by casting a blue Ro80 for a fairly prominent role in *The Protectors*, an early 1970s espionage series

Saint Lucia issued a stamp featuring the Ro80 in the 1980s celebrating 100 years of the automobile. (Phil Blake Collection)

LAST CHANCE SALOONS, 1968–77

Another collector's card from Edito Service. (Phil Blake Collection)

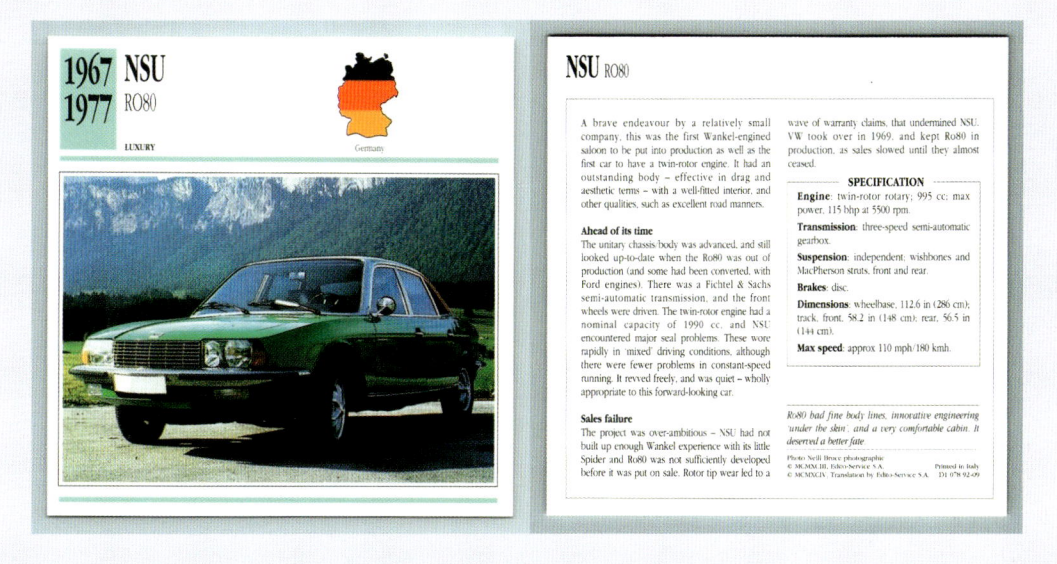

starring Robert Vaughn as the unsmiling Jensen Interceptor-driving Harry Rule. Registered YMJ621L, the NSU was issued to Rule's assistant 'the Contessa'. The story goes that the actress who played the character (the Contessa Di Contini, a wealthy aristocrat with a flamboyant wardrobe and a taste for fast cars) had trouble driving her character's original car, a Citroën SM.

In the UK, most people's first contact with an Ro80 was the Dinky version, the toy version (*Dinky Toys* number 176) with the battery-operated front and rear lights and 'luminous' seats. When *Ladybird* updated its *Keyword Reading Scheme* 'Peter and Jane' books in the early 1970s (giving the protagonists more casual hair cuts – and clothes – compared to their short-back-and-sides 1964 predecessors), they also updated the motor cars in the artwork; that an orange Ro80 was depicted driving down an English high street seemed to be an indication that the modern world had truly arrived even in the cosy mid-century landscape of Peter and Jane.

SIR JOHN WHITMORE AND OTHER FAMOUS Ro80 OWNERS

Prominent Germans who drove an Ro80 included actors Günther Schramm and Erik Ode, the television presenter Wim Thoelke and the politician Walther Leisler Kiep, as well as the reformed former Nazi Albert Speer, who had three. Simon Dee, the 1960s talk show host and DJ, did some promotional work with the Ro80, but it is not certain that he owned one.

In the 1990s, no less an eminence than the late Sir John Whitmore ran a Mazda-converted NSU Ro80. The former racing driver was best known for his success racing Lotus Cortinas both with the Ford works team and then with privateer Alan Mann. It was with Mann that Sir John won the European Touring Car championship in 1965. He was also well known for racing Mini Coopers and Ford GT40s: yet for road use he chose this twenty-year-old German saloon with a distinctly dodgy reputation.

A relaxed and friendly character who latterly earned his living teaching – and writing books about, performance coaching – I interviewed Sir John in 1996 about his 1975 maroon Ro80:

I tried one when they first came out and it appealed to me because the rotary engine was so smooth. As a director of David Ogle at the time I was interested in the futuristic styling too.

As well as the Mazda engine Whitmore had the suspension stiffened, yet he disapproved of driving quickly on the road and really wanted the Ro80 for its relaxing qualities.

I have a Sierra four-wheel-drive estate, but if I have a long journey to do I go to the NSU.

continued overleaf

■ LAST CHANCE SALOONS, 1968–77

POPULAR CULTURE, PROMOTION AND FAMOUS OWNERS *continued*

It is not known if Simon Dee, DJ and talk show host owned an Ro80, but he turned up for this publicity shot.

BROCHURES, PRESS PACKS AND HAND BOOKS
Although the Ro80 was featured in a variety of NSU and Audi-NSU range brochures, there were relatively few dedicated publications. The original 1968 brochure was a fold-out effort showing a pre-production car with the simulated wooden facia, a 'Wankel' script embossed on the steering hub and a different rear badge that looks suspiciously as if it has been added to the picture afterwards with artistic licence. The 1969–71 brochure *A New Experience in Motoring* shows a white car and is more graphically sophisticated than the original pamphlet.

The year 1971 saw the introduction of the '*Vorsprung Durch Technik*' Ro80 brochure showing an orange car. Created under the Audi-NSU regime, it has a much more lavish feel than previous catalogues, with six pages of full colour fold-outs. It is probably the only Ro80 handout that truly captures the essence of the vehicle. The English language translation was called *Success Through Engineering*.

Contents of an Ro80 folder including handbook, service book, radio instructions and guarantee.

The 1975–77 brochure is a half-hearted affair showing a blue car on steel wheels seemingly parked in a field. The text is brief and badly translated from German.

As supplied, the Ro80 came with a wallet containing the owner's handbook (there were at least three versions of this), a list of service stations, a service record book, a radio instruction pamphlet and in some cases a note detailing changes to spark plug specifications.

Lavish ring-bound press packs were published in 1967 and 1969 with photographic slides and black and white shots showing the Ro80 in a variety of scenarios: the new car gambolling through the German countryside at high speed, parked outside modern architecture and at the airport awaiting a young jet-setting couple; the fact that the man is wearing a trilby strikes an odd note next to the modern statement the car makes.

There are also in-depth technical descriptions and styling sketches in a publication that must be one of the first modern-style, comprehensive motor industry press handouts.

IN PERIOD TOYS AND MODELS

1/43rd Scale
Dinky (UK) Number 176 Diecast Working lights front and rear. Red, green, silver. Sold 1968–72.
Tekno 836 (Denmark) Diecast blue or gold opening front doors, bonnet. Sold 1968–72.
Mebetoys A37 (Italy) Diecast opening front doors and bonnet in silver, green or blue 1969; also produced under licence in USSR by state-owned toy company.

continued overleaf

■ LAST CHANCE SALOONS, 1968–77

POPULAR CULTURE, PROMOTION AND FAMOUS OWNERS continued

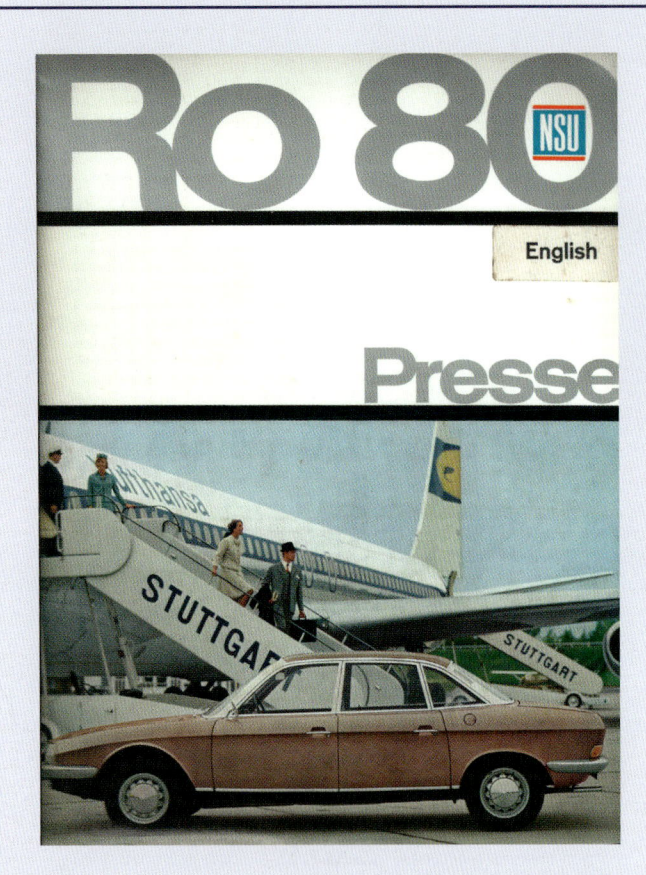

Cover of the first press pack.

1969/70 brochure showing latest colours.

Early brochure folds out to make a poster.

1971 brochure showing Audi influence in presentation and the famous tagline later revived for the C3 Audi 100.

LAST CHANCE SALOONS, 1968–77

Audi-NSU range brochure attempts to merge the two families.

**NSU Prinz 4L
=economy plus**

Two doors, four seater,
air cooled rear engine
598 cc 30 BHP (DIN)
75 mph top and cruising speed
0-50 mph 15.8 secs
49 mpg on **petrol (DIN 70030)

**NSU 1000C
=economy plus comfort**

Two doors, four seater, air cooled rear engine
996 cc 40 BHP (DIN)
81 mph top and cruising speed
0-50 mph in 12.0 secs
37 mpg on **petrol (DIN 70030)

**NSU 1200C
=economy plus
performance plus
comfort**

Two doors, five seater,
air cooled rear engine
1177cc 55 BHP (DIN)
90 mph top and cruising speed
0-50 mph in 9.4 secs

Also available in 1200 automatic
(with selective auto transmission)
1200 TT (1000C body with 1177 cc
Twin carb engine)

**Audi 75 Variant
=economy plus
spaciousness**

Three doors, five seater,
front wheel drive
1697cc 75 BHP (DIN)
93 mph top and cruising speed
will carry 1102 lbs load

continued overleaf

123

■ LAST CHANCE SALOONS, 1968–77

POPULAR CULTURE, PROMOTION AND FAMOUS OWNERS *continued*

**Audi 100LS
=luxury plus
performance**

Two/four door, five seater,
front wheel drive
1760 cc 100 BHP (DIN)
106 mph top and cruising speed
0-60 in 11.7 secs
Available in automatic
Foglamps and headrests
optional extras.

New for 1972

**Audi 100 Coupé S
=luxury plus
performance plus
style**

Two door fast-back, five seater,
front wheel drive
1871 cc 112 BHP (DIN)
115 mph top and cruising speed
0-60 in 9.7 secs

New for 1972

**Audi 100GL
=*more* luxury
plus *more*
performance**

Two/four door, five seater,
front wheel drive
1871 cc 112 BHP (DIN)
115 mph top and cruising speed
0-60 in 9.7 secs
Available in automatic
Foglamps and headrests
optional extras.

**NSU Ro 80
=luxury plus
performance plus
technology**

Four door, five seater,
front wheel drive
Double rotary piston engine with
2 × 497.5 cc chamber volume
Output 115 BHP (DIN)
112 mph top speed
0-60 mph in 12.6 secs
Selective automatic

The first-generation Audi 100 offered, on paper, much of what the Ro80 set out to achieve but in a less innovative way.

LAST CHANCE SALOONS, 1968–77

Price list for British Forces in Germany, valid as from 1 March 1969.

PRICE LIST FOR BRITISH FORCES GERMANY

(valid as from March 1st. 1969)

NSU Ro 80

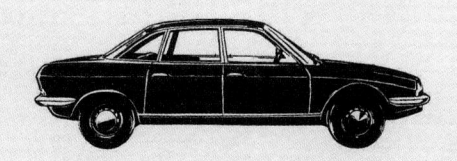

4-door sedan, NSU Wankel Rotary Engine, 2 x 500 cc. chamber volume, watercooled, 115 HP (DIN) = 130 HP (SAE), front wheel drive. Gearbox: Selective automatic with three speed ranges. ATE disc brakes front and rear, dual brake circuits, radial tyres. Standard interior equipment: Upholstery in cloth or vinyl, reclining seats. Also, 2 speed windscreen wipers, twin fog lights, revolution counter, warning lights, power assisted steering and others.

LHD MODEL	DM 12.900.--
RHD MODEL	DM 13.200.--

More information about extras and colour schemes for the Ro 80 is available on request.

continued overleaf

POPULAR CULTURE, PROMOTION AND FAMOUS OWNERS *continued*

Gama (West Germany) Diecast No 9670 opening front doors and bonnet. 1973 but reissued in 2000s.
Marklin No 1811 Diecast (West Germany), four opening doors and bonnet, reclining front seats in green or pink.
Jean Hoefler (West Germany) Plastic, green with cream seats.
Sablon No 7 (Belgium) 1969 Diecast opening front doors, bonnet and boot lid.

1/67th and 1/87th SCALE
Husky No 37 (GB) 1968–70 Diecast Blue. 1/66th scale, opening bonnet and detailed engine.
Corgi Junior (GB) No 37 1969–73 Purple, pink or Blue, Whizz wheels
Wiking (German) 1/87 scale, plastic in red, green. Blue and grey. Also available as a taxi.
Gama Minete 1/63 late 1960s–early 1970s. Diecast, opening bonnet and boot lid.

The famous Dinky model with working front and rear lights.

Italian Mebetoys, also produced under licence in the USSR. (Phil Blake Collection)

Husky 1/66th scale. (Phil Blake Collection)

From Tekno in Denmark, blue or gold. (Phil Blake Collection)

LAST CHANCE SALOONS, 1968–77

Hopes for a Wankel-powered follow-up to the Ro80 lay with the Audi 100-based cars powered by a new KKM 871 engine with 230bhp in some versions.

Twenty were built for evaluation, mostly for the use of Audi management who proved unwilling to relinquish them.

■ LAST CHANCE SALOONS, 1968–77

Audi took the safer route of 5-cylinder power, with turbo technology in the flagship 200 model pictured here.

If the Ro80 was doomed by the mid-1970s, the Wankel concept still had friends at Neckarsulm, although new boss Ferdinand Piech, fresh from Porsche, had severe concerns about the long-term viability of an engine with such poor thermal efficiency and thus thirst. Its simplicity and compactness remained, but the Wankel had never been cheap to make compared with reciprocating engines and its reliability prospects were still marginal in the eyes of the public. Piech had a hunch that turbo diesel power could be the way to go for big cars. He favoured a 5-cylinder engine for the next generation of large Audis on the basis that a six, teamed with front-wheel drive, was too long. So it was at the in-line five pot that technical resources were aimed, somewhat to the detriment of Wankel engine development.

Yet the irascible Austrian, grandson of Ferry Porsche, was willing to give the Wankel idea one last try, sanctioning a fleet of twenty Audi 100 C2 saloons in 1976 as test beds for a fuel-injected version of the KKM871.

Built to take on the BMW 5 Series and Mercedes W123, this second generation Audi 100 – created from the start to accept the Wankel engine – was built at Neckarsulm and effectively replaced not only the original 1968 Audi 100 but also – in 4-cylinder form – the VW 411 and K70. There were, in fact, plans for a cheaper VW-badged version.

The C2 Audi 100 was styled by Helmut Warkub in an angular style that allowed for a rather unremarkable 0.42 drag coefficient; Claus Luthe did the interior.

Such a car could have emerged as an alternative version of the Audi 200 at the end of the 1970s. The prototypes were shown at Frankfurt and at American and Japanese auto shows, more as a way of demonstrating the Germans' continued commitment to rotary power – for the benefit of licence holders – than as a serious production proposal.

Even so, there had been a faint hope that Citroën might adopt the design for the CX (871 engines were tested in the new big Citroën, but dropped from the programme at a late stage) and there was serious interest from builders of light aircraft.

Weighing 60lb (27kg) less than a Rover V8, the KKM871 had axial flow cooling to help tame heat build up around the spark plugs that could lead to cracking. With 230bhp, this lean burn unit with stratified charge injection technology and promising emission figures made a silky rocket-ship out of the slightly frumpy and angular C2 Audi 100, even when fitted with conventional automatic transmission. This was so much the case that the Audi board members who were allocated these special cars – and the bigger-engined Ro80s – proved unwilling to give them up long after the KKM871 project had died. A surprising number of these now highly-prized KKM871 engines escaped from Neckarsulm and found their way into Ro80s belonging to private individuals.

In 1982 Felix Wankel was presented with one of the twenty KKM871-powered Audi 100s to his fleet. Having sold his interests in the Wankel engine to the South African (but UK-based) business tycoon Tiny Rowland in 1972, Dr Wankel now split his time between research and animal welfare issues. He was still inventive well into his seventies, working late at the single-storey, glass-fronted research centre on Lake Constance at Lindau that he had designed himself.

After his wife Emma died in 1975, Felix Wankel continued to pursue his ideas. Latterly he was working on designs for gliders and an idea for a small rotary-powered boat that could be used like a family car to cross the Atlantic if necessary, refuelling at floating petrol stations. He was also designing a supercharger that he hoped would cure the fuel consumption problems endemic in the Wankel engine. He developed a valve for rotary compressors and filed a patent for a variable compression system for both rotary and reciprocating engines.

But Wankel's health was poor in his last few years: he was diagnosed with prostate cancer in 1984 and had a vertebra surgically removed in 1987, the year he filed his last patent. He died at home on 9 October 1988, just a few days after the passing of another great twentieth-century engineer, Alec Issigonis.

Audi NSU ceased production of the Ro80 in March 1977, clearing production capacity for the Porsche 924 on the Neckarsulm assembly lines. Only eleven cars sold in the UK this year, where the Ro80 had been on special order only for two seasons.

It had rapidly become a very expensive car in Britain, where the price had rocketed to over £7,000. In Germany the final Ro80s were almost unsaleable, their popularity not helped by the fact that prices of used versions were on the floor.

The last Ro80 off the production line, a silver car with gaudy 'rally stripes' was donated by Audi-NSU to the Deutsches Museum in Munich. In 1985, Audi NSU Auto Union officially became simply Audi AG.

In the world of motoring lost causes, the NSU Ro80 holds a curious position. It is too 'pure' a piece of engineering – too beautiful an object – to have the comedy value of a 1970s' British Leyland product or some terrible eastern bloc car. It was not even a straightforward commercial failure, given that it had a ten-year, 37,000-unit production run. It is a car that has inspired frustration and devotion in equal measure. Had the Ro80 been launched in 1969 or 1970 as a more fully developed and reliable product, the name NSU might still be with us today. With longevity comparable to a piston engine the success of the car as a whole – which was remarkably trouble free in all other respects – would have been assured.

The Ro80's superiority over its rivals in almost all aspects of behaviour was so clear cut in 1967 that it seemed to have

The UK was the best market for the Ro80 outside Germany, although only available to special order from 1975 to 1977.

■ LAST CHANCE SALOONS, 1968–77

The superb profile of the Ro80 captured many hearts even before the test drive; it still does today.

BELOW LEFT: **The flat floor and large glass area gave the car an airy, spacious feel. Velour seats were standard by the early 1970s.**

BELOW: **The latest dashboard, little changed from the late 1960s.**

been beamed down from another world, the product of a higher intelligence. It seemed barely plausible that a fairly minor player like NSU could have come out of nowhere with an automobile so consummately excellent: many have speculated that – like some sort of post-war, neo-Nazi peacetime super weapon – it must have been created for NSU by a consortium of the German motor industry tycoons secretly plotting to boost national pride with a 'world first' product.

A true last chance saloon for NSU, it was clear within a year or so of the Ro80's 1967 launch that it was going to lead to the loss of the company's independence as a car maker: a more positive spin on that inevitability is that the spirit of NSU and the Ro80 lives on in the modern Audi empire, particularly in its big saloon cars.

Given that Audi was really just a freshly rebranded incarnation of Auto Union (who had only recently kicked its two-stroke habit) NSU were bringing rather more to the table, not only in terms of product but also of the design talent that would go on to make Audi's reputation in the 1980s as serious competition for BMW and Mercedes. The Ro80 is the catalyst that lies at the heart of that sequence of events.

LAST CHANCE SALOONS, 1968–77

ABOVE LEFT: **Engine bay of a two-plug car showing the transistorised ignition unit and original plastic sheathing over the distributor.**

ABOVE RIGHT: **The flip side of achieving such good aerodynamics was poor through-flow ventilation at a time when even quite humble cars were improving dramatically. Vents on the 'C' pillars and additional knee-level fresh air outlets never quite made up for the lack of an air conditioning option.**

Period film and pictures of the Ro80 amidst mid-1960s West German city traffic – composed mostly of VW Beetles and ghastly chrome-encrusted Opels – tell you everything you need to know about how shockingly advanced this car looked when it was launched.

Ten years later it had grown into itself yet, somehow, not aged a single day. You could buy an Ro80 just to admire as a static exhibit – some have – but for me that would be a shame. Once experienced on the road, covering the ground with a uniquely relaxing and majestic poise, the Ro80 seems even more beautiful. With an ordinary engine it would have been a nice car, a good car. For better or worse it was the Wankel rotary unit that made it a great car.

ABOVE: **The definitive 110 watt Bosch headlamps gave a better lighting performance than the earlier type, where the feature line of the body flowed into the lens.**

■ LAST CHANCE SALOONS, 1968–77

THE COMPLICATED HISTORY OF DKW, AUTO UNION AND AUDI

For fifteen years after the war, two-stroke DKW and Auto Union cars were the obvious choice for buyers who wanted a vehicle that was upmarket of a Beetle, but also more interesting and credible than a gaudy German Ford or a tinny Opel.

These cars established many of the values associated with Audi today: good build quality, rational front-wheel-drive packaging (with the engine mounted longitudinally ahead of the front axle line), for the kind of stability and handling that earned them a fine reputation in international rallying.

Streamlined shapes and high gearing made these DKWs very much a product of a country where it was already possible to cruise at high speeds for long distances. DKW *is* Audi. Dampf Kraft Wagen was formed in 1904, albeit under a different name, initially producing pipe fittings before moving into military equipment. Then, in the 1920s, it became a significant manufacturer of two-stroke motorcycles, joined by an advanced range of 2-cylinder, transverse-engined, front-wheel-drive cars following in 1930. DKW was the dominant partner in the Auto Union alliance of 1932, having taken over the up-market Audi marque some four years earlier.

With no market for big middle-class cars at the time, Auto Union allowed the Audi name to lie dormant after World War II, before resurrecting it in the mid-1960s as a rebranding exercise for a new generation of four-stroke, 4-cylinder cars that would finally banish the two-strokes.

It was not dogma that kept DKW faithful to the two-stroke, because it did have its advantages in terms of fewer moving parts (no valves, no oil pump) and simplified maintenance (no need to change the oil!), which many still considered an acceptable trade-off for the inconvenience of adding oil to your fuel.

But in an increasingly affluent West Germany, this outdated technology was running out of credibility by the early 1960s. It was not easily adapted to the bigger, more powerful engines that the market was demanding, and it somehow had a whiff (literally) of poverty motoring about it that aligned it with the miserable Wartburgs and Trabants that the East Germans were driving.

Auto Union's first post-war car was the F89 of 1950, with a pre-war 700cc twin mounted longitudinally in a new chassis, all-independent transverse-leaf suspension and hydraulic brakes. The car had been previewed in 1939 as the three-cylinder DKW F9, Auto Union's answer to the Volkswagen, but only prototypes were built before the war got underway. Some 60,000 examples of this car, known as the *Meisterklasse*, were built before the *Sonderklasse* version appeared in 1953, using the 3-cylinder 896cc engine that had been seen before the war.

With its four needle-roller big ends and pressurised crankcase, this engine could take the new 3=6 DKW to 75mph (121km/h; nifty for a sub-1-litre car in the mid-1950s). The '3=6' name was a reminder that the power-on-every-stroke engine had the smoothness of a 6-cylinder. Widened by 4in (102mm) for 1956 and with a re-styled grille, this basic shape went through to 1963 and it was in this form that it became a familiar and successful rally machine and European Touring Car Champion in 1954.

From 1958 to 1963 the 'big' DKWs were branded Auto Unions. The re-proportioned 1000S four-door shared the same wheelbase as the Universal Estate version. In 1000S form, it has 50bhp and synchromesh on first – useful for a car in which you have to use the bottom ratio quite a bit to keep momentum going in hilly terrain. With its glamorous cream steering wheel and opulent seats, the four-door was promoted in its brochure as a car for gracious living, with mink stole-wearing ladies taking trips to the opera, an image that did not quite square with the trail of blue smoke that followed the 1000S everywhere.

A new 'Lubrimat' system for 1961 (automatically feeding oil into the engine, in proportion to revs and load) at least meant there was no more fiddling with cans of oil when the time came to fill up.

The 1000SP was the glamour car of the Auto Union line-up, a low two-seater coupé or a much rarer convertible with bodywork subcontracted to Baur. It was marketed as the connoisseur's choice – a luxury sports car with a more powerful 55bhp engine. It was claimed that the fins helped stability at speed, but they were really a fashion item that made the 1000SP look so much like a Thunderbird it was a wonder Ford did not sue.

LAST CHANCE SALOONS, 1968–77

The post-war DKW and Auto Unions continued with front-wheel drive and two-stroke engines.

Post-war, DKW maintained a proud tradition of commercials with the *Schnellaster* (Rapid Transporter), a front-drive van with a low loading floor. As the 1-litre Auto Unions and DKWs became more elaborate and up-market towards the end of the 1950s, they began to lose a traditional element for economy-minded buyers.

The 1960 DKW Junior was a successful attempt to regain the interest of this market with a cheaper, smaller model with more contemporary styling. The Junior begot the F11 and the F12 in 1963. The F102 was introduced in 1963. The curvy streamlining of the Sonderklasse was replaced by a rational, angular and glassy three-box look that foreshadowed Audi styling of the late 1960s and early 1970s but, surprisingly perhaps, the two-stroke was thought to have continued potential. It was still a triple, built along the same general principles, but up to 1175cc with 60bhp and more torque. This was a car with determinedly middle-class aspirations, with a large boot, reclining seats and five-seater capability. The inboard front discs would be favoured by Audi for decades to come.

continued overleaf

■ LAST CHANCE SALOONS, 1968–77

THE COMPLICATED HISTORY OF DKW, AUTO UNION AND AUDI *continued*

The F11 was a smaller-engined, more modern take on the two-stroke theme.

The Audi 90, derived from the F102, was a change of direction with a modern Mercedes-designed four-stroke power unit.

LAST CHANCE SALOONS, 1968–77

The F102 had two doors at first, a four-door following in 1964, the year Volkswagen bought Daimler-Benz's stake in Auto Union.

DKW production ended in 1966 and thus crossed over for a year with the 4-cylinder Auto Union Audi (note that 'Audi' was a model name at first, rather than make), precursor to the Audi 100 and the modern generation of cars from Ingolstadt. Its high-compression, Mercedes-designed engine was a legacy of that company's 88 per cent controlling interest in Auto Union between 1958 and 1964. In fact, this basic engine design was used by Audi well into the 1990s.

Tellingly, in a sixteen-page introductory brochure to the new car, there is not one mention of DKW, despite the fact that the new Audi was undeniably the old F102 lightly made over with a longer nose (to accommodate the bigger, canted-over engine) and rectangular headlamps.

These DKWs and Auto Unions seem emblematic of a period in which technical variety and difference in everyday cars was still celebrated; a time when, in the face of creeping blandness, you could still tell the maker of the car by the noise it made and, in the case of DKW, by the smell.

ABOVE: **Audi provided comprehensive instrumentation with rationally-placed switchgear.**

RIGHT: **Two-door versions of the Audi 100 provided the basis for convertible versions by Karmann and Crayford.**

135

■ LAST CHANCE SALOONS, 1968–77

COMOTOR AND THE CITROËN GS BIROTOR

With the same price tag as a DS23Efi (but a greater thirst) it should come as no surprise that Citroën only built 835 of its 1973–75 GS Birotor-based oddities. The surviving examples would doubtless be in therapy if they were people: the Birotor was disowned by its parent Citroën, who even tried to save itself the bother of having to supply parts and service for its unloved progeny by attempting to buy back, and destroy, all 835 of them. Around a third are thought to survive. Its commercial failure was one of the deciding factors in Citroën's bankruptcy (and subsequent takeover by Peugeot), not so much on the basis of those 835 cars but because of its joint investment with NSU in a company named Comotor.

Here, in a new factory thirty minutes east of Luxembourg, the two firms plotted to build rotary engines, Citroën having satisfied itself of the feasibility of a Wankel-powered car by doing a dry run of 267 specially adapted Ami coupés fitted with a single rotor 49bhp engine. Known as the M35, these were sold to 'special customers' for evaluation between 1969 and 1972.

With its various external drives for the hydro-pneumatics, the Birotor's peripheral port engine – transversely mounted and mostly obscured by the spare wheel – was ready by 1972. Although its general architecture was similar, internally, to the NSU, it shared nothing directly with the German car. Its lower power rating of 106bhp was presumably attributable to losses associated with the brake and suspension pumps.

With a rotary CX prototype waiting in the wings, it seems odd that Citroën chose the compact three-year-old GS as the basis for its first Wankel production vehicle when, presumably, buyers of the bigger car would have been more open to the idea of a powerful and technically advanced engine, even if it was rather thirsty. The Wankel-engined CX would have had two rotors rather than the widely hinted at three (for which there is little evidence such a plan ever existed), but it does seem that the big Citroën was designed from the beginning to take a rotary engine as it shared the outboard brake layout of the Birotor, a very similar front suspension design and engine bay architecture.

Little of the Birotor was interchangeable with a standard GS; beyond the obvious flared arches, five-bolt wheels and all disc brakes, much of the suspension and underpinnings were unique to the car. The fact that front brakes were outboard, rather than inboard, was just one of many differences. Most Birotors came in chocolate brown or light gold with a contrasting roof finish. The brown theme continued inside where, to justify a price 70 per cent higher than the most expensive air-cooled GS, Citroën gave the Birotor full carpeting, circular instruments and front seats with built-in headrests. On the centre console there was a button and a gauge to monitor engine oil levels, a reminder that rotary engine oil consumption is much higher.

Like NSU, Citroën adopted a semi-automatic, three-speed gearbox for the Birotor to mask the lack of low-speed torque and over-run snatch. Certainly no other GS had anything like the urge of the Birotor and, with its anti-roll bars and that smaller, lighter engine, there was less roll, understeer and tyre squeal to contend with.

Floating serenely along on its hydro-pneumatics, to have such an isolating big car ride in something so compact was one of the great features of these flat-four Citroëns. The Birotor would end up being the one and only production car to mix hydro-pneumatics and a Wankel engine.

THE C111 AND THE MERCEDES WANKEL ADVENTURE

In the late 1960s there was a belief that Mercedes might actually go into production with a rotary-powered car.

The Wankel was big news – virtually every manufacturer was developing a version of this new smooth, light and compact wonder engine – and as an image-boosting high-tech, mid-engined flagship, the C111 would have been a perfect launch pad for a Mercedes rotary power unit. Bruno Sacco, former head of styling at Mercedes, was quite clear about the seriousness of the C111 when I interviewed him in the late 1990s:

LAST CHANCE SALOONS, 1968–77

The C111 cars were intended as a follow-up to the 300SL gullwing.

Mercedes built three- and four-rotor fuel-injected engines for exotics on these mobile test beds.

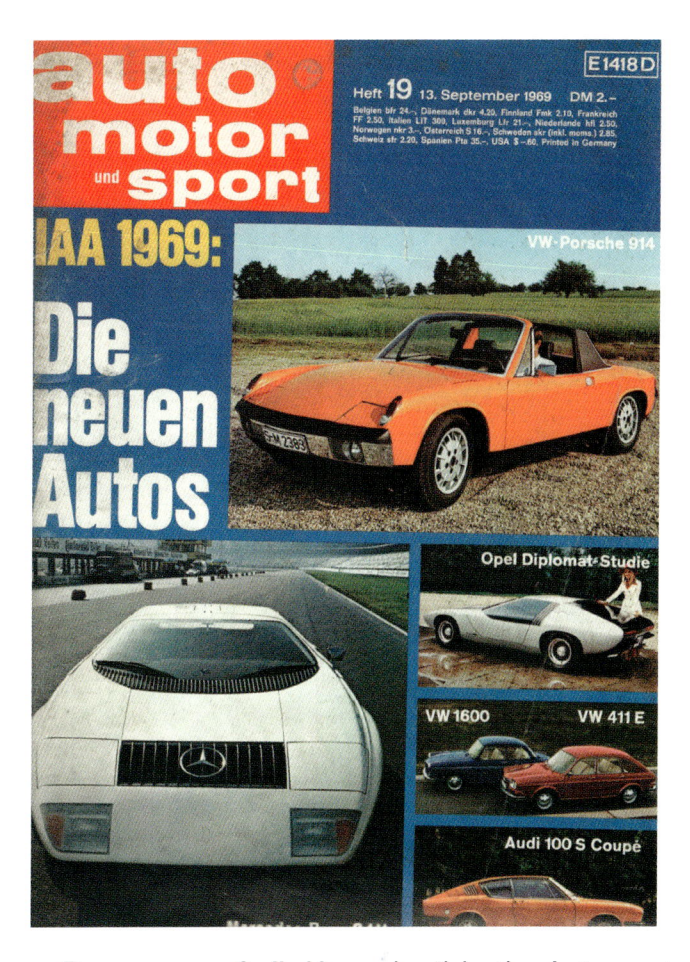

Press coverage fuelled buyers' anticipation, but no amount of money could persuade Mercedes to part with these cars.

When the design was commissioned it was meant to go into series production but it has been the setbacks in the development of the Wankel engine that prevented us from going into production. At the time our engine developers really believed in the Wankel, and if it had worked we would have had an ace up our sleeves, because it would have had great output and would have been superior and it would have been a surprise in the market for our competitors.

There was never any question of a racing career for the C111. This was intended to be a street-legal, comfortable civilised grand tourer with boot space and easy ingress and

Well thought-out interior contrasts would have made the properly engineered C111 unique among its supercar contemporaries.

137

exit. A flagship supercar that recaptured the excitement of the 300SL Gullwing.

Work had only started on the C111 at the beginning of 1969, yet Mercedes were happy to show the first car at the Frankfurt show in the autumn, resplendent in Sacco's new body and painted in silver rather than the orange that would become a trademark of the C111 later on. The chassis was a steel platform with bulkheads either end of the cockpit. The windscreen and rear window hoops were joined by a central bar for stiffness, but it also acted as a hinge for the gullwing doors. An early prototype had a rudimentary aluminium body, but Sacco's design was wrought in bonded and riveted glass fibre (another first for Mercedes), supplied by a manufacturer of railway rolling stock.

The first three-rotor, fuel-injected Wankel engine with a capacity of 1800cc (equivalent to 3800cc in a piston engine) produced 300bhp at 7,000rpm and was tucked down between the rear bulkhead and the wheels, with a ZF five-speed gearbox hung out behind the axle. Suspension was by upper and lower transverse links at the front, with semi-trailing arms at the rear, although these were later changed for transverse arms and long forward-facing links when the prototype was found to be unstable. The recirculating ball steering with its zero offset geometry was to be found later on in the production S-Class saloons of 1972. The 13 gallon (59ltr) fuel tanks were in the sills.

Although it was good for 170mph (274km/h) this three-rotor car – of which five examples were built – suffered from drive-ability problems, because the peak torque came in so high (5,000rpm). The only answer was to build a revised car with a longer wheelbase that gave room for a bigger four-rotor Wankel engine. Enter, at the 1970 Geneva show, the C111-II. Sacco had given his body a more refined, less brutal look with a lower waistline, larger side windows and a bigger screen. The bonnet treatment was different, with deep, scalloped ducts that allowed air to escape from the radiator intake at the front. The slats in the flying buttresses behind the cabin had been removed to good effect.

With 350bhp at 7,000rpm this C111 – offering the equivalent of 4800cc – was tested at 187mph (300km/h) and was hardly any heavier than its predecessor. 33 per cent more torque gave it much greater flexibility – 288lb ft delivered between 4,000 and 5,500rpm.

The public – and the press – loved the car and, as Paul Frère says in his book on the C111, 'Firm orders for such a vehicle, accompanied by blank cheques, came in from various parts of the world.' But as we know, it was not to be. By the time Mercedes had developed a Wankel engine they were satisfied would be reliable, events were overtaken by the 1973 oil crisis. Suddenly the thirsty Wankel was bad news and with ever more stringent anti-pollution legislation on the horizon its long-term future looked even bleaker. Mercedes-Benz now had the perfect excuse to abandon their rotary Wankel-engined plans, perhaps secretly relieved that they no longer had to face the huge cost of tooling up for series production. With the retirement of Rudolf Uhlenhaut and others of his generation, the idea now had fewer champions in Stuttgart.

Even so, the C111 cars continued as mobile test beds for several years. One was converted to diesel power in the mid-1970s for record breaking while another streamliner C111-III – also the work of Sacco – was built for more record breaking at Nardo in 1978.

I was privileged to be allowed to drive the four-rotor C111. For a prototype it was remarkably civilised and complete, with a production car feel to it. Rotary engines can sound slightly two-stroke-like at idle, but this one – with double the number of rotors most are blessed with – sounded smooth and sophisticated, but sufficiently different in a hard to define way. Like a cross between a V12 and a jet is the nearest analogy I could come up with. You would know there was something interesting providing the power even if nobody had told you. It was easy to drive, the big rotary engine having a consistency of its pull and a relentless surge

---

THE ROTARY VAZ 2101/LADA

The ubiquitous VAZ 2101 – better known outside Russia as the Fiat 124-based Lada – was available to certain 'special' home market police and KGB customers with rotary Wankel power from 1978 until well into the 1990s. Eight different models of the VAZ 2101 were available with Wankel engines in 70bhp (single rotor) and 120bhp (twin rotor) form. They were, naturally, faster than their piston-engined equivalents but tended to have a short 20,000km (12,430 mile) working life. Believed to have been 'inspired' by the Mazda 13B rotary engine, the Russian version came in up to twenty different variants including 3- and 4-rotor versions for the larger Volga/Vaz 431 cars (for the KGB) and heavy military applications producing an alleged 350bhp.

DETROIT AND THE WANKEL

American rotary licence holder Curtiss Wright had already demonstrated the Wankel's suitability for automotive use by fitting its RC 2-60 engine into a Ford Mustang prototype in the mid-1960s. The Ford Motor Company, after showing some initial interest, convinced themselves that the engine could not be made 'clean' enough to conform with up-coming legislation and dismissed the Wankel idea fairly early on as a mass-production proposition. Chrysler preferred to continue pouring millions into the ultimately fruitless Gas Turbine project.

However, General Motors' President Ed Cole saw a future for the Wankel as an engine that would help bring American cars down to size in the 1970s and, after eight years of hard negotiation, signed a $50 million agreement for a basic licence with Curtiss Wright and NSU at the end of 1970. This was – or should have been – a key moment in the mass acceptance of the engine. Ultra-conservative GM was the largest car maker in the world, whose stamp of approval would convince even the most sceptical about its future prospects. Knowing this, Cole was able to do a special deal with NSU whereby GM did not become a member of the information sharing Wankel 'Club', and did not receive – or require – access to technical information garnered by other Wankel-producing firms post-1970. Neither would GM share any of its own findings or pay NSU a royalty on each engine it produced. These engines would be simplified, highly productionised units rebranded GMREs and built by GM's Hydramatic Division who, as producers of its automatic transmissions, had great experience in machining curved components very accurately. It was common knowledge that General Motors were looking very seriously at producing rotary engines in high volumes and rolling out new models – or made-over versions of existing ones – throughout the 1970s. There was going to be a four-rotor, mid-engined Corvette, various two-rotor, front-wheel-drive vans and mid-size rotary saloons from the Chevrolet, Pontiac, Oldsmobile and Buick divisions. One of the first slated for a rotary make-over was the Chevrolet Vega, the 145bhp Wankel/GMRE replacing its somewhat hopeless 4-cylinder engine. Although it was later claimed that GM engineers had solved the Wankel's fuel economy and longevity issues, the twin factors of the fuel crisis, and Ed Cole's retirement, effectively killed off the GMRE. A knock-on effect of this was that AMC had to drop its plans for a rotary-engined version of its Pacer, which had been earmarked for a GMRE supplied by GM, at least until AMC could build its own.

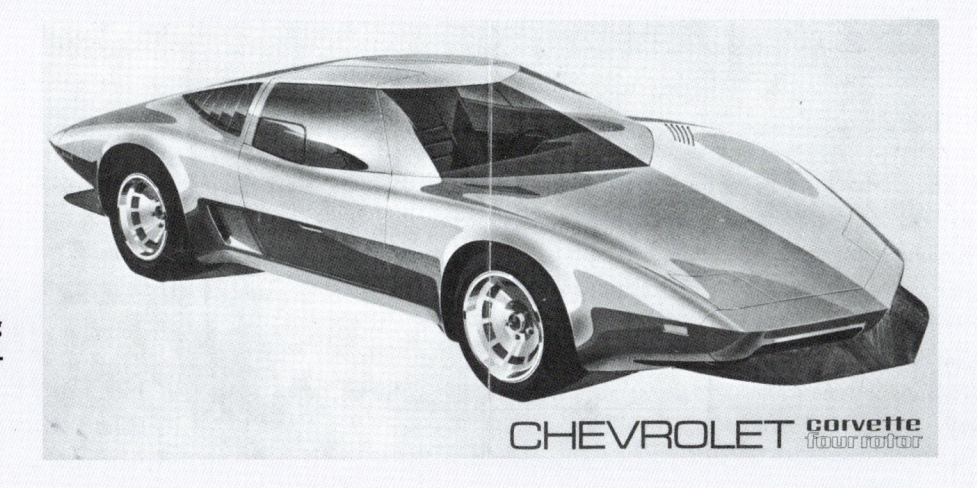

ABOVE: **Rotary power could only have improved the awful Chevrolet Vega.**

RIGHT: **By the mid-1970s, plans for a four-rotor, mid-engined Corvette were quite well advanced, including various two-rotor, front-wheel-drive vans and mid-size rotary saloons by other GM divisions.**

continued overleaf

■ LAST CHANCE SALOONS, 1968–77

DETROIT AND THE WANKEL *continued*

Had General Motors taken up plans to make rotary engines, they would have supplied them to AMC for use in its Pacer compact.

for the red line with no peak in the delivery. The smoothness and strength of its delivery were addictive, as was that noise: a whistling jet-like hum that added to the futuristic feel of the car and made your neck hairs bristle every bit as convincingly as any four-cam V12.

The gearbox was friendly, the ride supple and saloon-like and the shell of-a-piece. Through urban curves and autobahn slip roads it whisked along with the stable assurance and confident poise you would expect from a thoroughly developed mid-engine car.

A curious footnote to the C111 story is the rotary-engined Mercedes SL built for Felix Wankel. In the early 1970s Dr Wankel was still looking forward to taking delivery of a C111 that had been half-promised to him by Mercedes. It never arrived, but Wankel had a back-up plan in the form of a brand new 350SL (he took delivery of one of the very first in September 1971) and a four-rotor M950/4 engine. He paid for both with his own money, although Mercedes at first refused to sell him one of the twenty development four-rotor engines, until he convinced them it was for a boat project rather than a car.

As usual Wankel himself did not get his hands dirty. The rotary-engined 350SL was developed by Dankwert Elermann at the Wankel institute at Lake Constance. Elermann adapted it to use a 300SEL 6.3 exhaust system and a manual SL gearbox with an appropriately beefed up twin-disc clutch. Because the Wankel was 130lb (59kg) lighter than the V8, modified front springs and shock absorbers were used. The only outward differences were the rotary badges on the bonnet and boot lid and a rather crude looking front spoiler. It probably needed it: on 320bhp Felix Wankel's SL was good for 150mph (241km/h), 0-60 in 6.9 seconds, 100 in 15 seconds and zero to 125mph in 25 seconds. Those who drove it in-period could only compare its smoothness, power and flexibility with a V12. Felix Wankel never drove it (he never learned to drive), but apparently took great delight in instructing his driver to hose-off lesser V8-engined Mercedes encountered on the road at every opportunity. Today it lives in the Mannheim Museum of Industrial Technology alongside an NSU Wankel Spider, an Ro80 and a prototype rotary KKM871-engined Audi.

Ro80-BASED CONCEPT CARS BY PININFARINA AND BERTONE

The Ro80's styling was so universally admired that few saw any virtue in gilding this particular lily: in many ways it

LAST CHANCE SALOONS, 1968–77

ABOVE LEFT: **Pininfarina's curious reinterpretation had some interesting features but sank without trace after a couple of European motor show outings.**

ABOVE RIGHT: **Interesting if not exactly beautiful, the 2 Porte + 2 had rear-hinged 'suicide' rear doors.**

ABOVE LEFT: **Bertone's mid-engined Trapeze, designed by Gandini, was shown at Paris in 1973.**

ABOVE RIGHT: **The big wrap-around screen had a single wiper and the six rectangular headlights lived under a pair of retractable covers.**

was a shape that put the efforts of even the Italian styling houses to shame. However, if anyone was going to rise to the challenge of reinventing the style of one of the world's best-looking cars it was likely to be Pininfarina, who displayed an intriguing if not conventionally beautiful three-box saloon on the Ro80 running gear at the Paris Salon in 1971. It was also seen at Turin and Brussels that year but afterwards disappeared into the Pininfarina museum collection. Today the 2 Porte + 2 lives in the Audi Museum at Ingolstadt.

LAST CHANCE SALOONS, 1968–77

The name related to the seating layout, front seats close together, the rears either side of the engine: passengers could stretch legs either side of the front seats.

Created by Paulo Martin, whose career-defining Fiat 130 coupé made its debut at the same show, the 2 Porte +2 had a severe profile that foreshadowed some 1980s Cadillacs and the 700 series Volvos. The rectangular lights looked similar to the 130 coupé's and the neatly integrated black rubber bumpers were an early taste of Martin's treatment on the Lancia Monte Carlo of 1975. There were side-impact beams in all four doors. The back doors, which could not be opened without opening the fronts first (and only from the inside) were rear-hinged 'suicide' type. Its other 'party trick' was that the main section of the roof folded down behind the rear seats (manually) without taking up any boot space. Inside, the seats were trimmed in bright red velour and while the dashboard was a roughly similar shape to production Ro80s, the treatment of the instruments and light finish were totally different, as was the Alfa-style steering wheel. Electric windows were fitted. Some motor show dream cars are not really cars at all but immobile models: 2 Porte +2 was a running vehicle.

The car's flanks were broken up by a contrasting darker section – first black then grey – and the wheels were just the standard steel Ro80 type, although the 2 Porte +2 has also been shown with fancier wheel covers.

The mid-engined Trapeze was shown at Paris in 1973 and looked like a softer take on the Bertone Lancia Stratos: both were designed by Marcello Gandini. The name related to the clever seating arrangement with the front seats placed close together and the rears placed either side of the compact engine with the occupants able to stretch their legs either side of the front passengers. The big wrap-around screen had a single wiper and the six rectangular headlights lived under a pair of retractable covers.

More original than the Pininfarina car, Bertone's effort would have made a certain kind of sense as an alternative to the factory saloon. Sadly, by 1973 the fate of the Ro80, and the rotary engine, was sealed as far as Audi were concerned.

WHAT THE PAPERS SAID

Looking purely at the stopwatch readings, the Ro80 has only medium performance. But in practice it feels rapid and once underway it is untroubled when maintaining high speeds. Poke it along and it can feel decidedly sporty... The engine is so smooth it makes you wish for full automation with a good kick-down. There is no disputing, however, that the semi automatic does its job with aplomb once you master it.

CAR giant test Ro80 v Jaguar XJ6 v BMW 525, August 1974

There is a very special feel about the Ro80, a feel which I think attributable to the unworldly remoteness of the utterly smooth and blissfully quiet Wankel engine: in the absence of awareness of the engine, and in the absence of any significant wind noise or road shock, one has more sensitivities at one's disposal for appraising the fit and support of the seats (quite magnificent these), the quality of the ride, the accuracy and alacrity of the steering, the progressive and sensitive brakes. What with all these properties, how could one not judge this car as one of the very best?

L. J. K. Setright, **CAR**, 'Throttle Bending', April 1974

There are grounds for thinking that the NSU Ro80 is one of the world's most misunderstood cars.

Autocar, 'Buying Second-hand', 26 November 1977

In 22 years as a motoring scribe I still rate the NSU Ro80 as one of the three best cars I have run, and the only one that I really hanker to own. Best not only for driver appeal, comfort, civility and engineering concept but also, against all the odds, reliability too.

Roger Bell, **Old Motor**, February 1981

Ro80-BASED ODDITIES

Due to the nature of their construction the small rear-engined NSUs had long been popular as a basis for one-off or short-run, rear-engined sports cars, and there were attempts to revive this idea with the Ro80, gullwing doors being a consistent theme. In fact the Tara, first seen in 1971, started life as a four-door coupé based on the NSU 1200 in 1966, created by a 16 year-old Frenchman called Dominique Billotte. His 1971 iteration, with a glass-fibre body, was rotary engined and even had an Ro80 dashboard. Billotte could not capture the interest of any major producers and sold the project to Tony Russell.

It was re-issued in 1981 – now Porsche powered and branded as the 'Nancy' – but has since disappeared without trace.

At the 1973 Geneva show, Franco Sbarro, prolific Italian-Swiss creator of superior neo-classical replicas and one-off concept cars, showed a white, wedge-shaped coupé called the SV1, a 'safety car' with a tubular chassis and a roll cage, that was supposedly powered by two 150bhp Ro80 engines and fitted with a plumbed-in sprinkler system for the engine bay. It was built for the Polish–French aristocrat and noted dandy Stanislas Klossowsky and, at the 1974 Geneva show re-presented with an orange paint job: it did not look any prettier. Slightly less offensive was the Gmachmier Ro80 shown at the Geneva and Tokyo shows in 1975. Huge gullwing doors gave access to a full four-seater cabin. It was powered by a turbocharged Ro80 engine with an alleged 200bhp. Felix Gmachmier of G-Design in Munich was a former Audi stylist.

The Gmachmier Ro80 shown at the Geneva and Tokyo shows in 1975.

Huge doors meant gullwing operation was a must.

■ LAST CHANCE SALOONS, 1968–77

FUCHS ALLOYS

The famous design created for Porsche in the mid-1960s.

LEFT: **Five-bolt, 14-inch forged alloys as fitted to the Ro80 as an option.**

The Otto Fuchs company was formed in 1910, making brass components for German industry and, in the 1930s, began working in aluminium, principally for the aviation sector. Post-war it supplied synchro rings to VW and titanium components for aerospace manufacturers. The still family-owned and operated business began making wheels when approached by Porsche in the early 1960s. They specified a new wheel that had to be at least 3kg lighter than the then current steel type in the name of unsprung weight. Intended for the new 'S' version of the 911, it also had to be strong, which meant it had to be cast rather than forged with no welding or riveting, as these types of construction had proven too fragile in testing. A wooden model was created of a 4½ x 15 in early 1965 by Fuchs and, after tweaking by Porsche into the now familiar 'impeller' or cloverleaf design, made its debut on the 911 Targa at that year's Frankfurt Show.

Public reaction was so positive that Porsche put in an order for 5,000 units and the Fuchs Felge subsequently became standard on the new 911S of December 1965. In fact it is hard to picture any early 911 without them. The VW-Porsche 914 was optionally available with a similar design.

Greatly focused on the benefits of reducing unsprung weight, NSU wasted no time in approaching Fuchs to create an optional 'five clover' wheel for the still secret Ro80, 14 inch with a 5J rim and a five-bolt fixing and to be shod (as was the standard steel wheel) with Michelin XAS asymmetric tyres, the first mass production tyres designed to run at 130mph (209km/h). These beautiful wheels became available in 1968 and were always optional on the German market; in the UK they were part of the standard specification after 1972. The physical makeup of the Fuchs wheels was 97 per cent aluminium, 3 per cent wrought alloy, with magnesium and pure silicon to increase strength. The 1972 Fuchs alloys for the new Mercedes S-Class brought cast alloy wheels into the mass production sector and orders from BMW, Opel and Audi soon followed. Today Otto Fuchs AG, still family owned, makes wheels for many of the more upmarket European brands.

A TRUE SUCCESSOR? THE AUDI 100/200 C2 1982–91

The Audi 100 of the 1982–91 generation, built at the Neckarsulm plant, is often cited as the true inheritor of the Ro80 legacy in that it was a large, tastefully styled, pleasingly finished front-wheel-drive German saloon focused on the best possible aerodynamics and extracting high performance out of small engines, in this case no larger than 2.2/2.3 litres.

Voted Car of the Year in 1983, it was made famous in the UK by a slick television advertising campaign that revived the *Vorsprung Durch Technik* slogan first used by NSU for the Ro80 in 1971.

There was a hint of Ro80 about its rising-wedge profile but, while the shape has aged well, could anyone honestly say the C3 Audi 100 truly recaptured the beauty and fascination of its rotary-engined predecessor? The 0.30 drag coefficient was not intuitively arrived at, but was the result of many wind tunnel hours combined with detail innovations like exotic flush glass, wheel covers, wipers and door handles. The roomy interior was a masterclass in fit, finish and use of materials – in fact the car as a whole was a high point in build quality for Audi under the watchful glare of Audi boss Ferdinand Piech. However, it shared the vice of poor ventilation with the Ro80, so air conditioning was a must. Quattro four-wheel-drive technology was the major C3 innovation for those who required it, but basic drive trains and architecture were inherited from the C2, which meant in-line, canted over 4- and 5-cylinder engines – the latter available as the high-specification Turbo as the 200 – and a range of five-pot diesels. With over one million produced, the C3 Audi 100/200 could not be counted as anything other than a success. With durable galvanised bodywork (another innovation) they looked set to be a regular sight on the road for decades, yet they now seem to be all but extinct – probably rarer than the Ro80.

The aerodynamic Audi saloons of the 1980s inherited some of the Ro80's flavour, if not its charm.

■ LAST CHANCE SALOONS, 1968–77

STUART BLADON RECALLS HIS *AUTOCAR* Ro80 LONG TERM TEST CAR

In 1971, my friend the late Erik Johnson, who was press officer of Mercedes-Benz, arranged for me to have one of the new Audi 100 models on loan to Autocar on long term test. They had been very impressed with my reports on running one of the first of the Audi Super 90s imported to Britain. Those were the days when the make was unknown here. People used to admire it and say: "Ordy? Who makes that? Is it Japanese?"

Mercedes-Benz had the concession for Audi cars, but only a few weeks after my Audi 100 had arrived the concession was snatched away by NSU. Immediately all Audi sales material and advertising had to be scrapped, and my short-lived long term test ended when the car was reclaimed.

Shortly after this I was contacted by the newly formed Audi-NSU (GB) Ltd to say they thought I had been badly let down by the sudden end of my Audi 100 test, and they would like me to accept one of the new Ro80s on a long term loan to Autocar.

Only two days after it arrived in March 1971 I set off with four of us on board for a lengthy tour of the NSU factories in Germany to prepare an article on the new NSU-Audi structure and to witness production of the Wankel engine. I came to like the Ro80 very much indeed, appreciating the excellent visibility due to its deep windscreen and slender pillars, and the impressive stability, ride comfort and ventilation. To overcome the low-speed roughness of the Wankel engine, all Ro80s had semi-automatic transmission, so gear changes were made effectively clutch-less, and at traffic halts the engine would be ticking over through a torque-converter, to pull away as soon as the driver opened the throttle. I was quickly familiar with this, and as always with an automatic transmission I used my left foot on the brake pedal, but drivers unfamiliar with it would be caught out and press down on what they thought was the clutch pedal but was actually the brake.

After hearing a shriek of locked wheels when anyone unfamiliar with the car moved off from a traffic halt, I had to tell them to put the left foot well away from the pedals or they will have someone run into the back of them.

After running the car for six weeks I made an appointment to take it down to NSU at Shoreham to cure increasing problems with misfiring and, worst of all, terrible smoke from the exhaust when the engine was cold. Surprisingly the car was confiscated (if that's the right word, since it was theirs) to be replaced with another one, which arrived in July 1971. The new one disappointed, having a bad flat spot in acceleration, stiff steering although it was a ZF power steering system, and its smoking when cold was even worse than with the earlier car. I used to be embarrassed in the morning to look in the mirror and see the blue haze left behind.

At 1,400 miles [2,250km] the clutch started to remain engaged, so one had to remember to slip into neutral before coming to rest. After attention at Normand Continental, the NSU London dealers, the clutch was replaced but exhaust smoke continued, and there was frequent difficulty with the sparking plugs oiling up. I used to carry spares with me, and with much practice could jump out and change the plugs in three minutes. After sand blasting they were then re-usable, which was just as well since they cost ten times as much as normal sparking plugs.

It wasn't all bad news and when I took it up to Scotland to cover the 1971 Glasgow Motor Show I appreciated the effortless cruising at 80–85mph [129–137km] with almost total lack of mechanical noise or vibration. Fuel consumption was consistently around 20mpg [14.12ltr/100km].

In June 1972, with the car now over a year old and 20,000 miles [32,200km] covered I began to notice a knock from the engine, and a date was fixed for me to take the car back to Shoreham for complete engine strip down by the excellent Mike Hoppis, and it was found that the centre bearing had failed. This was apparently a known fault and a new crankshaft of later design was fitted, which increased the oil flow to the centre bearing. The whole job of engine out, dismantle, repair and reinstall was completed in time for me to drive back home the same day.

From then on the Ro80 ran well though still with the disgraceful smoking from the exhaust after a cold start, and in November 1972, with the mileage now over 26,000 [41,840km] it was felt that, again, we had nothing more to learn from the Wankel engine and the car was gratefully handed back to NSU. It had always been a safe, comfortable and enjoyable car to drive or travel in, but the engine let the car down in terms of fuel and oil consumption in relation to its performance.

LAST CHANCE SALOONS, 1968–77

At the launch of the Jaguar XJV12 I was confronted by the late Harry Mundy, who had been technical editor of Autocar *for some ten years before moving on to become chief engineer of power units at Jaguar. "Well, Stuart," he said, "what's your erudite opinion of the Wankel engine now that you've been running one for – how long is it?"*

"Four years, on and off," I replied. "I'm afraid it hasn't come up to the initial high expectations. The disadvantages of extreme exhaust pollution, disappointing economy, lumpy low-speed running and lack of bottom-end torque far outweigh the advantages of compactness, low weight, and smoothness at high speeds." Harry was always argumentative, but this was one of the relatively few occasions when I heard him reply: "I agree."

Stuart Bladon and family with the *Autocar* long-term NSU.

Ro80 and its replacement, an Opel Commodore.

147

PETER ROBINSON ON ROAD TESTING THE Ro80 IN AUSTRALIA

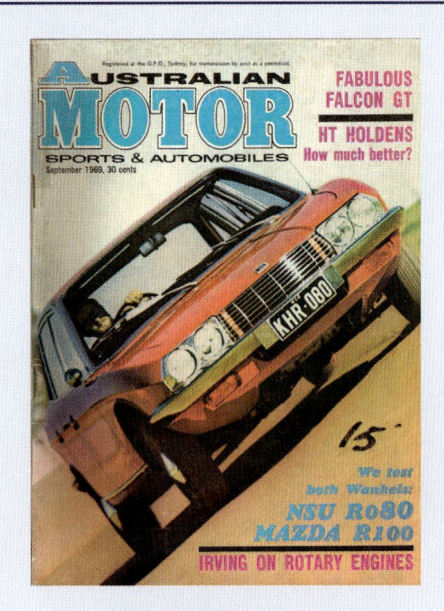

I road tested the NSU for Australian Motor Sports & Automobiles magazine (September 1969) and rather went overboard. Ignore the (then unknown) engine problems and the Ro80 was a brilliant car in terms of refinement, the quality of the power steering (the best I'd tried to that point), the refined ride, spacious interior and, not least, it helped that I loved the purity of the styling. It was the first car since the DS to establish a new and unique design direction. Ventilation was an issue in Australia and I pondered how the car would be with a five-speed manual gearbox.

In 1972, a neighbour offered to sell me his Ro80 after the engine stopped with around 28,000km [17,400 miles] on the odo. Cost $(A)1000 and I couldn't resist. I investigated rebuilding the engine and took the plunge in the late 1980s, but the rebuild didn't work and the car sat at a Sydney specialist garage when we left to live in Italy in 1988. After getting to know the Audi people, I asked to interview Herbert Brockhaus, the head of NSU testing in 1967, who was the director of engineering services at Audi. I wrote an Autocar Heroes column (18 Sept 1996) about the bloke, who could not have been more honest and charming. I asked Herbert about finding parts for my car. I have also attached the resulting letter from Neckarsulm. Further investigation revealed the cost was somewhat outrageous, so I didn't go ahead.

TOP: **Peter Robinson fell in love with the Ro80 after testing it in 1969.**

ABOVE: **The Ro80 was eagerly anticipated in Australia.**

RIGHT: **Like the UK, Australians got the quad circular lights at first.**

Helpful note from Herr Brockhaus of Audi, 1991.

NSU GMBH NECKARSULM

Telefax Nr. 010-3930725209

NSU GmbH Postfach 1144 D-7107 Neckarsulm

Peter Robinson
European Editor
Autocar and Motor
42 Contrada
S. Piedro Calino 25040

Italien

Ihre Zeichen	Ihre Nachricht vom	Unsere Zeichen	Datum
	03/06/91	Pl/eh	June 6, 1991

Information on NSU Ro 80 spare parts

Dear Mr. Robinson,

Mr. Brockhaus asked us to support you in your search of spare parts for your NSU Ro 80 manufactured in 1968.

AUDI NSU AUTO UNION AG discontinued the Ro 80 production in 1977 so that unfortunately neither spare parts nor exchange parts for this car have been available regularly ex factory since 4 years.

The only chance we see that you may acquire NSU Ro 80 spare parts is to contact Mr. Witzelmaier, Talstraße 26, 7121 Ingersheim, Germany. He has a special repair service for NSU Ro 80 engines and it may be possible that he is able to supply you with an exchange four-spark-plug engine and with the required door sealing frames.

If you are only interested in buying the rubber frames of the lower parts of the doors please contact Mr. George Stoelen from the NSU Club Belgium, who has remanufactured these parts. His address is: George Stoelen, Mgr. Raeymaekersstraat 34, B-2235 Westmeerbeek, Belgium.

In addition we suggest to contact Mr. Michael Marold, P.O. Box 54, Castlemaine, 3450 Victoria, Australia.
He is a real NSU enthusiast and owner of some NSU Ro 80 cars. It may be possible that he can help you in a less expensive way than purchase from Germany or Belgium would mean.

Yours sincerely,   cc: I/E-7 Herr Brockhaus

N S U   GmbH

                                                  i. V.

P. Lutz   R. Plagmann

NSU GmbH   Geschäftsführer: Telefon (0 71 32) 31-13 45   Sitz der Gesellschaft Neckarsulm   Bankverbindung
NSU Straße 24-32   Peter Lutz   Telex 7 28 811   Eingetragen im Handelsregister   Baden-Württembergische Bank AG
D-7107 Neckarsulm   Telefax (0 71 32) 31 13 69   des Amtsgerichts Heilbronn Neckar   Neckarsulm
                                       Teletex 7 132 450 Audid   unter HRB Blatt 2982   Konto-Nr 815 625 00 00
                                                                                                         BLZ 620 300 50

■ LAST CHANCE SALOONS, 1968–77

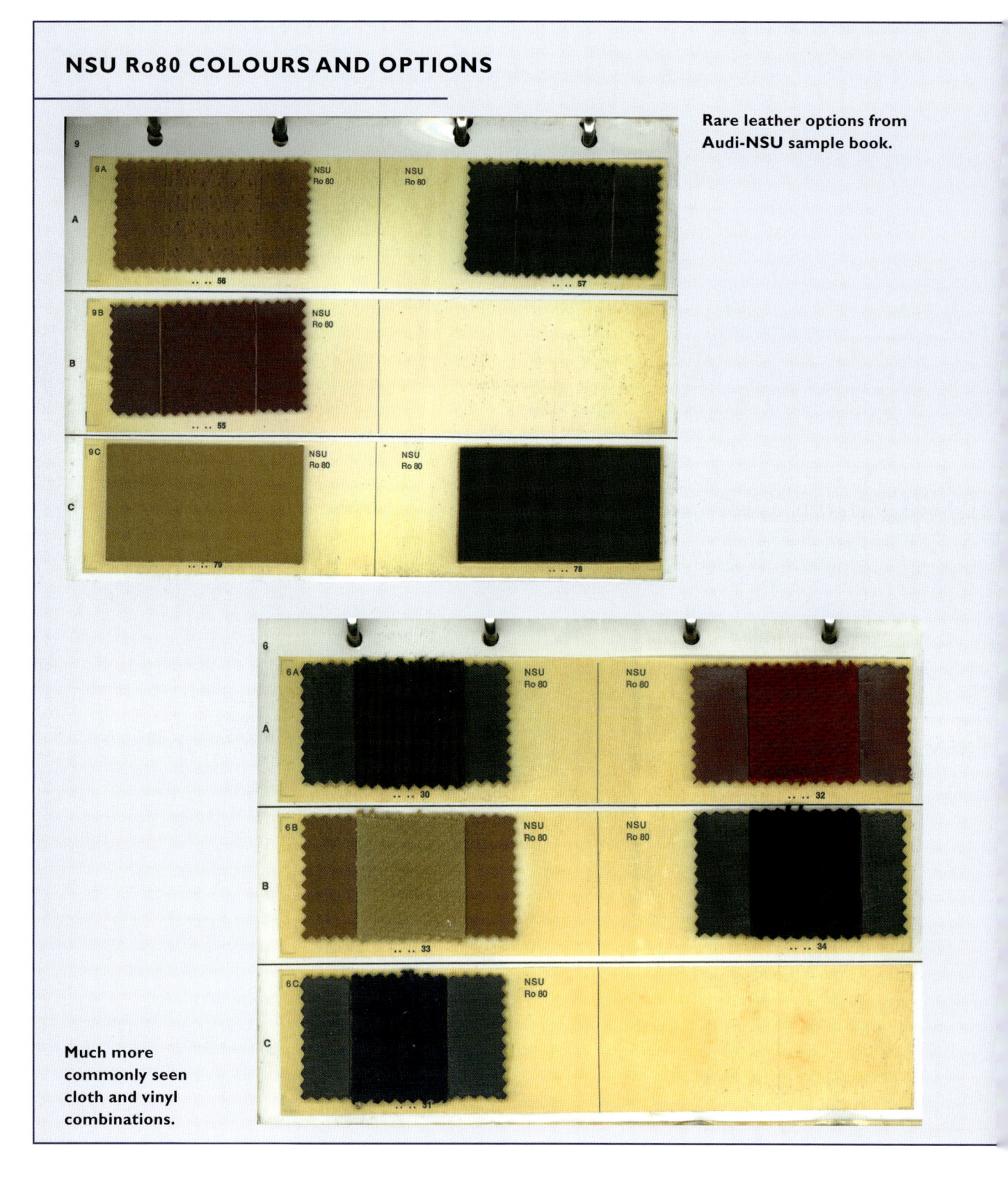

NSU Ro80 COLOURS AND OPTIONS

Rare leather options from Audi-NSU sample book.

Much more commonly seen cloth and vinyl combinations.

150

LAST CHANCE SALOONS, 1968–77

Sepia metallic, 1967–69.

BELOW LEFT: **Targa Orange 1968–71.**

BELOW RIGHT: **Padma Green 1968–71.**

continued overleaf

151

■ LAST CHANCE SALOONS, 1968–77

NSU Ro80 COLOURS AND OPTIONS *continued*

White 1968–71.

Iberian Red 1971–76.

Banana Yellow and Rally offered on late cars.

152

LAST CHANCE SALOONS, 1968–77

Alfa Red.

Signal Green 1975–77.

continued overleaf

■ LAST CHANCE SALOONS, 1968–77

NSU Ro80 COLOURS AND OPTIONS *continued*

ABOVE: **Variations on red included Colorado, Brocade, Iberian, Mars and Maroon.**

Marathon Blue Metallic, 1973–77.
AUTHOR'S COLLECTION

LAST CHANCE SALOONS, 1968–77

Cosmo Blue, 1971 only.

Agate Brown 1973–74 (model years)
Agate Brown Metallic 1973–74 (model years)
Aero Blue Metallic 1972 (model year)
Alaska Blue Metallic 1973–74 (model years)
Alfa Red II 1967–71 (launch colour to model year 1971)
Atlantic Metallic 1975–1976 only (model year)
Atlas White 1973–76 (model years)
Aqua Blue 1975–77 (model years)
Bahama Blue Metallic 1977 only (model year)
Bermuda Green 1973–74 (model years)
Brocade Red 1977 only (model year)
Cadiz Orange 1975–76 (model years)
Ceylon Beige 1975–77 (model years)
Champagne Beige* 1969 to (model year) 1971
Clementine 1972 only (model year)
Colorado Red Metallic 1973–74 (model years)
Corona Yellow 1972–74 (model years)
Cosmo Blue* 1969 to (model year) 1971
Derby Red* 1967 only
Delft Blue 1973–74 (model years)
Diamond Silver Metallic 1977 model year only
Durba Green* 1968 only
Gemini Metallic 1972 (model year only)
Glacier White* 1967 to (model year) 1971
Iberian Red 1971–76 (model years)
Hunting Green* 1967 to (model year) 1972
Kansas Beige 1971 model year
Copper Metallic 1977 model year

Lotus White 1972 model year
Maladent Metallic 1975–76 (model years)
Marathon Blue Metallic 1973–76 (model years)
Maroon 1974 model year
Mars Red 1977 model year
Nevada Beige 1972 model year
Opal Green 1972 model year
Padma Green 1968 to (model year) 1971
Pastel White 1971 model year
Phoenix Red 1975 model year
Polar White 1977 model year
Rally Yellow 1977 model year
Smoke Blue 1972–74 model years
Reseda Green Metallic 1977 model year
River Blue 1971–72 model years
Sagunto Blue 1967 to (model year) 1971
Sahara Beige 1973–74 model year
Black* 1967 to (model year) 1977
Sepia Metallic* 1967–69
Signal Green 1975–77 model years
Silver Metallic* 1967 to (model year) 1971
Emerald Green 1972 model year
Spanish Green 1973 model year
Targa Orange 1968 to (model year) 1971
Taxi Ivory 1975 model year
Tibet Orange 1972–76 (model years)
Deep Sea Green 1971 model years
Titian Metallic 1975–76 model years
Tropic Green 1974 model year
Light Turquoise Metallic 1974 model year
Turquoise Green Metallic 1972–73 model years
Coralle 1973–76 model years
Banana Yellow 1975–76 model years
Tizian Metallic 1975–76 model years
Island Green 1977 model year
Fish Silver* 1967
Silver Grey* 1967
Silver Grey Metallic 1971 model year
Bristol Grey* 1967
Florida Grey* 1967
Oppok Yellow* 1967
Rauhreif* 1967
Maya Metallic 1975–76 model years

continued overleaf

155

NSU Ro80 COLOURS AND OPTIONS *continued*

OPTIONS

STEEL SUNROOF MANUAL OR ELECTRIC OPERATION (1968–77)

REAR FOG LAMPS
Not available until model year 1975. Standard from model year 1976 on.

HEAD RESTS
Front: option until model year 1972. Standard from model year 1973 on, in Germany. Other countries may be different. Rear: option from model year 1974 on.

ELECTRIC RADIO ANTENNA

AUTOMATIC SEAT BELTS
1967–model year 1972: Option front or front and rear. Static belts only until 1977. Model years 1973–77: Front automatic seat belts standard. Rear static seat belts option.

METALLIC PAINT

ALLOY WHEELS

RADIOS: Typically fitted
Blaupunkt
Hildesheim/Frankfurt/Köln
Becker Monte Carlo/Europa/Grand Prix

SEAT TRIM
Cloth (1967–model year 1971)
Velour (1972–77 model years)
Leatherette (1967 to model year 1977)
Leather (1967 to model year 1973)

*Note: At NSU identified its new models by 'year of construction', but at Audi they went by 'model year', which always began after the factory holidays in the summer of the previous year. So, 'model year 1972' means summer 1971 to summer 1972. If a colour was available from Audi from 1972, then that means 'from model year 1972', so from summer 1971 on.

CHAPTER SIX

BUYING YESTERDAY'S FUTURE

The estimated number of NSU Ro80s remaining worldwide is 3,000 to 3,500 cars so, while they are not a common sight on today's roads, finding one should not be difficult.

The general guidelines when it comes to buying an NSU Ro80 are much the same as any other steel-bodied, unitary construction fifty-year-old motor car. As the Ro80 changed relatively little in its decade-long production run, one should always buy on the basis of condition rather than colour, specification or year of manufacture.

It feels like a cliché to say 'Buy the very best car you can afford', but this is always a good plan, particularly as really good Ro80s are not expensive in the great scheme of things.

ESSENTIAL CHECKS

If your budget does not run to a truly spotless example, then it is generally better to buy an honest project than a superficially respectable car that, in the end, will require the same amount of effort to get right but will cost you more to buy in the first instance, merely because the paintwork looks prettier.

The choice these days is, generally speaking, between these 'honest projects' and the really good examples: rust – and the general ravages of time – have swept most, if not all, of those dangerous 'in-between' cars away.

As with most classic cars, the market values originality. While nobody really expects one of these cars to still have its original 'matching numbers' engine, the rotary is now much more of a known quantity than it was in the 1970s and 1980s.

Modern techniques can make the Wankel just as reliable – perhaps even more reliable in some cases – than an equivalent piston engine of its era.

Bodywork

Rather than getting too hung up on the reputation of the rotary engine you should, in the first instance, make your judgements about any potential purchase on the basis of the condition of the bodyshell, because this will be by far the most expensive and time-consuming thing to put right.

It is worth remembering that the 1974–75 cars are thought to be more vulnerable to rust because they were built – during a steel crisis – out of poor-quality recycled steel.

Another general rule of thumb is that sunroof cars tend to leak and cause the roof to start rusting.

Blocked drain tubes and a broken sunroof seal eventually let water in that seeps down to other parts of the car, while at the same time maintaining a 'reserve' of water that can find its way out when the car leans over in a tight corner; a friend of mine discovered this one evening when, on throwing the NSU hard into a left-hand hairpin, a pint of this rusty cocktail emerged from the roof lining and went down the back of his neck. This is very complicated to put right: usually, a roof off a donor car is the only solution.

Structural rust is the most significant issue, beginning with the front longitudinal beams, which are no longer available, difficult to repair and critical to the front suspension geometry. Examine the entire length, particularly around the anti-roll bar mountings, the arches under the drive shafts, the rear ends under the car's floor and the water run-offs, which were plugged – for no obvious reason – on 1975 model year cars.

Next, check the front fairing or apron: the areas between the fog lamps and the wheel arches, the corners of the rectangular section and the welded radiator support are all susceptible to corrosion. Reproduction sheet metal – or a plastic fairing – can be used to fix this. Shock absorber housings, front and rear, should be examined and the air intake

■ BUYING YESTERDAY'S FUTURE

Trouble spots
1. Front valance and the box section behind it
2. Chassis legs (£100 used): notably anti-roll bar mounts; under driveshafts; rear ends
3. Air intake plenum chamber
4. Strut mounts on inner wing
5. Wheelarches front and rear
6. Three-part sills
7. Around sunroof; corners of front and rear screens
8. Doors, especially bottoms
9. Rear strut mounts and inner wheelarches
10. Boot floor

Extensive potential for corrosion, but no worse than many other cars of its era.

vent – with its built-in windscreen wiper motor mechanism – can harbour corrosion.

Check the sills, particularly the ends and jacking points, the wheel arches front and rear and the plate between the front wheels. The A-pillars need a gap on the underside for the water from the sunroof and engine bay to escape. This is often missing or blocked with underseal.

The floor above the exhaust silencer is best viewed by removing the rear seats and the floor underlay. The lower edges of the doors rust, the middle of the lower black painted section and inside the lower parts where dirt and water accumulates if the vent is blocked with underseal. An insulation pad is stuck to the inside of the door, which absorbs water.

Look at the boot floor near the wheel boxes and the double-skinned sections with exhaust mounting bracket underneath.

You can spot leaks around the windscreen and rear window by rust blisters underneath the aluminium trim of the window seals. A warped parcel shelf usually means a leaking rear window. Signs of rust above the front footwell vent nozzles are also indicative of a leaking windscreen.

If the windscreen or rear window has not been watertight for a while then the window frames of the bodywork will usually be rusted through. Corrosion in the boot (including spare wheel well and rear wheel arches) is often due to a leaking rear window.

Dampers get weak and leak: corrosion affects suspension arms, and rear shock absorber housings, which are only accessible after removing the parcel shelf.

The rear panel and the side struts between the wheel housing and the bumper brackets should also be examined for accident damage. If the front floor pans are bent, then the triangulation point for the body jig has probably been used as a jacking point.

The sills are a three-part closed box section that merges into the floor. The weak points are hidden by underseal,

158

carpeting and the anodised exterior trim, but you can check them by shining a light into the vents by the back doors. Sills are not available but can be fabricated. The Swiss club offers repair panels for rear wheel arches. Good doors are difficult to find (and usually expensive) but can usually be repaired. Boot lids and bonnets are fairly easy to find in good or easily repairable condition.

Outer Trim and Glass

The bumpers last well but chrome on the door handles was always fairly poor quality. Early four-plug cars had a pleasing aluminium grille, which was replaced by a plastic type on later cars. The anodised trim tends to lose its shine and is difficult to revive, although cleaning with WD40 can provide a temporary solution.

Windscreens can show a 'milky' effect on the sides. The Ro80 screen is curved vertically and horizontally but replacement screens often are not curved on the horizontal axis. The curvature of an original windscreen should flow perfectly with the line of the roof. If it does not look right it probably will not fit properly either.

Engine

Many NSU Wankel engines nowadays run over 100,000 miles (160,934km) without any problems. They tend to quietly 'fade away' rather than fly apart. I have been luckier than most. On one occasion the bonnet cable release on my first Ro80 broke and I ran it around for days on end without checking oil or water. The temperature gauge indicated the latter was low but I had no alternative other than to keep driving, and suffered no ill effects. So much for the supposed fragility of Dr Wankel's brainchild.

Keeping the plugs clean was the secret to reliability – I occasionally had to heat them up in the oven if I did not have a clean spare set. Careful warming up from cold – and then liberal use of the rev range wherever it was safe and prudent to do so – was also important.

The handy trick of running a business card through the distributor points if the engine starts to lose power (they are very sensitive to even tiny specs of muck) usually works.

The condition of the trochoids and the side plates and also the sealing elements – the 'apex seal' and 'side seals', which are responsible for the compression – are critical.

The health of the engine can be fairly reliably (but not conclusively) assessed using a special compression tester for Wankel engines.

Good engines have a peak pressure of over 7bar in every compression 'spike'. The values of the individual spikes of compression should not differ from each other by more than 0.5bar. The differences in the compression values can tell an expert if the side seal, apex seal or trochoidal surface is worn.

The idle speed should be at 1,200rpm when the engine is warm. If much higher, it was likely raised to conceal a weak engine. Do a stall test by pressing the brakes, shift to first gear and apply full throttle. If the engine does not reach a speed

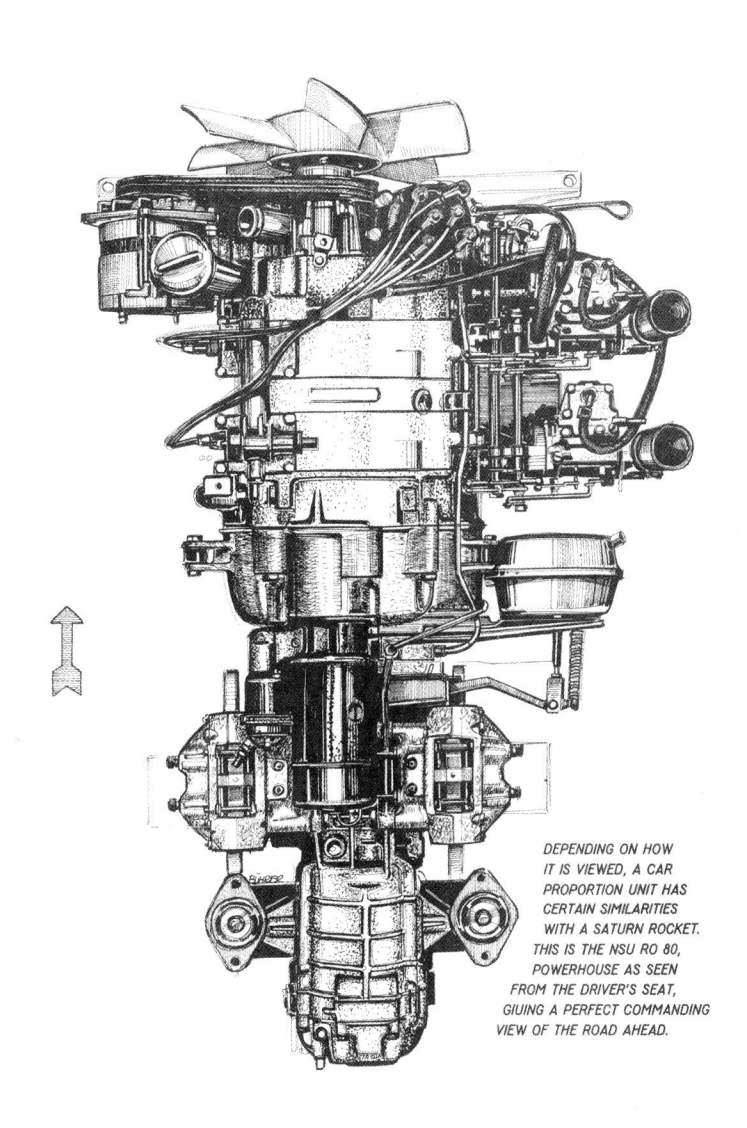

DEPENDING ON HOW IT IS VIEWED, A CAR PROPORTION UNIT HAS CERTAIN SIMILARITIES WITH A SATURN ROCKET. THIS IS THE NSU RO 80, POWERHOUSE AS SEEN FROM THE DRIVER'S SEAT, GIVING A PERFECT COMMANDING VIEW OF THE ROAD AHEAD.

Plan view of the engine, smothered by out-of-scale ancillaries.

SPARK PLUGS

The difference between the various original spark plugs is in the gap between the electrodes and the heat value. The requirements for a four-spark plug engine – with coil ignition – are different than for a two-spark plug engine with electronic ignition. Conventional spark plugs – especially with coil ignition – could not cope with the heat generated in the Wankel combustion chambers or the sooty deposits. Today, almost all Ro80s use the electronic ignition. The original Bosch and Beru spark plugs have not been available for some time, although new old stock items can be found. Motorcycle plugs can be used, using an adaptor produced by the Ro8- Club International. If an engine refuses to fire, or runs badly, cleaning the plugs is usually all that is required. Because they run hot all the time, the plugs in the Ro80 have a hard and relatively short life and cleaning is not always entirely successful.

Avoid power-pack jump-starting your Ro80 as this can 'blow' vital components in the ignition unit and make the car impossible to start unless the unit is overhauled. Fitting the biggest battery that sits comfortably in the space provided is always a good idea.

The original Beru and Bosch plugs have not been available for some years, but new-old stock items can still be found.

ABOVE RIGHT: **Conventional spark plugs could not cope with the heat demands of the rotary engine, which is the reason for the wide, flat nose of the original plugs as a means of dissipating the heat.**

RIGHT: **The Bosch transistorised ignition boosted the ignition spark for improved starting and cleaner running.**

BUYING YESTERDAY'S FUTURE

The condition of the trochoids, the side plates and the sealing elements – the 'apex seal' and 'side seals', which are responsible for the compression – are critical. 1. Radial oil seal between eccentric shaft and end housing. 2. Radial oil seal between the eccentric shaft and piston. 3. Intermediate compression chamber. 4. Gas Seal.

of 2,000 to 2,200rpm, then it is tired. If it reaches noticeably higher speeds, the clutch is slipping. Do not do this test too often – and only briefly – so as not to damage the mechanics.

The idle speed while free-wheeling should be 1,200rpm. Select a gear while the car is stopped under brakes and release the gear stick. The rpm should only drop by about 250–300rpm. Next, stop the car with the foot brake: again, the idle speed should be 1,200rpm. Select first gear, release the gear stick and fully turn right or left without opening the throttle and hold it under tension. The engine should not die.

Check if the engine, gearbox and brakes (including the compensator) are leaking. A well-maintained Ro should be relatively 'dry'. Look for oil-tight drive shaft gaiters by the drive shafts as well.

Gearbox

Gear selection should be easy and take-up smooth; adjustment will fix most problems, although a squealing gearbox will need to be replaced or overhauled. The micro switch in the top of the gear lever, or the vacuum servo, are the favourite culprits if you cannot get a gear. You can adjust how sharply the change is taken up by way of a screw on the vacuum unit. Torque converter seals can leak and bearings can be noisy. With rough handling it is possible to jam the lever into one of the gears for which the only solution is removal of the gearbox.

Electrics and Ignition

The electronic ignition module is not available new but can be repaired and is worth fitting to earlier engines. Otherwise, the electrics are fairly good with the fuses easily accessible in the glove box: if something stops working it is usually

---

SPARES

Although the Ro80 was infamous for years due to its engine troubles, these are, today, not such a deal breaker. Repairable engines from dismantled cars are occasionally available for scrap value while overhauled units can be found at prices far below those being asked for certain exotic piston engines. In fact if you buy a V4-converted car with a view to going back to rotary power you might be surprised at how much your unwanted Ford engine is worth in an on-line auction.

New – or original replacement – engines are offered occasionally and are, naturally enough, much more expensive but not prohibitively so. Experts can overhaul practically any engine with new parts nowadays. Thanks to the internet – and the efforts of the various clubs – the spares situation is probably better today than it was twenty or thirty years ago; the Ro80 Club International even has an on-line shop and has service items professionally remanufactured regularly. These include newly-coated engine housings, ceramic apex seals, new shock absorbers, new brake discs, or new fabrics for the seats and much more. It is odd to think that these cars were so (relatively) common on British roads in the 1970s that for many years a salvage yard, Autosave of Bury, Lancashire, specialised in breaking them with a weekly advertisement in *Exchange and Mart*: 'always 33 Ro80s in for breaking'.

Artwork of the floorpan showing outline of exhaust system, suspension and the flat floor.

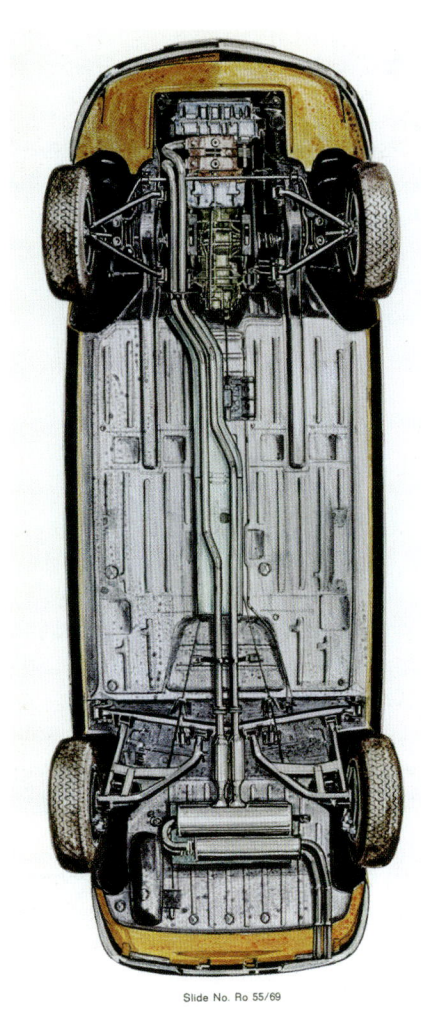

X-ray eyes see through cars as well as humans. One glance shows the healthy disposition of space in the NSU Ro 80.

Here we have turned the NSU Ro 80 upside down so that anybody can see, at leisure, the whole car from the bottom. Front-wheel drive, wheel suspension fore and aft, and above all the smooth clean line of the Ro 80's underside are there to be studied.

The Ro 80's drive (with NSU/Wankel dual RC engine), in longitudinal section, shows the compact design made possible by the economical size of the powerplant.

Slide No. Ro 55/69

down to a blown, loose or poorly-connected fuse. Check if the intermittent wiper and wash/wipe functions are working. The ancillary engine components are conventional items, similar or the same as those used in other contemporary piston-engined vehicles. If any of these fail, replacements are available for sensible prices either new or in good condition. The only expensive parts are the spark plugs: but, on most Ro80s, at least you only need two of them.

Suspension and Brakes

MacPherson strut top bearings can wear and generate knocking sounds, while dampers get weak or leak – betrayed by a soggy ride when driving. Corrosion can affect suspension arms, rear discs, the load-sensing valve for rear braking and the small handbrake drums. The wishbones of the front and rear suspension and rear shock absorber housings can be seriously corroded if the water drainage holes are blocked.

The front and rear shock absorber housings are also vulnerable. While the front ones are easy to see when the bonnet is opened, the rear housings are only accessible under the parcel shelf and inside the wheel arches. After a long period of standing, the brakes – especially the rear brakes – can seize up. The necessary parts are (with the exception of the rear axle brake force limiter) still available. The four-pot ATE inboard disc calipers share their seals with BMWs and should give excellent braking if not seized from lack of use. The braking force limiter can be overhauled. With original equipment Michelin XAS tyres now available, there is no excuse for not having correct period-looking rubber.

Interior

The seat covers can, especially if the car does not have tinted glass, become very faded and fragile. Watch out for the upper edge of the backrests, especially the rear seats.

BUYING YESTERDAY'S FUTURE

Later velour-type seats are not as hard-wearing as vinyl.

Dark colours are the most vulnerable. Poor quality seat fabrics are more of a problem than worn seat foam; this can be repaired. Original upholstery fabric cannot be found any more; for some patterns, the Ro80 Club International has replacement fabric. Plastic (faux leather) seats are usually in better condition, but not everyone likes them, as they get very warm in summer.

Door cards and floor carpets are usually not hard to find in reasonable condition. Dashboards are sometimes brittle due to too much sunlight. The front window winder mechanism can give trouble, failing to seal properly at the top when they rise at the wrong angle, but these are easy to repair with replacement parts.

DRIVING AND OWNING

Even today a good Ro80 is a special, silky serene experience everyone who is interested in cars should try at least once.

You soon get used to the clutchless semi-auto if it is set up correctly. First, if you have never driven an Ro80 before, be sure to tuck your left leg out of the way, just in case you subconsciously mistake the brake for a clutch pedal. The brakes are potent and this is something you will, hopefully, only do once, as the results can be quite dramatic.

Get familiar with the starting ritual. From cold, if your Ro80 has the downdraught carburettors with automatic choke proceed as follows:

- Ignition key to 'Farht' (drive).
- Slowly depress accelerator pedal all the way and release.

- Start without accelerating.
- Warm engines start best at half throttle with no pumping.

If you have horizontal carburettors with manual choke (cold):

- Pull choke out all the way.
- Start without touching the accelerator pedal.
- Push choke back about three-quarters of the way in.
- Depending on the driven distance, push the choke back further; it should be completely pushed back after 1 kilometre.
- Do not use the choke if the engine is warm, as the engine will flood instantly.
- When it gets warmer in summer, the choke is barely needed even during a cold start, at most shortly whilst starting.

You can, of course, pull away in top gear should you wish to abuse the privilege of having no valves to worry about. There are three forward ratios – NSU liked owners to think of them as 'speed ranges' rather than gears – with '1' left and down. Blue exhaust fumes (burnt oil) appear if there are worn oil seals, but should disappear after a short time.

The oil pressure indicator should go out as soon as the engine reaches more than the idle speed. The engine coolant temperature should always remain in the 'thin white area' of the thermometer while in normal driving mode. The 'thick white area' should only be reached in warm weather during prolonged climbing of steep inclines. The red area should ideally never be reached.

Keep an eye on your oil level, as the Wankel engine naturally burns the stuff. Check the dipstick every time you brim the fuel tank as a rule of thumb and look at the coolant level at the same time, but take care removing the cap if the engine is hot.

The main thing to remember about these cars is that they need regular use. Relative quietness and stable high-speed cruising make the Ro80 a delight on a long trip – a rare attribute among cars of this vintage in the 21st century – but in hot weather you may curse the lack of effective ventilation.

Do not be afraid of driving your Ro80 hard (once the engine is up to temperature) as timidity with the throttle pedal tends to lead to fouled plugs: the revs – and the gearbox – are there to be used, but be prepared for regular outings to the petrol station.

Be prepared, also, for lots of very positive attention from people in all walks of life, a surprising number of whom will know exactly what you are driving and will probably want to talk to you about it.

PHIL BLAKE, THE Ro80 SPECIALIST

Phil Blake's first recollection of setting eyes on an NSU Ro80 was when he was a 15-year-old boy in South London.

There were three in a driveway on my paper round. Even back then they stood out as something different. Then I saw a magazine with a Ro80 on the front cover and bought it. It mentioned the NSU Owners Club so I contacted them. Being young and enthusiastic they made me an honorary member!

The following year Phil found himself in an Ro80 on the way to Germany with friends Clive and Christine Thomas, heading to the International NSU Treffen in Neckarsulm: Clive was the technical guru of the now disbanded Ro80 Club GB.

After that trip I was well and truly hooked. At the age of 16 I got my first moped, meaning I could travel to the Thomas's house a few miles from me, and help Clive with stripping and repairing Ro80s. Phil bought his first Ro80 from Clive around the same time, way before he got his first driving licence. That first Ro80 had a tired engine, and there is no doubt it was a pain in the neck: poor starting, lack of power and constantly stalling. But we lived at the top of a steep hill, so every time my mum and dad went out me and my mates would get the thing started by rolling it down and then go and have a drive around the town – if we had the two quid to buy a gallon of petrol. When I bought my next one, which had a healthy engine, it was an absolute revelation.

The days of poor reliability are now a distant memory.

I have covered countless miles in Ro80s on international trips and holidays and on the only occasion I ended up stranded by the side of the autobahn, it was completely my fault. Doing 100mph-plus on aged Michelin XAS tyres resulted in two blowouts leaving me without a spare. I've never made that mistake again!

Working with Clive, and on his own, Phil accrued a lot of Ro80 expertise – and a lot of cars.

They were dirt cheap or even free. I could never bear to see a salvageable Ro or useful parts go to waste. I've no idea how many have gone through my hands but current ownership count is around thirty. The most I've ever paid for one in the early days was £1,500, because it had a new engine in it. But mostly they were either free or maybe fifty quid: yet amongst those cars I've picked-up some really good ones.

As well as earning a part-time living repairing and restoring this German marvel, Phil now looks after the technical advice for the NSU Owners Club. Having moved out of London, Phil has been able to indulge his passion but also get himself organised with a workshop and ample storage for project cars. While he acknowledges there are not really enough Ro80s out there to run a full-time business, he has been able to turn his hobby into part of how he makes his living these days.

I can carry out repairs and engine rebuilds for customers and although I try not to take on full restorations due to the time involved, I can assist owners along the way with various aspects.

Parts availability for the Ro80 is better than ever.

I have a good stock of used parts and the Ro80 Club International is now re-manufacturing many previously unavailable parts. With this comes the availability of refurbished rotor housings and ceramic apex seals. The ceramic seals have proven to show no evidence of wear on the housing surface after a test engine was stripped for examination at 20,000 miles.

After decades of being far too cheap, Ro80 prices have risen of late with some cars on the continent fetching upwards of €30,000. Phil says UK cars rarely come up for sale and often sell before going onto the market. But they remain good value.

The oldest Ro80 is now 55 years old and the youngest 45. That's 55 years of owner and specialist experience learning what to do – and what not to do – to achieve good reliability from the NSU Wankel engine.

Phil, who remains as enthusiastic as ever about these magical saloons, is always happy to chat Ro80s and advise any potential buyers who might be cautious of taking the plunge.

There are cars running around these days with several hundred thousand kms on an engine. And yet at any mention of the Ro80, every internet expert will be straight on the keyboard ranting about engine failures and Ford V4 conversions. The most common question being asked by the public being 'has it got the original engine in it?' The reality is that hardly any remain with the Ford transplant these days. I know of two that have been converted back to Rotary within the last two years, and I have just started converting a car back for a customer that had an Essex V6 in it at one time, hence the butchering of its front end. It is already proving immensely rewarding getting it back to looking like it should, but also replacing one of the world's roughest engines, with one of the world's smoothest.

FORD V4 AND V6 CONVERSIONS

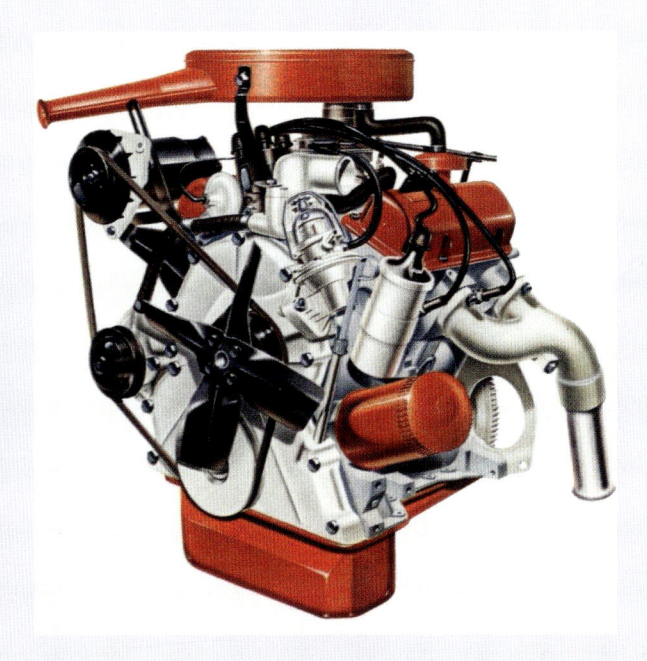

The ubiquitous Ford V4, favoured engine of 1970s' Ro80 engine swappers.

The Ford V4/V6 and Audi-converted Ro80s are few and far between these days and the best that can be said for them is that they can sometimes provide the basis of a good car for somebody who wants to go back to original NSU rotary power if they have remained otherwise complete and relatively sound. The Ford V4 conversions of the late 1970s and 1980s – undertaken in the UK by the likes of the The Ro80 Centre on the Albert Embankment at London SE1 and Hurley Motor Engineering in Coventry – can sometimes be found, although are now pretty scarce. Mated to the original gearbox they were restricted to about 100mph (160km/h). The Capri-specification 96bhp V4 – supplied new, in a box, from Ford – only weighed 35lb (15.8kg) more than the rotary engine, so the handling was not too badly affected: but there was a depressing price to be paid in smoothness and refinement. About 100 cars were known to have been converted in the UK by the end of 1977. At £675–700, it was a big saving over the £900 (not including labour) that Audi NSU dealers wanted for a new rotary engine at the time. A few people opted for the much heavier Ford Essex V6 conversion, giving better acceleration but still no more than 100mph. However, it was a more complex swap that involved drastic alterations to the radiator position and spoiled the handling, and at a price that was not far behind what NSU wanted for a new rotary unit. But when the prices of new rotary engines dropped – and the car moved into the realm of 'classic' rather than an everyday use vehicle – the V4 conversion business went into decline. If you go for a Mazda 12A 2.3 litre swap, it should be neatly done with tidy electrics and without the give-away oversized sump. British specialists Rotechniks developed a good conversion in the 1990s and many are still running well.

NSU Ro80 PRODUCTION FIGURES AND PRODUCTION HISTORY

PRODUCTION HISTORY SEPTEMBER 1967–MARCH 1977

September 1967, Frankfurt: NSU Ro80 launched. Limited imports into the UK with left-hand drive. Early version with four-plug engine (two spark plugs per rotor), engine compartment painted black, light grey or black headlining, door sills without anodised side panels, smooth door panels with two-coloured B-pillar cover.

September 1968, Frankfurt: Engine compartment same colour as bodywork, new interior door panels, anodised side panels on door sills. First right-hand-drive UK imports with four circular headlights: Ro80 wins 'Car of the Year' award.

September 1969 Frankfurt (1970 model year): Plastic radiator fan instead of aluminium, auxiliary halogen headlamps behind radiator grille. Annual production peaks at 7,811. Now known as Audi-NSU Ro80 after merger.

September 1970 Frankfurt (1971 model year): Single-plug engine (one spark plug per rotor), high voltage capacitive ignition (HKZ = *Hochspan nungs-Kondensator-Zündung*), windscreen wipers with intermittent action, halogen main and auxiliary headlights with flat diffuser glass, plastic radiator grille, dashboard indicator lights and buttons with symbols. Three-plug ignition box, better seats, child-proof locks on rear doors, flush-fit sun visors in new flame-resistant headliner.

September 1971 Frankfurt (1972 model year): Audible warning system fitted to guard against over-revving. Chassis number moved to the right-hand suspension strut. Cars are now being produced at the rate of 300 per week.

September 1972 Frankfurt (1973 model year): Blower and exhaust reactor for post-combustion, single-pipe exhaust, downdraught carburettor with automatic choke and different air-inlet housing (Switzerland: from 1974 on), HKZ ignition unit on metal plate in engine compartment, electric rpm gauge (Switzerland: from 1974 onwards), rpm warning buzzer, front suspension spider out of aluminium alloy instead of cast iron.

September 1973 Frankfurt (1974 model year): Brake discs with spacers and adjusted drive shafts, Audi seats without height adjustment.

ABOVE: **Unusual view shows how the Ro80 did not have a bad angle. Claus Luthe wanted to continue feature lines in the bonnet on to the roof, but it would have interfered with the planned sunroof option.**

Early UK press shot of one of the handful of left-hand-drive cars imported before 1969.

BUYING YESTERDAY'S FUTURE

ABOVE: **Press shots emphasised the driver appeal of this agile saloon.**

LEFT: **The shape suited strong colours like Targa Orange, offered 1968–71.**

RIGHT: **1975 model year changes evident here: new badge, bigger lights and rubber bumper inserts plus new Banana Yellow colour.**

September 1974 Frankfurt (1975 model year): Coolant expansion tank out of plastic, rev counter and speedometer with larger numbers, generator with integrated voltage regulator, improved automatic choke.

September 1975 Frankfurt (1976 model year): New rotor oil seals, enlarged rear lights with integrated rear fog light, rear number plate above instead of below bumper, rubber profiles on bumpers, car boot lock moved to lid, new plastic Ro 80 badge on boot lid.

September 1976 Frankfurt (1977 model year): Oil injection circuit with non-return valve, strengthened gearbox for intended power increase from chassis no. 0871 000 334 (from gearbox no. 38 348).

March 1977: Ro80 production ends.

continued overleaf

NSU Ro80 PRODUCTION FIGURES AND PRODUCTION HISTORY *continued*

Annual Production Numbers and Prices
1967	354 (306*)
1968	6,066 (5,333)
1969	7,811 (8,219)
1970	7,200 (6,698)
1971	2,916 (3,411)
1972	4,203 (4,432)
1973	4,074 (4,004)
1974	1,286 (1,181)
1975	1,311 (1,518)
1976	1,795 (1,937)
1977	386 (203)
TOTAL	37,402 (37,242)

* Figures in parentheses are sales quantities

Production year	List prices (DM, incl. VAT)
1967	14,150
Jan. 1968	14,190
Sept. 1969	14,862
Dec. 1969	15,500
Nov. 1970	16,500
Jan. 1972	17,590
Feb. 1973	17,990
Aug. 1973	18,190
Aug. 1974	19,800
Aug. 1975	21,520
March 1976	22,695
March 1977	23,620

TOTAL UK SALES: 3,614

UK list prices by year (Pounds Sterling including PT)
Feb 1968	£2,249
May 1969	£2,279
March 1970	£2,444
March 1971	£2,589
June 1972	£2,593
April 1973	£3,079
Oct 1974	£3,531
April 1975	£3,531 (special order only)
April 1976	£4,500–5,000 (special order only)
Feb 1977	£7,765 (special order only)

APPENDIX

THE WANKEL 'CLUB'

Most of the world's major manufacturers were developing Wankel engines by the early 1970s. In the USA, 80 per cent of the motor industry had signed an agreement: in Japan it was 71 per cent, but European manufacturers – at 44 per cent – were more cautious.

Together with various partners, Felix Wankel had formed Wankel Gmbh in 1958, earning 40 per cent (later 36 per cent) of the royalties. In 1971 he sold his share to Tiny Rowland of Lonrho for DM100 million.

On acquiring an agreement, a company had to pay a joining fee to Wankel GMBH. The fee was calculated on the basis of what type/size of Wankel engine it wanted to produce, but also when the licence was acquired because, with the passage of time, the fee became greater as the pool of knowledge about the technology grew. For example, Curtiss-Wright are thought to have paid $2½ million in 1958, but GM paid a massive $50 million in 1970. On joining, licensees were entitled to all the existing technical knowledge about the engine from all the other members, except GM who, in turn, had no access to the technical improvements obtained after the filing of their agreement on 10 November 1970. Toyo Kogyo were under no obligation to share any information with other Japanese Wankel Club members. The engine was protected by six basic patents that were due to expire between 1978 and 1984 depending on the territory.

Dr Felix Wankel and his brainchild.

■ THE WANKEL 'CLUB'

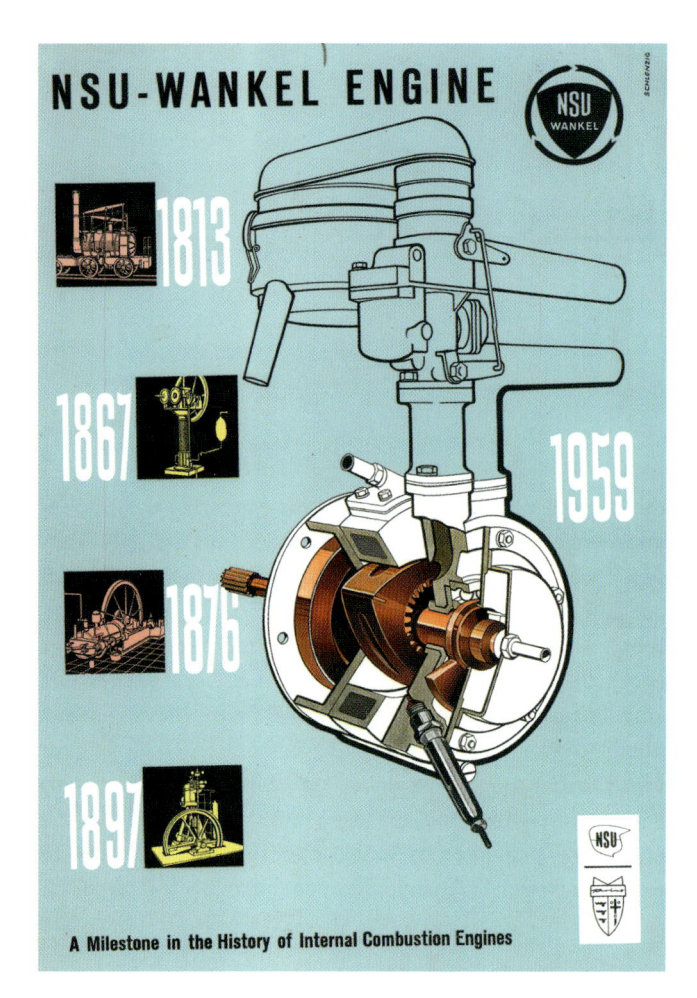

Launch book for the Wankel Rotary concept, 1959.

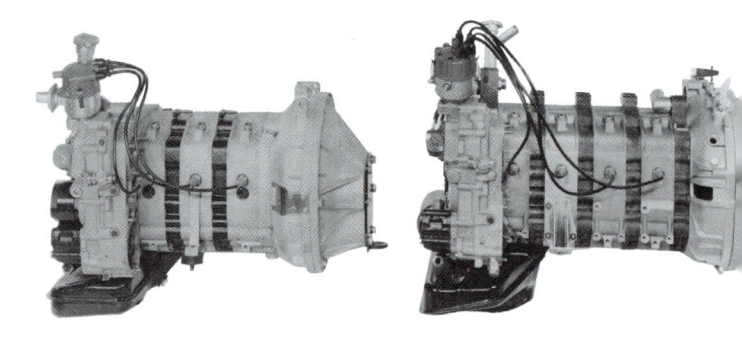

Mercedes-Benz three- and four-rotor Wankel engines.
AUTHOR'S COLLECTION

NSU/WANKEL

1962

PLM 150 air cooled engine with oil cooled rotor

Messrs. Magirus at Ulm and the Bros. Bachert at Bad Friehall, Germany, developed experimental portable fire pumcorporating 150 cc NSU/Wankel engines. The particular used for this purpose was air cooled with the exception rotor, through which lubricating oil circulated. This PLM engine developed 13.5 BHP, its relatively low weight resulfire-pumps which, although exceeding by 22 lb. the 88.2 lb. lated in the German TS 2/5 specification, gave it a performapproaching that of the larger and far heavier TS 4/5 specifi

Photograph No. D 7 (18x24 cm)

RIGHT: **Details of the Magirus rotary water pump unit from 1962.**

170

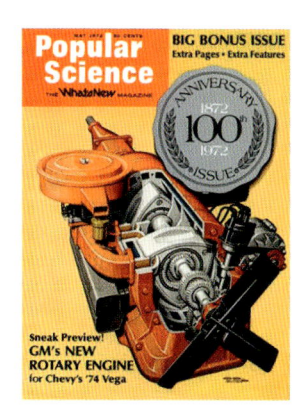

THE WANKEL 'CLUB'

ABOVE: *Popular Science*.

LEFT: **Wankel** licence-holders **Curtiss-Wright** fitted a two-rotor, 185bhp engine in a Ford Mustang in 1965.
AUTHOR'S COLLECTION

The two- and four-rotor, mid-engined **GM** concept cars started life in the late 1960s as potential alloy-bodied replacements for the front-engined **Corvette** – code name **XP-897** and **XP-897GT** – and almost made production, albeit with conventional V8 engines.
AUTHOR'S COLLECTION

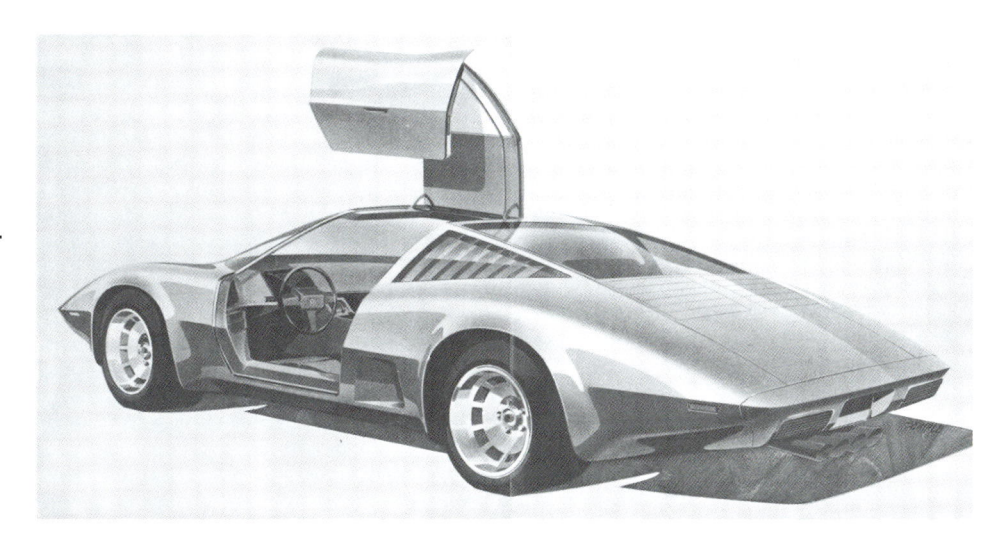

RIGHT: The single-rotor 1969–71 M35 was sold to 267 hand-picked Citroën customers as a prototype purely for appraisal.

■ THE WANKEL 'CLUB'

Mazda launched the Wankel concept with the charismatic Cosmo in 1967 and sold 1,178 of them through to 1972.
AUTHOR'S COLLECTION

Citroën illustrated its full commitment to the Wankel idea with the Birotor in 1973. Sharing surprisingly little with the GS, its launch was poorly timed to coincide with the fuel crisis and Peugeot's takeover.
AUTHOR'S COLLECTION

Alfa Romeo's interest in the Wankel engine is less well known, but they experimented with the idea between 1962 and 1973 and fitted engines into a Spider and a 1750 saloon similar to this one.
AUTHOR'S COLLECTION

THE WANKEL 'CLUB'

RIGHT: **The motorcycle designers were attracted to the compact, light rotary engine. The pictured Yamaha RZ201 got close to production in 1972.**

FAR RIGHT: **Rolls-Royce worked on the so-called 'cottage loaf' diesel-fuelled rotary engine for ten years, a project to produce a lightweight military unit using a second rotor as a compressor.**

DATE	LICENCE	APPLICATION
21/10/58	Curtiss-Wright Corp (USA)	All applications
29/12/60	Fichtel and Sachs AG (Germany)	Industrial/Marine
25/2/61	Yanmar Diesel Co Ltd (Japan)	100bhp petrol, up to 300bhp diesel applications except cars/motorcycles and aircraft
27/2/61	Toyo Kogyo Ltd (Japan)	Up to 200bhp for all land vehicles
4/10/61	Klockner-Humboldt-Deutz AG (Germany)	Unlimited Diesel applications
26/10/61	Daimler-Benz AG Germany	Internal combustion engines, at least 50bhp
20/10/61	MAN Maschinenfabrik (Germany)	Diesels, unlimited application
2/11/61	Fried. Krupp (Germany)	Diesels, unlimited Application
12/3/64	Daimler-Benz AG (Germany)	Diesels, unlimited application
15/4/64	Alfa Romeo (Italy)	Internal combustion engines unlimited applications 50 to 300bhp
17/2/65	Rolls Royce Motors Ltd	Diesel and Hybrid (Great Britain) engines 100 to 850bhp
2/3/65	Porsche KG (Germany)	Internal combustion engines 50 to 1,000bhp for passenger cars and racing/rally vehicles
1/3/66	Outboard Marine Corp (USA)	Internal combustion engines 50–400bhp, marine applications
11/5/67	Comotor S.A (Luxembourg)	Internal combustion and hybrid engines 40–200bhp, land vehicles
12/9/67	Johannes Graupned (Germany)	Internal combustion engines for models/toys 0.1–3 bhp
29/8/69	Savel Ltd (Israel)	Internal combustion engines 0.5–30bhp industrial application
1/10/70	Nissan Ltd (Japan)	Internal combustion engines 80–120bhp for passenger cars
10/11/70	General Motors Corp (USA)	All applications except aircraft
24/11/70	Suzuki Motor Company Ltd (Japan)	Internal combustion engines 20–60bhp for motorcycles
25/5/71	Toyota Motor Company Ltd (Japan)	Internal combustion engines 75–500bhp for passenger cars
29/11/71	Ford Werke AG (Germany)	Internal combustion engines 80–200bhp for passenger cars, station wagons
27/7/72	British Small Arms Ltd (Great Britain)	Internal combustion engines 35–60bhp for motorcycles
28/9/72	Yamaha Motor Company Ltd (Japan)	Internal combustion engines for motorcycles 20–80bhp
4/10/72	Kawasaki Heavy Industries (Japan)	Internal combustion engines for motorcycles 20–80bhp
3/2/73	American Motors (USA)	Gasoline engines 20–200bhp

SOURCES AND FURTHER READING

The Wankel Engine by Nicholas Faith (1976)

The VW Story by Jerry Sloniger (1980)

NSU Wankel Spider road test *Motor* 22/5/1965

NSU Wankel Spider long-term report *Autocar* 3/9/1965

Serious Contender *Motor* 9/9/1967

NSU Ro80 introduction, technical description *Autocar* 7/9/1969

The NSU Ro80 *Autosport* 8/9/1967

NSU Ro80 technical description *CAR* 9/1967

Car of the Year – or Decade? *Motor* (road test) 3/2/1968

NSU Ro80 Car of the Year *CAR* 03/1968

NSU Ro80 Road test *Autocar* 8/2/1968

NSU Ro80 Road test *Autosport* 22/3/1968

NSU Ro80 v Citroën ID20 *Autocar* 1/5/1969

Hard Week with Ro80 *Autocar* 14/8/1969

NSU and the Wankel Engine *Motor* 7/3/1970

NSU v Rover v Opel v Citroën v Jaguar *Motor* 14/03/1970

Ro80 Reassessment *CAR* 8/1970

TrailBlazer, White Elephant or Both? *CAR* 6/1972

NSU Ro80 final report at 23,000 miles *Autocar* 31/8/1972

NSU Ro80 v Citroën DS *CAR* 7/1973

Yesterday's Car of Tomorrow *What Car?* 9/1974

NSU Ro80 road test *Autocar* 13/6/1974

NSU Ro80 road test *Motor* 22/6/1974

NSU Ro80 v Jaguar XJ6 v BMW 525 *CAR* 8/1974

NSU Ro80 long-term report 20,000 miles *Motor* 28/9/1974

Classic Ro80? *Thoroughbred* and *Classic Cars* 08/1975

Swings for Roundabouts (V4 conversions) *Autocar* 03/12/1977

NSU Ro80 Buying secondhand *Autocar* 28/11/1977

Last Ro to Riva *CAR* 11/1977

Where's the Wankel Now? *Autocar* 22/4/1978

NSU Ro80 Cars to Keep *Old Motor* 02/1981

NSU Ro80 v Citroën DS *Classic and Sportscar* 01/1983

The Rotary Club Outing *Supercar Classics* 02/1991

Where's the Progress? *CAR* 06/1991

NSU 'The Great Cars' *On Four Wheels* No. 77

INDEX

aerodynamic properties, Ro80 7, 64
Air Comfort System 79
air-cooled engines 30–35
AUDI 100/200C2 145
AUDI, history of 132–135

Bercot, Pierre 12
Blake, Phil 164–165
Brockhaus, Herbert 12
Bunford, Max 12
buying guidelines, NSU Ro80
   driving and owning 163
   essential checks
      bodywork 157–159
      electrics and ignition 161–162
      engines 159, 161
      gearbox 161
      interior 162–163
      outer trim and glass 159
      spares 161
      spark plugs 160
      suspension and brakes 162

C111 and Mercedes Wankel adventure 136–140
Car of the Year award, NSU Ro80
   by Autovisie 9
   by CAR in 1968 9
Citroën 136
Cole, Ed 12
concept cars by Pininfarina and Bertone 140–142
Curtis-Wright 43

DKW and Auto Union cars 132–135
Drehkoibenmotor 40

driving and owning 163

essential checks on buying
   bodywork 157–159
   electrics and ignition 161–162
   engines 159, 161
   gearbox 161
   interior 162–163
   outer trim and glass 159
   spares 161
   spark plugs 160
   suspension and brakes 162

Fiedler, Fritz 12
Ford V4 and V6 conversions 165
Frankenburger, Victor 12
Froede, Walter 12, 71

Gmachmier Ro80 143

Hasenmuhle Programme 109–110
von Heydekampf, Gerd Stieler 12, 17
Hoeppner, Ernst 12
Hurley, Roy 12
Hutzenlaub, Ernst 12

Keppler, Wilhelm 13, 40
KKM619 115
KKM871 116
Kleines Kettenkraftrad 19
Kreiskolbenmotor 42

Lotz, Kurt 13
Luthe, Claus 66–68, 67–68

INDEX

Matsuda, Tsuneji 13
Mazda Cosmo 80–82

Neckarsulmer Radwerke 15
NSU
    air-cooled engines 30–35
    125 and 250cc Rennsport racing bikes 16
    baby, driving the 24
    Fiats 18
    pedal bikes 16
    Prinz 4 26, 28
    Prinz II and III 26
    Prinz 1000L 28, 30, 32
    Ro80 (see Ro80)
    roots of 15
    Type 32 19
    VW connection 17–21
    Wankel Spider 44

Otto Fuchs company 144

Paschke, Dr 13
Praxl, Ewald 13, 59, 61
Prinz 4 26, 28
Prinz II and III 26
Prinz 1000L 28, 30, 32

Ro80
    aerodynamic properties 7, 64
    based oddities 143–145
    buying guidelines 157–163
    car of the year award 9
    colours and options 150–156
    concept cars by Pininfarina and Bertone 140–142
    developments 104–106
    doubts 87
    driveable prototype 73
    the driving 10
    eccentric shaft 72
    end of rotary dream 116, 129–131
    engine developments 70–72
    exhaust emissions 71
    fatal flaw 8
    Gmachmier 143
    Hasenmuhle Programme 109–110
    history of 7
    internal competition 101–104
    key players in 12–13
    labour intensive 66
    the launch 73–79
    looks 83–86
    modern saloon 86–87
    performance figures 107–108
    production history 166–168
    road testing in Australia 148
    rumours 65–66
    scale model of 9
    selective semi-automatic transmission 88–90
    shortcomings 110–111
    specifications 1967–1977 92–94
    stability 64
    Stuart Bladon review 56–58, 146–147
    technical niceties 8
    timeline 14
    Which? magazine 91
Rowland, 'Tiny' 13

Sports Prinz coupé 7
Stuart Bladon review
    on *Autocar* Ro80 146–147
    on the Wankel spider 56–58

Wankel club 34, 43, 169–173
Wankel, Felix 13
    acute spatial imagination 37
    club 169–173
    DKM motor 40–41
    history of 37
    KKM engine 42–43
    in Nazi party 40
    rotary pumps and engines 37
        operation of 38
        vs. reciprocating engine 37
Wankel Spider 7, 43, 44
    autocar's Stuart Bladon on 56–58
    factors to buy 54–56
    first thoughts on 48–52
    Frankfurt launch 52–54

Yamamoto, Kenichi 13